MBAplanet

Stuart Crainer and Des Dearlove

MBAplanet

the insider's guide

to the business school

experience

FINANCIAL TIMES
Prentice Hall

an imprint of **Pearson Education**

London • New York • San Francisco • Toronto • Sydney • Tokyo • Singapore • Hong Kong
Cape Town • Madrid • Paris • Milan • Munich • Amsterdam

PEARSON EDUCATION LIMITED

Head Office:
Edinburgh Gate
Harlow CM20 2JE
Tel: +44 (0)1279 623623
Fax: +44 (0)1279 431059

London Office:
128 Long Acre
London WC2E 9AN
Tel: +44 (0)20 7447 2000
Fax: +44 (0)20 7240 5771
Website: www.business-minds.com

_____

First published in Great Britain in 2001

© Pearson Education Limited 2001

The right of Stuart Crainer and Des Dearlove to be identified as Authors of this Work has been
asserted by them in accordance with the Copyright, Designs and Patents Act 1988.

ISBN 0 273 65018 1

British Library Cataloguing in Publication Data
A CIP catalogue record for this book can be obtained from the British Library.

10 9 8 7 6 5 4 3 2 1

Designed by designdeluxe, Bath
Typeset by Northern Phototypesetting Co. Ltd, Bolton
Printed and bound in Great Britain by Biddles Ltd, Guildford & King's Lynn

The Publishers' policy is to use paper manufactured from sustainable forests.

HBS does not permit reporters and/or film crews on campus, in classrooms, or in residence halls. Anyone wishing to talk with reporters should arrange meetings off campus and should understand that when they are being interviewed they do not serve as spokespeople for the Executive Education Programs of the School.

HARVARD BUSINESS SCHOOL POLICY

about the authors

Stuart Crainer's book credits include: *Key Management Ideas*, *The Management Century*, *The Ultimate Business Library*, *The Tom Peters Phenomenon*, and many more. He writes a column for *The Times* and the American Management Association's MWorld, and contributes to magazines worldwide including the BA in-flight publication *Business Life*, *Strategy & Business*, *Business 2.0*, *Across the Board*, *Hemispheres*, and *Internet Business*.

Des Dearlove is author of *The Ultimate Book of Business Thinking*, *Key Management Decisions* and co-author of *Architects of the Business Revolution*. Des has a long-established column in *The Times* where he has also been a commissioning editor. He also contributes to a variety of international publications including *The Industry Standard*, *Across the Board*, *Strategy & Business*, *Human Resources*, *Time*, *Silver Kris* and *Business 2.0*.

Stuart Crainer and Des Dearlove are the authors of *Generation Entrepreneur*, *Gravy Training*, *MBA Planet* and *The Ultimate Book of Business Brands*. They are editors of the *Financial Times Handbook of Management* and the founders of Suntop Media.

contents

acknowledgments

The original idea for *MBA Planet* came from the ever fertile mind of RIchard Stagg of Financial Times / Prentice Hall.

We were greatly aided in researching the book by Stephen Coomber who now knows more MBA students than anyone else on planet MBA.

Our colleague at Suntop Media, Georgina Peters, offered a constant stream of informed criticism and applied invective.

This book would not have been possible without the many students, former students and b-school employees who gave freely of their time. It's not possible to list them all but a special thank you to: Saud Abbasi, Zeyn Adam, Mike Allen, Jaime Antunez, Roberto Arana, Vicky Arcos, Andy Arends, Erik Barmack, Rajesh Bhatia, Susie Block, Jeff Bocan, Lauren Vanessa Buck, Alicia Bywater, Christopher H. Cheng, Christos Constandinides, Nolan Empalmado, Ram Fish, Roger Fortune, Jose Garza, Elizabeth Golluscio, Tim Gordon, Emily Granada, Andrew Grinstead, Eric Happel, Dan Harris, Katy Hart, Shannon Hawbaker, Mark Hicken, Jennifer Himelfarb, April Hingst, Megumi Ikeda, Bryan Jaffe, Brian Jaroszewski, Michael Jauss, Eelco de Jong, Virginia M. Justicz, Subramaniam Karthik, Marshall King, Jon Kinsey, Jennifer Lemming, Anu Mannar, Mark McDonald, Amit Mehra, Tony Micele, Joe Mitchoff, Mary E. Murphy, Charles Naylor, Julie Neenan, Mark Permann, Michele E. Previte, Peter O'Brien, Karen Roy, Alexis Rozman, Esther Schuller, Emmanuelle Skala, Kirill Slavin, Steven So, David Socks, Nancy Spector, Anne Therese Stephens, Sarita Talwar, Erin Toole, Nestor Torre, Mark Underwood, Robert Uyan, Michelle A. Veith, Cristobel von Walstrom, Adam Wellman, Pat Wilburn, Sean Lilly Wilson, Liz Zale.

We welcome comments from other MBA students for future editions of this book. Please send your comments to www.mbaplanet.com

introduction

Don't take the experience too personally. B-school culture requires making you feel privileged to get in, humbled by doubt in your ability to succeed, and confident in your superiority as a result of passing through the institution. It's a process that repeats itself every two years, regardless of whether you are in it or not.

CHICAGO STUDENT

A great deal has been said and written about the Master of Business Administration (MBA). It has been described as a 'union card' for senior management, and 'the greatest career step-up mechanism in the world'. These and other erudite phrases tripped off the tongues of deans of top b-schools in the course of our research. Deans, of course, are adept at talking up the MBA in general, and their own version of it in particular. It goes with the job. In this case, they are probably right. The MBA is a remarkable qualification.

In the business world the MBA is drooled over. Instant salivation. MBAs from the top schools are the golden graduates. They are wooed by the top companies; fought over by the leading consulting firms; and offered large joining bonuses by the richest investment banks. Failing a major recession, this is likely to remain the case for the foreseeable future. The popular image is of bright young men and women educated to the hilt who step off campus and into high-powered jobs.

The MBA, then, is a marvellous thing. It's a great way to improve your long-term career prospects. It facilitates job mobility, enhanced earning power, an entry into general management, a platform to switch careers, and a grounding in the latest business techniques and theories. It can also be a springboard for those who want to start their own businesses, or run the family business. Venture capitalists, too, like MBAs. A growing problem for them is the dearth of entrepreneurs with a solid knowledge of the basics of running and building a business. The MBA offers that knowledge on a salver. An MBA degree, in short, is a very useful piece of paper.

But the MBA is more than just a diploma and a headful of knowledge. It's a once-in-a-lifetime experience – and a real roller-coaster of one to boot. When we looked at the shelves of books devoted to the MBA we found they were full of directories, guides and other worthy tomes offering advice on how to choose the right course, prepare for the GMAT exam, and get the best job afterwards. Many were written by distinguished commentators on the subject. They quoted business school deans, leading recruiters, and even the occasional student. But what they didn't do was describe the MBA experience from the student's perspective. They didn't ask current students what it was really like, or how they managed the workload. They didn't ask them about shortcuts or tips to cope with the pressures of b-school life. They certainly didn't ask them about the social life, the partying, and the other aspects of b-school that make it such a challenging, mind-expanding – and, yes, fun – time. We set out to put that right.

The good, the bad, and *MBA planet*

Our idea was to write a rough guide for MBA students. A manual to help them not just survive but positively thrive in the pressure-cooker atmosphere of an MBA program. We wanted to know what the students really thought about their experiences – which courses were good, which were lousy. Which professors they rated highly, and which were duffers.

We wanted to understand how they approached their studies. Which classes they cut; how they bluffed their way through classes they hadn't prepared for. We also wanted to know how they balanced academic and extra-curricular activities; how they kept old friendships and personal relationships alive, while making new lifetime friends.

In short, we were curious about the whole MBA experience – from start to finish. Naturally, that included how they selected their schools, tackled the GMAT, and navigated the application maze. But there's more to it than that. We were curious about the expectations of b-school that today's students have, and their aspirations. How they reorganized

MBA aspirations change over time. The Fuqua School at Duke University is one of the few b-schools to track the views of MBA students. In 1987, when it first surveyed students, junk bond king Michael Milken was the most admired person in the world, and his company Drexel Burnham Lambert the most admired company. Milken has since spent a spell in prison. His current company Knowledge Universe is big in the education world.

For the last six years, the most admired person has been Bill Gates (whose wife Melinda went to Duke) with Microsoft the most admired company.

their lives in preparation for the MBA. How they coped with the culture shock in the first semester. How they got on with their fellow students. How they approached finding a job at the end of it all. And especially, what advice they had for those following in their footsteps.

Some of their comments confirmed the popular image of the MBA. Some did not. Some gave rave reviews of their schools, and their peers. 'I went into business school with the expectation that it would be an arduous experience with "I can't call my parents ever," "I'll never be able to afford to eat," type of ideas. It hasn't been like that at all. Of course, money is tight, but I've made great friends, I'm taking interesting classes, and I'm in a position to do whatever I want with my life,' said a Yale MBA. 'Chicago is a special place for special people. I have a wonderful social life, and have met many good friends,' said a Chicago student. Others were scathing. 'The level of academic difficulty here is a joke,' one Kellogg student told us. 'It's really made me question the quality of the American undergrad and high school education.' A student at Stern had this to say about his peers: 'The only thing that has failed to live up to my expectations is the attitude of many of my classmates. To my dismay many of them are suffering from a deficit of intellect and motivation.'

Harsh words. All in all, it paints a fascinating picture. If you're thinking about taking an MBA, we think you'll find it instructive.

Who did we ask?

We were selective. We contacted only students at the very top schools. These, we figured, were bright people; the elite of the MBA world. We talked to them on campus, and away from their schools, and we sent out copious e-mails, and generally tried to get under the skin of the top business schools. It was by turns a frustrating, entertaining, irritating, uplifting, time-consuming, and humbling experience. It convinced us that the average

MBA student we've been reading about for years does not exist. Far from being clones, we found that MBA students are a hugely diverse bunch. This is as it should be. The future business leaders must be drawn from a wide cross-section of society.

The trouble with b-schools is that many take a cookie cutter approach to MBA students. They get hold of bright people and then try to stamp the school emblem on their forehead. Too often they put their academic image above all else. They are so concerned about slipping a couple of notches in the rankings that they don't always take the opportunity to learn from their customers. They would like prospective students to feel awed by their impeccable credentials. As the quote at the start of this section suggests, students are supposed to feel honored if they are offered a place. We see it differently. We see a symbiotic relationship. Without good students, the top b-school would be no different from the second- and third-tier institutions. The top b-schools rely on attracting the brightest and best. It was their views that we sought.

The idea was to by-pass the schools themselves. To go straight to the people who really know – the students. They are the customers, after all. Some b-schools were concerned about our intentions. We had frosty replies from schools seeking to protect the privacy of their students. Our questions had been drawn to their attention by worried students. At least, that's what they said. We politely explained what we were doing and why. We told them that we wanted to communicate directly with their students, rather than have the schools filter their comments. As a result, the observations we received were uncensored by the powers that be. Many students had nothing but praise for their schools anyway. Others were less impressed. Some students were quizzical, too, about what we were up to. We explained and asked for their co-operation. We told them we would respect what they told us in confidence. That is a promise we have kept.

Many of the students who contributed to *MBA Planet* have yet to complete their courses. Their quotes are anonymous, as are those from former students who asked for their names to be withheld. In other instances, we have used our own judgment, preferring to err on the side of caution, if we felt that by identifying a student we might cause embarrassment to them or jeopardize their b-school careers. Embarrassing the schools is another matter.

MBA Planet examines the b-school experience through the eyes of the people who really matter – the students. It doesn't pretend to be a comprehensive directory of all the b-schools in the world – there's plenty of those already. Nor, for that matter, does it claim to be the last word on the MBA phenomenon. Rather, it is a snapshot of the views of MBA students today and a route map for the students of tomorrow.

We are grateful to those past and present b-school employees – from the dean down – who helped us in this endeavor. But most of all we'd like to thank all of the students who took time out from their busy schedules to talk to us, and who made this book possible. It goes without saying that the book's shortcomings are down to us. This is just the start. We hope, in time, to make *MBA Planet* the single most useful resource available to prospective MBAs. To make that a reality, we will depend on each new intake of students to tell us about their experiences. If you think it's a worthwhile endeavor, we'd appreciate your help.

So why not visit the MBA Planet community at www.mbaplanet.com, where you'll find a world of MBA advice and an opportunity to tell us, and those who follow you, more about the MBA experience.

www.mbaplanet.com
Stuart Crainer and Des Dearlove
August 2000

why do an MBA?

*The MBA is the most remarkable step-up mechanism
ever invented. Business schools take people of infinite
variety and give them a tremendous platform for
opportunity. If you do well, the opportunities are
fabulous. For a 25- or a 30-year-old, it's a great way
to change your life. There aren't too many
mechanisms around which allow that.*

PAUL DANOS, DEAN OF THE TUCK SCHOOL, AT DARTMOUTH COLLEGE

MBA magic

So, you think want to take an MBA? You want to turn your back on a good job and regular salary to bang your head against a bunch of books, with no guarantee of a job at the end of it? You want to go through the dislocation of packing your life up and moving to a new place, maybe halfway round the world, with no idea where you might end up? You're prepared to risk losing touch with your family and friends and putting incredible strain on your relationships with your nearest and dearest in order to meet a bunch of new people you aren't even sure you'll like? You want to give up a Monday through Friday existence, to study seven days a week? You want to step out of the world you know and into a twilight zone of case studies, assignments, and exams? You want to go back to school and be poor again? Worse, you want to borrow a shitload of money to do it and have a student loan hanging over you for years?

No one's forcing you. It's up to you. It's your decision. But are you sure you're up to it? It's a big step – especially at your age. You were just starting to find your feet and now you want to throw it all up in the air again. You're sure you want to do this? OK, just checking. If your mind's made up, you may as well get all the help you can. Others have walked the path that lies ahead of you. They'll tell you that the MBA is a rollercoaster ride. There are some good bits and some not so good bits. There are some long ways round and there are some shortcuts. This book aims to put you straight. Think of it as your personal rough guide to surviving and thriving at business school. Think of it as a friend – but a friend who doesn't pull her punches. Think of it as anything you like. Here's what it is: an amalgam of thoughts, comments, tips, warnings, and advice from former MBA students. They have no reason to kid you. Why not listen to what they've got to say? Who knows, they might just save you some time and trouble. Reinventing the wheel went out with the Stone Age.

First, the commercial break. In the pantheon of degree courses there has never been another qualification quite like the Master of Business Administration (MBA). It is, quite simply, the premier business qualification in the world. For those aspiring to a career in senior management, it has no equal. No other degree has its cachet, its glamor – or its mythology. If you want to crank up your career, switch jobs, or simply make more money, the MBA is the qualification for you.

Elevated from modest beginnings in the US in the early part of the century, today the MBA is the fastest growing postgraduate qualification in the world. Its appeal transcends national borders. In the past decade, the number of students graduating with MBAs in the UK, for example, has increased fourfold – from about 2,000 in 1986 to its current level of more than 8,000. But it is little more than a drop in the ocean compared to the number of MBAs graduating from North American schools each year.

Today, there are close to 1,000 business schools in North America offering the MBA qualification. In all, the American business schools now graduate between 80,000 and 90,000 MBA students every year, with another 20,000 graduated from schools in Europe and Asia. That means that more than 100,000 MBA graduates step off-campus and into the business world each and every year. That's a lot of people. Along the way, the MBA has become a career transformer – a stepping stone from a functional training into general management; a passport to job mobility; a union ticket to move between business sectors; and a grounding for a new breed of entrepreneurs who are themselves transforming the business landscape.

An MBA now figures prominently in the career plans of a growing number of high-flyers. For them, the question is no longer whether to do an MBA, but where and when. Many students no longer see the qualification purely in terms of climbing the career ladder. They see it as an opportunity for personal development – individual growth. Dot-com mania, too, has gripped the imagination. That will pass, but the fundamental changes that it represents are likely to be more lasting. Many of the fundamentals of business are still as important as, or more important than, they ever were. But the changing business environment, the rise of the internet and the new entrepreneurial *Zeitgeist*, also makes understanding new issues arising from e-business and the new economy essential. The traditional MBA is having to adapt to remain relevant. The fact is that companies, even traditional old-economy employers, now require managers who are more entrepreneurial. At the same time, shifts in employment patterns and changes to the business landscape mean that permanent jobs and the old career ladder itself are increasingly under pressure.

A growing proportion of MBA students now want to start their own businesses, or join new companies. Business start-ups are now attracting many of the best and brightest minds.

Says a Fuqua student: 'Old-guard companies (insurance, industrial, consumer goods) that don't project an innovative, forward-thinking image have had – and will have – little success in recruiting at Fuqua. The new economy has told us that creativity and innovation don't come from paying your dues or climbing up the corporate ladder – just the opposite. And that's not going to change anytime soon.'

The stampede to the new economy may be over stated. But it does highlight important changes both to the curriculum and to the aspirations of students.

The MBA has continued to evolve as the business world has evolved. Today that evolution has turned to revolution. The new challenges posed by e-commerce, e-learning, e-strategy, e-marketing and the like, are forcing business schools to re-evaluate and revise the traditional MBA. But amid the noisy hype that accompanies the new economy, many of the basics remain the same. In the frenzy that surrounded the dot-com gold rush, MBAs continued to be taught arcane but useful business first principles. Unfashionable concepts such as cash flow management, return on investment, and the p-word – profits – were drummed into students. But new subjects were also added: e-commerce, e-marketing, e-strategy, e-just-about-anything-you-care-to-think-of.

The MBA: past, present and future

Some history. Amid the fireworks celebrating the new millennium, the MBA slipped quietly into its second century. The forerunners of the modern MBA were created at the start of the twentieth century by the newly established US business schools. Back then, the likes of Harvard Business School, the Wharton School at the University of Pennsylvania, and the Graduate School of Industrial Administration at Carnegie Mellon University were pioneers. The very idea of academic institutions dedicated to training young managers was a novelty. Many in the fusty world of academia raised their eyebrows at the very notion of management as an academic discipline. (Some still do.) The early courses the business schools taught became the basis of management as we know it today. The emphasis then was on finance.

The new schools, many of them inside famous universities, had a mission. They wanted to create a science of business which would lay the foundations for a new profession. In short, they wanted to put management on the map. The MBA became the embodiment of that aspiration.

In 2000, the Tuck School of Business at Dartmouth College in New Hampshire celebrated its centenary. Today Tuck is one of America's blue-chip business schools. When it was founded in 1900, Tuck was the first graduate school of management in the world (the first recognizable business school was the Wharton School at the University of Pennsylvania, founded in 1881). In that same year Tuck offered the first ever graduate program in management. Although not an MBA in name, Tuck awarded the first postgraduate business degree in 1902. (Originally it was a 'three two' program, with three years' undergraduate study at Dartmouth followed by two years at Tuck.) It paved the way for the modern MBA.

For its centennial year, Tuck found itself in the happy position of selecting from 3,000 applicants to fill 191 MBA places. A lot's changed since those first students enrolled at Tuck, but the core subjects would have been familiar to those early management scholars. 'They would have learned accounting, marketing, managing people, and other basic disciplines,' says Paul Danos, dean of Tuck. 'The program was surprisingly international even then. There were language courses and courses in international finance. In a sense, it was quite global at that time – more global than a lot of programs that came after.'

The subjects may seem similar, but the context has changed beyond all recognition. Its growing popularity and changes to the business environment have transformed the way business education is taught. One school in particular had a huge impact on the evolution of the MBA – Harvard Business School was founded in 1908, and awarded its first master's degree in management in 1910. For decades it led the way. This started with the development of the case study method, which was established in 1924, and was later exported around the globe.

Interest grew rapidly. Among American schools, the next 60 years were characterized by an attempt to bring academic rigor into both business school research and the classroom. In the 1950s and 1960s, the classic two-year American MBA model established itself both at home and further afield. The first year was devoted to the core disciplines and the second year offered more specialization through a choice of electives. Originally, most students enrolled immediately after taking a first degree. That is now changing, as more US schools insist on some work experience prior to taking an MBA.

The Harvard case study method (an approach which originated in the law schools) started the move to more experiential learning, something that has been built on by other schools. 'The big waves were the move to using real case studies, which allowed students to apply what they had learned,' says Tuck's Danos. 'Then in more modern times the big change has been to more experiential learning through real projects with real clients.'

In Europe, however, a different sort of MBA model emerged. INSEAD was started in Paris in 1958 by a former member of the Harvard faculty, and this international business school is now based at Fontainebleau. IMD, based at Lausanne in Switzerland, traces its origins back to 1946. In the UK, Henley, Ashridge and Cranfield were joined by London and Manchester Business Schools (LBS and MBS) in 1965. But although some of the new schools copied the two-year American model, a distinctively practical European approach was apparent at schools like INSEAD and IMD. They eschewed the US model in favor of a one-year MBA program aimed at students with some work experience under their belt.

European schools placed much greater emphasis on work experience prior to entering their MBA programs. As a result, students at these schools tended to be slightly older, with a minimum of two or three years of management experience. The European schools also included a more practical focus, with many including in-company projects as an integral part of the MBA qualification. American schools, by contrast, were more concerned about participants' academic ability, placing greater emphasis on high GMAT scores and often accepting applicants with little or no work experience.

The 1960s and 1970s were characterized by two different approaches. The American schools continued to pursue academic kudos, while the continental European schools concentrated on staying close to the real world of business.

By the end of the 1970s, the MBA had cemented its place, but its apotheosis came in the 1980s boom. Suddenly it seemed that recruiters couldn't get enough of the new business school graduates. The inevitable recession that followed in the early 1990s restored a semblance of reality. Since then the gap between the top American and European schools has begun to close. Schools such as LBS and INSEAD are investing more in research, while US schools are trying to get closer to the corporate world.

Technology has also brought changes through the addition of distance-learning. 'The evolution has meant not only a change in delivery but also in study material – there has been a switch to live case studies from the traditional case study material,' says Professor Colin Eden, director of the Strathclyde Graduate Business School in the UK.

The student profile has also changed. Success has upped the ante for MBA applicants. Landis Gabel is the associate dean of the MBA program at INSEAD. He took his MBA at Wharton in 1967. According to Gabel, the growing stature of the MBA now attracts the very brightest students.

The competition to get into the top schools has become much more intense. When I applied to do my MBA at Wharton in the late 1960s, a lot of the really smart people were applying to Law School or Med School. Now I think the top business schools draw from among the very best of the cohorts. Students have also gotten older. Twenty years ago, most US schools were looking at students straight from college. I was 22 when I took my MBA. Now the average age is older. INSEAD has always attracted older students, but the average age now is 29. At the US schools, too, students are coming with more business experience and more life experience.

Paul Danos agrees: 'The original MBA programs were for people straight out of college. One of the biggest changes in recent years is that the top US schools have now gone for a work experience requirement. The average age of an MBA student is now 27 years old. That's a gigantic change.'

According to Danos, however, there has been a more fundamental shift in the classroom.

The biggest change is the notion of working and learning in teams. If you went back to the early days of business education you'd find people working as individuals. Today, much of the learning is done in teams. The shift is from passive classroom learning to working with other people who have different strengths. That reflects what happens in the real world of work.

Through it all, the core MBA subjects have remained surprisingly unchanged. The basics of marketing, operations, organizational behavior, finance, and strategy endure. 'If you look at the curriculum, in a sense it really hasn't changed that much,' notes INSEAD's Gabel. 'The core of a business education is still pretty much the same. You learn some pretty enduring principles. In 1967, I took a couple of math and stats courses, a couple of marketing courses, a couple of accounting courses, some organizational behavior courses and a bunch of electives. What has changed is the electives. Thirty years ago there weren't e-commerce or entrepreneurship courses.'

Talking to MBA students the change of emphasis is clear. 'In the past MBA students wrote their strategy reports on traditional industries, most of ours are on start-ups,' says one American studying at INSEAD. 'A company like Amazon.com gets people excited.' Indeed it does. Whether it will continue to arouse MBA passions or become a case study of an early new economy road-kill remains to be seen.

Why do people take an MBA?

The reasons for taking an MBA are as diverse as the people who enrol. Many students take a broad view of what an MBA will do for them, seeing it as a career anchor in the choppy waters of change. For some it's an easy decision. 'For me, it was a no-brainer as I was sort of in a go-nowhere job and have quadrupled my salary in two years, but there are others who were making close to or over one hundred thousand dollars a year who give that up for the allure of the MBA,' explains one Chicago MBA.

For many the primary drive is to create the classic bridgehead to move from a specialized discipline into general management. A student at Vanderbilt University's Owen School, for example, wanted to break out of a functional role: 'After six years in marketing, I realized that I wanted to make a change in my career. As a math major in undergrad, I had little exposure to the business world and was unsure of the choices that were available to me. Business school was a perfect opportunity to see a wide range of professions and careers. I also determined that unlike other graduate degrees, an MBA would quickly pay for itself after graduation.'

'I was an engineer at Intel and was getting involved in project management roles; I liked the multifarious responsibilities of the teams in which I became involved. I thought formal business training would help me to move from engineering or engineering management to more of a strategic management role,' says a Tuck student.

For others an MBA represented a natural career progression, like the Haas (Berkeley) student who told us: 'I came to business school with a specific purpose. While I was a change management professional in Andersen Consulting, I saw the importance of business acumen for doing strategic human resources work. I immediately identified that business school was the fastest and best way to expand my knowledge of business areas such as finance, accounting, operations, and so on, so that I may continue successfully with my career.'

Some are seeking to switch careers, or sectors: 'I wanted to make new opportunities for myself. B-school seemed like a great way to transition from the public sector to the private sector,' says a University of Michigan student.

For others it's more to do with filling in gaps in their earlier education and professional experience. 'I decided to go to business school because I knew that I needed to round out my understanding of business. Sounds simple, I know. But, I studied international politics and political economy as an undergraduate and a graduate student, and I worked as an information systems consultant. At work, I realized that the analytical and strategic thinking that I brought to any discussion about international politics should be extendable to discussions of business strategy, but that I lacked the skills and tools to do this. So, I went back to school to learn about marketing, finance, and strategy in order to better understand why companies choose certain strategic directions,' reports a student at MIT Sloan.

For others this is combined with other motives. 'I decided to go to business school for a variety of reasons. However, two stand out,' one MBA student at Chicago told us.

One, I was unsatisfied with my undergraduate education. I didn't learn the important concepts and business skills to be employed by the best companies, even to get in the door. That is an indictment of the classes I had and the reputation of the school I attended. Second, the business I was working for went through financial distress, winding up in bankruptcy and eventually liquidation. The important point of that story is the business was a family business and I couldn't do anything to see the problems coming, nor could I do anything when those problems arose. I didn't have the financial, accounting, or marketing skills to help the company change direction, see problems ahead of time, and return to profitability. And I wanted desperately to help if the situation ever arises again.

Some regard it as the chance to get serious, and consolidate their careers. 'My career had been very diverse and I felt the need to bring it together,' said a student at London Business School. While for others it is the natural precursor to starting their own business. 'I chose to go to business school in order to learn enough about business to start my own,' says a student at Columbia.

Others are simply widening their horizons. 'I decided to go to b-school because I had been working in the internet space for four years and was a little weary of all the buzz and hype surrounding this field,' explains a Stanford student. 'I figured that if I ever wanted to switch careers, an MBA made sense. I figured that if I ever wanted to start a company, an MBA would help me raise capital. And I guessed that if I ever wanted to work abroad, I'd need contacts and credibility … In short, unless I wanted to continue to do exactly what I was doing, I saw an MBA as a way of expanding my options, yes? Also, I am currently developing a business idea that's essentially an aggregation play on all the fanzines out there like yidtalk.net.'

You don't have to know why. Others have even less clearly defined goals. 'B-school was never my aspiration, I wanted to go to medical school. I decided at one point that it wasn't for me, and there was a period of time that I had no idea where I was going. My cousin suggested I apply to b-school. I thought about it, and it made sense to me, because an MBA is a good degree to have, I can do a lot with it, it's only two years, and it will be easier to find a job with it. I'm looking forward to second year, because I will have much more free time, and I am looking forward to being involved with school more,' a student at Ivey told us.

It was ever thus. It is surprising how many people admit to taking an MBA because they simply couldn't think of what else to do. 'Why did I decide to get one? I was in a pickle and it was the best way out that I could think of,' says Peter Robinson, former speech writer for President Reagan, and author of *Snapshots From Hell*, a chronicle of his MBA experience at Stanford. 'I had spent six years in the White House, most of the 1980s. Good friends had gone on to law school, gone on to business school, gotten established in journalism, and I had gotten established as a Presidential speechwriter, and there's just not much of a market for them. I thought about going to law school; read, in fact, Scott Turow's book, *One L*, which helped to persuade me that law school was not for me.'[1]

Robinson wasn't the first – and certainly won't be the last – to fall into business school simply for the wont of any better ideas. Management guru Tom Peters did much the same 20-odd years before. 'I didn't know what to do after the Navy. I didn't have any better ideas than doing an MBA,' he says. It was a move not exactly fired by a burning interest in the subject he would be studying. 'I went to business school because that's what people were doing. My half-dozen best friends had decided the MBA was hot. The MBA became a popular phenomenon at the time and two-thirds of my buddies went to Harvard,' says Peters.

While most b-school students are not drifters who find themselves reading Porter on competitiveness because they haven't the wit to think of something better to do with their lives, nor are they right-wing, market forces fanatics. Those that slip onto MBA programs are less inclined to be capitalist ideologues than was once reputedly the case. If current MBA students remember Gordon Gekko at all, they are more likely to criticize than idolize him. Indeed, business ethics is now a core part of many MBA programs – a change the schools say has been driven by student demand. Outside classrooms, too, the talk is more likely to be about 'stakeholders' and 'corporate citizenship' than 'asset stripping'.

The 1980s created a mythology which now bears little relation to reality. 'The idea of the grasping MBA is a caricature,' says George Bain, former dean of the London Business School. 'There are a few exceptions of course. On the whole, though, most people who take an MBA are career-changers. They want to have an experience that will change their lives.'

Today's applicants see business school as more than simply a place to have their ticket punched as they pass through on their way to a better job. Gruelling as the MBA workload is, where once they thought only of staying the distance, a growing number of today's students want to enjoy the ride as well. Increasingly, it is more than just the promise of a salary hike down the road that motivates them. The opportunity to re-discover student life, meet new people, and take some time out for themselves has special resonance for many.

To some extent, this may reflect the older age profile of today's MBA students. Many have notched up enough years at work to make them appreciate the pleasures of student life. One recent survey of MBA students found that the typical MBA student is now more likely to be in their early 30s than in their 20s; is likely to hold a first degree in engineering, social sciences, or life sciences; and to have between six and twelve years' work experience under their belt.

Not surprisingly, among this group, the two most popular reasons given for taking an MBA were to 'enhance marketability and salary', and to 'facilitate a change in career'. Important as they are, however, it seems these factors are only part of the story. A number of students talked about 'personal fulfillment' and the desire to 'continue study' as important motivations.

It is a universally acknowledged truth that every ambitious manager is in need of an MBA. Well, actually, not quite. Over the years, business schools and the MBA in particular have attracted their fair share of critics. Take these asides on the merits of the top French school, INSEAD, and its reputation for working students until they are ready to drop. 'INSEAD is the most high-powered finishing school in the world. Most MBAs find the time to ride in the forest of Fontainebleau, perfect their skiing and negotiate their way around a wine list,' noted one article in, of all places, the society magazine, *Harpers & Queen.*[2]

One European telecommunications company CEO quipped: 'They are all graduated like identical bunny rabbits. They are very charming, very personable, very intelligent, and incapable of actually doing anything. INSEAD graduates are like robots. Their brains seem to be disconnected from their bodies.' Another critic at a London investment bank said: 'They are totally obsessed by process. We try not to hire them but they infiltrate the place as consultants.'[3]

Another source of criticism is, predictably enough, people who have been successful without attending a business school. Their homespun wisdom usually regurgitates the university of life argument in one form or another. 'I am not impressed by diplomas. They don't do the work. My marks were not as good as those of others, and I didn't take the final examination. The principal called me in and said I have to leave. I told him that I didn't want a diploma. They had less value than a cinema ticket. A ticket at least guaranteed that you would get in. A diploma guaranteed nothing,' said Soichiro Honda, founder of Honda.[4]

With surprising understatement, former Chrysler CEO, Lee Iacocca noted: 'Formal learning can teach you a great deal, but many of the essential skills in life are the ones you have to develop on your own.' More opinionated was the late Avis chief and author of *Up the Organization,* Robert Townsend. 'Don't hire Harvard Business School graduates,' he warned. 'This elite, in my opinion, is missing some pretty fundamental requirements for success: humility; respect for people in the firing line; deep understanding of the nature of the business and the kind of people who can enjoy themselves making it prosper; respect from way down the line; a demonstrated record of guts, industry, loyalty down, judgment, fairness, and honesty under pressure.'

More recently, Bill Gates, Virgin's Richard Branson and the Body Shop's Anita Roddick have all been much quoted examples of those who missed out on business school but went on to reach the summits of business success. 'A great advantage I had when I started the Body Shop was that I had never been to business school,' says Anita Roddick. (Interestingly, Roddick helped create a quasi-business school, the New Academy of Business.) Similarly, 1-800-Flowers founder, Jim McCann, says that the company would have not got off the ground if he'd been to business school – 'I would have thought too much about why the deal couldn't be done,' says McCann.[5]

What is more surprising is that some of the most vituperative criticism comes from business school insiders. Oddly enough you won't find their comments in MBA brochures. The strategy guru Henry Mintzberg is a long-term critic of MBA programs (despite teaching at McGill in Canada and France's INSEAD – though not on MBA programs). 'The idea that you can take smart but inexperienced 25-year-olds who have never managed anything or anybody and turn them into effective managers via two years of classroom training is ludicrous,' he says.[6]

The venerable Peter Drucker is another long-term critic of business schools. 'The business schools in the US, set up less than a century ago, have been preparing well-trained clerks,' he wrote as long ago as 1969.[7] More recently, he has predicted the decline of business schools noting that, 'Business schools are suffering from premature success. Now, they are improving yesterday a little bit. The worst thing is to improve what shouldn't be done at all.' To finish the demolition, Drucker has roundly dismissed Harvard: 'Harvard, to me, combines the worst of German academic arrogance with bad American theological seminary habits.' Drucker, who sees himself as an outsider, has eschewed the well-worn route to business school faculty life. Instead he prefers the relative obscurity of California's Claremont College.[8]

Is the MBA still the best option?

The MBA remains the classic business school qualification. A key strength is that it is a general degree, designed to provide an overview of all the different business functions. But the growth in e-business raises important issues for the classic MBA. Some see the new economy as a potential threat to the future of the MBA. Clearly the new economy raises important issues for business schools, including whether the traditional MBA offers the right training, and whether business school professors can keep up with a new generation of business hotshots.

Take people like Glen Meakem, chairman, CEO and co-founder of the Pittsburgh-based company FreeMarkets. After working at Kraft General Foods, Meakem took an MBA at Harvard, graduating in 1991. After graduation, he joined McKinsey and Company. In 1994, he left the consulting firm to become manager of the corporate business development group at GE. Today, FreeMarkets is one of the most successful b2b marketplaces on the web. Basically, a reverse-auction site for industrial buyers and sellers, the company has facilitated the sale of $7.6 billion worth of goods, including $2.2 billion in the second quarter of 2000. Analysts predict it could turn a profit by 2002. Meakem's vision dates back to the early days of the net. While working for GE in 1994, Meakem witnessed the chaos and inefficiency of industrial auctions, where suppliers of custom-made machinery parts and other items were bought and sold. He came up with the idea of FreeMarkets and pitched it to GE. But the mighty GE passed on it. So, in 1995, when Priceline.com was barely a glint in Jay Walker's eye, Meakem and Sam Kinney, a former McKinsey colleague, set up FreeMarkets.

The straight, plain vanilla, no frills MBA is no longer the only option. Frills abound. Today there are specialist masters to consider, too. For example, the UK's Ashridge Management College launched a Masters in Organization Consulting in September 1998; Strathclyde Graduate Business School launched an MSc in Leadership in 1999.

Be aware, too, that there is some debate at present over whether the MBA should remain a general degree or take on a more specialized focus. There are a growing number of specialized variations on the market, including programs which are MBAs in name but are aimed at specific industries and disciplines.

A growing number of b-schools are joining the specialist-MBA parade, especially in Europe. These include some curious recent additions. Italy's most famous business school SDA Bocconi offers an MBA with specializations in fashion and design, for example, while British schools offer MBA degrees in church management (Lincoln) and soccer (Liverpool).

Others are more mainstream. In 1997, City University in London began offering an MBA with a specialist stream in the management of technology. Manchester Business School (MBS), which launched an MBA for lawyers in 1997, will begin a new MBA in entrepreneurship for owner-managed and small or medium-sized enterprises next January.

In Holland, Nijenrode is launching a new Financial and Insurance Services MBA, a two-year program that takes students – who must have ten years' work experience – to other campuses in Europe, including the De Vlerick School voor Management at the University of Ghent, Belgium.

But schools in other parts of the world, for example, are also going for specialization. In North America, joint degrees are a fact of life – Montreal's McGill University has offered a five-year medicine and management program, or MD-MBA, since 1996. Nanyang Business School in Singapore has an MBA with specializations in accountancy, banking and finance, business law, hospitality, and tourism management. Where general management lies amid this profusion of specialist knowledge is increasingly difficult to determine.

The profile of MBA students is changing as a new generation of ambitious young managers pack their bags and head for b-school. 'Fifty years ago MBAs dreamed of running General Motors; ten years ago they dreamed of working at Goldman Sachs; five years ago it was McKinsey. Now they dream about running their own company,' Antonio Borges, the former dean of INSEAD told us recently. He's right. In particular, many MBAs are hungry to join new-economy start-ups. Market corrections mean that, for now, some of the fizz has gone out of the dot-com bottle, but the party is far from over. The TMT sector (technology, media and telecoms) is set to remain a major engine of economic growth for the foreseeable future. The MBAs we spoke to want – or more accurately, expect and demand – to be a part of that.

In the corridors of business schools today the talk is all about e-commerce and the internet. In the library and in the student bar, MBA students huddle around lap tops, and speculate about the new wealth creators or their business plans. The buzz is palpable. Where once they coveted a job with a Wall Street star like Goldman Sachs or a place among the consulting elite of McKinsey or Bain, many now want to work for Yahoo!, Amazon.com or Dell. Many have an e-commerce business plan of their own, and dream of creating their own online empire. 'There was a time when all the smart MBAs went into consulting and investment banking,' observes Professor William Sahlman of Harvard Business School. 'Now they're becoming entrepreneurs or zipping off to Silicon Valley to join an existing team, where they can turn the cranks and pull the levers that make the new economy thrive.'

Statistics confirm the shift. In 1998, nearly one-third of MBA graduates from Harvard Business School joined high tech or venture capital companies. In 1995 the figure was a mere 12 per cent. Even recent stock market jitters have done little to damp down the enthusiasm. Research in the US suggests e-commerce will rise to $64 billion in Europe alone by 2001, from $1.2 billion in 1998. A US Department of Commerce report predicts nearly half the American labour force will be employed by IT producers or heavy users by 2006.

This raises a number of issues for business schools, including whether the traditional MBA offers the right training for the internet economy, and whether business school professors can keep up with a new generation of business hotshots. In America, which leads the e-commerce race, big name schools such as Stanford, MIT and Harvard act as magnets for venture capitalists. These and others are vying with each other to convince students that they are the most progressive in this exciting new area. The Haas School of Business at Berkeley pioneered the idea of a business incubator to help MBA students launch their own internet business. Others schools are following suit.

At the same time, US schools have been beefing up the e-commerce content of the MBA program. There are two basic approaches: bolt-on electives in specialist areas such as e-commerce and the internet; and the integration of on-line business practice into the core syllabus – for example, studying e-commerce business models as part of the strategy module. At present, most schools do a little of both. They are also ramping up opportunities for students to develop their own business plans, including business plan competitions.

In Europe, LBS and Cranfield School of Management have created business incubators for MBA students. The aim is to create a launch pad for internet businesses.

The Cranfield incubator – with the trendy title CranfieldCreates.com – which became fully operational in 2000, supports students with internet business ideas to launch and beyond. Start-ups benefit from shared office space at the Cranfield Innovation Centre, prototype web design and hosting; and access to seed finance through a network of business angels and venture capitalists. Says Gerard Burke, seconded full-time from Information Systems Group to lead the incubator: 'The excitement surrounding e-business is not just hype. It stems from recognition of its vital role in all our futures. The new incubator is all about doing it for real, rather than taking a course. The only business school with something similar is Berkeley in California.'

Elsewhere, students are organizing themselves. For example, London Business School MBA students formed an E-Club to co-ordinate and promote entrepreneurship within the School. LBS graduates can apply to Sussex Place Investment, a corn seed fund available to London University graduates and backed by major banks. Professor Stephen Drew, recently recruited from America by Henley Management College to lead a new 'e-lective' in e-commerce, is another who believes the impact of the internet requires an urgent response. 'Most schools are trailing along in its wake because it has happened very quickly and business schools, like many institutions, resist change and are short of resources, time and skills. The UK schools are probably ahead of the Europeans, but lagging on the North Americans. We are in a catch-up situation – which is both an opportunity and a threat.'

Drew believes that schools that don't respond quickly risk being left behind. 'I would expect to see e-commerce as a key part of the MBA curriculum at most reputable schools in the UK within two years. Those who fail to follow suit will lose students and reputation.'

Some schools major on the technology dimension. At City University Business School, a specialist MBA (e-business) focuses on the business implications of new technology. The course builds on the work of previous years in assessing the business value of each new wave of IT developments. But there is another part of the dot-com equation for business schools. After years of assiduously building relationships with multinationals, bankers and consulting firms, they now have to reach out to the companies leading the new economy – and increasingly to venture capitalists – and convince them to recruit their MBAs.

For many venture capitalists, the influx of professionally trained managers in the dot-com world can't happen quickly enough. 'Like movie plots, there's a finite number of business plans – probably about eight,' says David Hart, of London-based Brainspark, one of Europe's leading incubators. 'A successful company needs a good idea, but success has more to do with the management team.' This will be music to MBA ears.

B-school: good and bad

The general consensus among students, not surprisingly, is that taking an MBA is a thoroughly worthwhile way to spend a couple of years. There are some sacrifices involved, naturally, but most of those we spoke to said it was an enriching experience – in more ways than one.

We asked them what, if anything, has failed to live up to their expectations? Many said the experience had exceeded their expectations. 'Before business school, I thought that an MBA was sort of a hardship someone had to go through so he/she could get the degree at the end of the two years and get a better paid job. Very untrue. It is a time of transformation and personal development, education, network building and a lot of fun,' says a Haas student.

'Business school has completely exceeded my expectations. And that is not something I say very often. It is an all-consuming, overwhelming experience. The intensity makes it hard and valuable at the same time. You learn more than the academics – if you open yourself to the possibilities,' says another at the Fuqua School at Duke University.

Others admitted they were less than ecstatic about some aspects of the program, or had mixed emotions. 'I expected more from my fellow students – to be more aggressive in pushing the envelope in class discussions. On the flip side, I learned more from my professors than I expected to – largely due to their personal experience, and the high number of opportunities to interact outside the classroom on projects and in extra-curricular activities. Socially – it has been great.'

Don't kid yourself, taking an MBA is not an easy option. Along with the grind of academic work, there are sacrifices to be made. For some people these are about short-term financial hardship, while for others the downside is all about relationships with old friends and partners. Comments from students confirm that the experience is not without its downsides:

> The personal sacrifices are all about foregone salaries. – MIT student

> Long distance relationships are tough, and in fact, most of the people I know who came here with girlfriends/boyfriends back home have subsequently broken up despite their best intentions. Business school, specifically the first year, becomes all encompassing and at times, you don't even realize its happening. – Chicago student

> I left an exciting, lucrative career, moved to Boston (my fiancée is in New York). I feel, however that the sacrifices will be worth it in the long run. – Harvard student

> The obvious ones of moving across the country and sitting on the sidelines for two years while the business world motors on. I guess also being in b-school forces you into an early midlife crisis (why am I here? why am I even in business?). – Stanford student

> Obviously, I had to sacrifice two years of salary. Beyond that, I had to give up movies on the weekend and days spent reading novels. But the rewards I've received (both academically and personally) have far outweighed the sacrifices. – Owen student

> You'll spend much less time with old friends and family members, at least at first. And you'll probably be somewhat cash constrained. – Columbia student

> Giving up two years of income and, being away from my fiancée. Life without a television. – forlorn Michigan student

> Some people give up sleep. – Michigan student

One or two felt uncomfortable being scrutinized by their fellow students. One woman at Chicago said the worst part was: 'Being watched. The conservative student-body of 20-somethings is starved for gossip. Sixty per cent of the first-years live in the same building and watch each other. Available, single women are under 10 per cent of the student body. As a result, potential gossip curbs public behavior. Regardless of my three-year relationship with my boyfriend, I've been reported as having sex with classmates and my current male room-mate.'

The same student also found surprising benefits: 'Best part? No wait in the Ladies rest room, any time.'

Criticism from others revolved around academic life. 'Due to the free market that determines class availability, I was "shut out" for three of my six quarters of bidding. In other words, I was unsuccessful in winning the classes that I wanted and I had to scramble among left-over classes to get a schedule. Bidding impacted my ability to secure classes of interest,' says a Harvard student.

Those expecting a vacation were also disappointed. 'I thought I'd have more personal time to hike, ski, etc. but I've found it very easy to get oversubscribed in both academics and activities. But that's not a problem for everyone I suppose,' reports a Tuck student.

More profound criticism was also offered. 'Too many people (faculty and students) believe that there is a quantifiable answer to everything – that all subjects are either black or white … or perhaps black and red, if you know what I mean. I expected a more healthy discussion of the gray issues, a sort of a liberal arts school environment where groups of students debate issues of interest. Whether it's that we're too busy or the mindset of students is more analytical than philosophical, I don't know. I had just hoped for more enlightened, thoughtful – and even perhaps contentious – discussions about the real issues facing our world,' says a philosophical Fuqua student.

Not everyone wants to learn, either. 'Some of the students don't seem to take it very seriously, and that bugs me. So many people surf the web throughout every class and don't participate at all. I expected to learn from some of my classmates, but that hasn't really happened as much as I'd hoped,' reports a Columbia student.

'From an academic standpoint, there's a pressure to make everything quantitative (classwise). Although this isn't bad, it puts pressure on someone like myself who isn't inclined to work that way. Socially, the only possibly negative thing I can say is that Yale can be kind of cliquish (if that's a word),' says a student at Yale. (And we're not sure that it is.)

Another Chicago student seemed to sum it up: 'I didn't come from a background where people went to business school, so I had no idea what to expect when I got here. Standing back a minute, I have spent two years in a great city, had a breadth of wonderful classes (a few clunkers in there, but everyone has those), made some great friends and forged strong relationships, got a good summer internship and a great permanent job, and have improved the potential of my future life a million times by just spending the ninety thousand dollars to get the degree, which I will make up in three years of working at a great job anyway. There are people who claim not to have learned that much or didn't get the job they wanted or had trouble making lasting friendships, but I believe those very few people are the outliers, not the norm.'

Endnotes

1   TV interview with Peter Robinson.

2   *Harpers & Queen,* October 1997.

3   'INSEAD: is its MBA any good?', *The European,* 2 October 1997.

4   Crainer, Stuart (editor), *The Ultimate Book of Business Quotations,* AMACOM, New York, 1998.

5   Bruce, Katherine, 'How to succeed in business without an MBA', *Forbes,* 26 January 1998.

6   Mintzberg, Henry, 'The new management mind-set', *Leader to Leader*, Spring 1997.

7   Drucker, Peter, *The Age of Discontinuity*, Heinemann, London, 1969.

8   The feeling is mutual. Academia has not embraced Drucker. 'Only now in my very old age has academia been willing to accept me,' he says.

which b-school?

The differences between the top schools have to do first and foremost with culture. That is, where and how do you want to live (city, suburb, or rural hamlet) and who you want to live and study with. The answers to these questions more than any other should determine where you choose to go to school.

COLUMBIA STUDENT

Buying the brand

Choosing the right MBA program is a complex process. It depends on many factors, including future plans. The changing business environment makes it vital for students to ensure that their chosen course fits their longer-term aims. 'The question for prospective students is what is their life plan?' says Antonio Borges, the former dean of INSEAD. The questions couldn't be much bigger.

Think of it as due diligence. Familiar to venture capitalists, due diligence is the examination of an investment proposition, lasting for a period of several months. There are two distinct phases to the due diligence process. The first is a rough analysis of the business plan or prospect (or MBA program). It is at this point that the prospect stands the most chance of being rejected. Rejection may be because it is not a good fit with the VC's investment strategy. Or the VC firm may not think much of the longer-term prospects.

If the business survives the rough analysis there will be a closer inspection of all the elements of the business plan. This includes examining the financial and technological aspects of the new venture as well as interviewing the management team. Since you're considering a major investment in an MBA, it's not a bad way to view target b-schools. Your professor of entrepreneurship would approve. (And if there isn't such a professor don't bother applying.)

As the business school market has become more mature, the leading employers have become much more selective about which schools they recruit from – a fact that students are only too aware of when they apply. Choosing an MBA course is a bit like choosing a car. Much depends on how fast you want to go, how much money you have to spend, and what you plan to do with it later. As with cars, too, other people – especially employers – put great store in the badge on the hood. With competition for places intensifying, getting into the top schools is getting tougher all the time.

An MBA from a top school carries more clout with employers and peers than one from a lesser-known institution. (Obvious, we admit.) The cost tends to reflect that. Just as cars have the same basic components – four wheels, engine, and steering wheel – the same is true of MBAs. Programs consist of core management subjects including finance, marketing, economics, IT and organizational behavior, and a choice of optional extras called electives. Finally, there is usually a dissertation or an in-company project. The business school brand is the added extra which can make the difference.

With more and more MBA graduates out there, choosing the right school is increasingly important. Schools also have strong associations with certain disciplines. Kellogg, for example, is highly regarded for marketing. Chicago is famous for turning out number crunchers. INSEAD prides itself on being international. The London Business School is renowned for finance and global strategy. The Sloan School at MIT is big on the technology side, e-business, and has a good name for finance. Columbia, too, is strong in finance, but is also associated with real estate and entrepreneurship (and has good links with media and film schools). Stanford excels in all things new economy, while Californian neighbor Anderson is big on the entertainment industry and entrepreneurship.

Business school reputations are all important. It's the same with all branded products; and make no mistake, it's branded products that the top business schools sell. The top schools talk about teaching quality and internationalism as if they are a magic dust that's sprinkled on their products to differentiate them from other providers. If the business school experience was just about the learning, then a student could go to one of the many up and coming business schools in Europe, Asia or the US. In terms of the teaching, some are probably as good as their more famous brethren. But to get the luster of real business school gold, you have to go to a school with a big name. If there's a mantra for the business school applicant who wants to ride the career elevator it has to be: reputation, reputation, reputation.

The top schools put a great deal of effort into their marketing. Lavish brochures and showcase events are just part of the pageantry. The trouble is that the wrapping can sometimes get in the way of the content. The discerning MBA hopeful should look beyond the marketing. The top schools attract the top faculty. That's a fact of academic life. They also confer stature on their alumni.

As a result, the famous business schools are sensitive about what is written about them. Deans have been known to call journalists to petition for more coverage. They can also turn nasty if they don't like the coverage they do get. Business schools live on their reputations more than most organizations. They know that it's the school's credibility (and the size of its MBA program) that will bring the top recruiters onto campus – recruiters like to fish where they know there are well-stocked rivers. But the process starts well before graduation. The top schools attract the brightest applicants. They also offer the key to the killer networks.

It is reputation, too, that will ensure the investment lasts. What really matters with a business school qualification is that it keeps its currency. No one wants to pay all that money, go through all that pain, all those late nights, to find that a few years down the road the treasured qualification isn't worth the paper it's written on. What alumni really want is a business school that treats its own brand like gold. One that guards its good name.

The problem for business schools is knowing how best to safeguard their reputations. Here they face another dilemma. The more prestigious the school, the more difficult it is to change direction. But failure to keep up with the pace of change in today's business world inevitably leads to obsolescence. So what schools tend to do is to tinker, but not really change anything much until they face a crisis. Continuous improvement is something they talk about in class but is rarely discussed out of it. It took the recession of the 1990s, for example, plus widespread and increasingly vocal criticism from the business community, before the leading US schools recognized they had to do something, to become more relevant and more responsive.

Even the famous Harvard halo slipped for a while. By the late 1980s, its failure to change with the times and its bureaucratic systems meant that HBS looked in danger of sleep-walking off the edge of a cliff. It took the appointment of an energetic new dean in Kim Clark to shake things up. Clark was an insider. He knew what needed fixing. In his first

Research by the Economist Intelligence Unit among MBA students indicates broad agreement in North America and Europe about the factors that influence their selections. Reputation predominates.

Students' views of importance of factors:

	North America (%)	Europe (%)
Reputation of school	31	34
Program content	19	20
Location	12	17
Quality of teaching	10	10
Published sources	11	8
Recommendations from friends	3	6
Teaching methods	4	4
Costs of tuition/living costs	7	2
Careers services record	2	1
Starting salary of graduates	2	0

six months he invested more than $11 million in IT, an area where HBS was slipping behind its rivals. He also initiated a major overhaul of the school's flagship programs including the MBA program.

In this, Harvard was just playing catch-up with other US schools. Wharton and Columbia, had already taken the decision to overhaul their curricula. The other leading schools followed. Reputations were at risk. In Europe, too, there was a period of soul-searching at the start of the 1990s, with all the major schools introducing changes to their MBA programs.

How important are rankings and accreditation?

The most talked-about barometer of b-school reputations are the rankings published by a variety of magazines and newspapers. Some people place a lot of emphasis on the b-school rankings. The best known are those compiled by *Business Week* and *US News & World Report*. The *Financial Times* now provides the only truly global ranking.

Business schools have a love–hate relationship with rankings. Whenever the topic comes up, deans say they hate, loathe and detest them; that the methodology used for compiling them is flawed; and that comparing schools and programs from different countries and traditions is like trying to compare apples with pears. But there is a much more deep-seated reason for their distaste. They don't like losing.

Whenever a new ranking is threatened the deans of the top business schools are fearful that their school will slip a few places. Once the results are published, it's often a different story. The schools that come out well have been known to rave about the rankings and to spend the next two years bragging that they beat their rival in this or that important area, whether it's the size of their graduates' starting salaries, or the number of teachers with PhDs. Any glimmer of a competitive advantage is seized upon, and used to bolster the school's image.

The fascination with rankings is not unique to business schools, of course. American law schools have been the subject of unofficial league tables for years. In fact, the top US law schools and the leading business schools have much in common. Both offer gateways to enormous wealth and power. Choosing the right school is vital.

The problem here is that there is no officially sanctioned league table or pecking order for business schools. Given the highly competitive nature of the market, and the American obsession with who is no. 1, this has inevitably created a vacuum that magazines and newspapers have been only too ready to fill. Today, there are literally dozens of these. (The enterprising John E. Wehrli has even gone to the trouble of creating a ranking of the rankings.)

Among the best known is the annual ranking published by *US News & World Report*. But without a doubt the most influential is *Business Week* magazine's ranking of the Top 25 US schools. What is remarkable is the clout these media-based rankings carry. The very idea that a magazine or newspaper should be the arbiter of quality in this sector is faintly ludicrous. Yet publication of the *Business Week* rankings is a cause of sleepless nights for the deans of America's leading b-schools.

Updated every two years, places in the *Business Week* ranking are based on the responses of students and corporate recruiters to a survey questionnaire. 'Let the customer speak. That is the philosophy behind *Business Week*'s rankings,' noted the editorial which accompanied the 1998 results. For a magazine, it is a massive undertaking.

Business Week's Top 25 ranking runs as a cover story every two years. The poll has gained much notoriety, and sells many copies of the magazine – the b-school issue is reportedly the year's biggest seller.

The practice is now spreading to Europe. Some believe US-style rankings may make some sense in America, where management has been taught for 100 years, and where companies have been recruiting from b-schools since after World War II. US MBA programs are broadly similar. But that's not the case in Europe. Many Europeans are appalled at the prospect of a US-style survey crossing the Atlantic. They have heard that American MBA deans often think only of rankings in the six-month run-up to publication.

'The problem in the US is that people try and please the rankings, instead of doing right by their students,' says one European placement director.

'Deans shouldn't report to magazines, but to their programs,' adds a former director of placement and admissions at a leading European school. 'The whole thing has got out of hand.'

Early attempts to rank European schools failed to produce a credible equivalent to the best-known American versions. Several were sabotaged by business schools, either threatening legal action or refusing to participate. Published for the first time in January 1999, new global rankings by the *Financial Times* are changing the gentlemanly game.

Rankings come in many shapes and sizes. But all have one thing in common: they are just one way to judge a business school. You should weigh their findings against what the school says, what its students and alumni tell you, the views of the business community, and your own feelings.

The other side of the rankings question is whose figures are they based on anyway? It depends on which criteria you look at. But in one critical area at least, the number of job placements and starting salary, the answer is less than reassuring. The figures fed into the highly sophisticated statistical methodologies come from that most reliable of sources – the business schools themselves. But no one audits the numbers. While some people may not have a problem with this, including many of those who compile the rankings, others do. This has led to the creation of an organization dedicated to ensuring the figures in the great job placement race are accurate.

The MBA Career Services Council (CSC) was created to keep everyone on the straight and narrow. Funded mainly by US business schools, it is currently engaged in the worthy task of evaluating and refining a set of standards its constituent schools can use to report salaries, total compensation and job offers for graduates. This is of more than academic interest.

Rankings are worth looking at if for no other reason than because they may influence the perception of your potential employers. But if you're going to base your decision on them, read carefully, and weigh the other criteria with them to get an overall, balanced picture.

More important is the question of accreditation. Accredited courses are those which have been approved by independent accrediting bodies. Look more seriously at these. The top schools are all accredited by major bodies like the AACSB (American Assembly of Collegiate Schools of Business), the British Association of MBAs (AMBA) or the European Quality Improvement System (EQUIS), the new European standard. This will be your quality guarantee. France, Italy and Spain also have national assessing organizations.

Return on investment

What many business school applicants really want to know is what the pay back will be on their qualification. Ronald Yeaple, a professor at the Simon Graduate School of Business at the University of Rochester in New York state, tried to oblige. While other rankings tied themselves in knots about the quality of teaching, in true MBA spirit Yeaple went for the jugular: Return on Investment (RoI).

In doing so, he may have been the first person to take a hard-headed look at the value of a business education. In 1994, he wrote a book called *The MBA Advantage: Why It Pays to Get an MBA*, in which he ranked 20 top US business schools according to the financial return they gave their graduates. It represents perhaps the best attempt to get to grips with the whole business school phenomenon.

The so-called 'MBA advantage' of each school was the cumulative amount that a typical member of the class of '92 could expect to earn in the five years following graduation, after subtracting tuition fees and what the student would have made without the MBA.

The ranking that emerged presented a very different view of business schools. Certainly it was an alternative to the more righteous rankings such as those produced by *Business Week*. This was a ranking for those with their eyes on the dollar signs.

Northwestern University in Illinois, for instance, achieved only sixth place in Yeaple's book, despite being top in the *Business Week* rankings. Yale University, which hadn't even made the *Business Week* list, rose to fifth. Yeaple's calculations didn't pull any punches. All that counted was just how big or small the payback from an MBA was. It confirmed what many already suspected.

Five years after graduating from b-school, a typical Harvard graduate (Yeaple's No. 1 school) had an MBA advantage of $133,647, while a typical graduate from New York University – Yeaple's lowest-ranked school – had one of only $4,121.

Once adjusted for taxes and the return on the extra money over time, the differences were even more stark: five years after graduation, the Harvard MBA was up by $148,378, while the NYU graduate actually lost $3,749 by attending business school. Game, set and match to Harvard.

One year or two?

An important decision for applicants considering a full-time program is: one year or two years? The two-year MBA is the classic US model and is still offered by most North American institutions and by a handful of Europe's leading schools, including the London Business School, IESE in Barcelona and SDA Bocconi in Milan.

Schools offering two-year programs say that managers need the second year to grow. 'When we look at what companies are wanting from us, we feel we can't deliver without a certain amount of time. Hence the two-year program,' says Eduardo Abascal, IESE's MBA director. At McGill, in Montreal, where the MBA runs for 20 months, course director Alfred Jaeger also defends the longer, North American model. 'You need at least nine months to give a foundation. And you need electives, especially if you have a particular interest to pursue. If not, you get the basic set of skills set up by someone else.' But while some students find four semesters over two years more comfortable than four terms in one year, others do not have the time. Most European schools, including INSEAD and IMD, offer one-year MBAs. There is a market for both. Career-changers probably want to specialize, so might need two years. If you have a particular interest, you'll want to go to a school that offers it. Make sure it's in the curriculum before you go.

There have been suggestions of late that the urge to join the dot-com bonanza has resulted in an increase in the number of students dropping out of two-year programs after the first year. London dean John Quelch dismisses such concerns:

> I think it's a temporary situation. As the froth on the Cappuccino dissipates we'll see a return to normality. The sense of urgency to punch one's ticket and get out there will pass. There may still be some students who want to just get the MBA certificate as fast as they can, but they wouldn't come to LBS. Our mantra is 'transforming futures'. I just don't believe in an MBA course where you are recruiting four weeks after arriving. There just isn't the time for reflection that is part of the MBA experience. The market for the 21-month MBA will remain robust.

Where in the world?

Clearly, a school's location is important – unless you really want to spend two years locked in a room with an occasional foray to a lecture theater. Some students put it near the top of their list of reasons for choosing a school. Asked why she chose Columbia, for instance, one student told us: 'The location in New York City. I really didn't want to spend so much time in lovely but boring Evanston (Kellogg) or filthy-delphia (Wharton).'

Choice of location also extends beyond national borders. Some people prefer to study in their own country, while others deliberately target a business school in another country as a stepping stone to an international career or exposure to different business cultures. It's worth thinking about. Don't just assume that because a school says it is international it really is. Some MBA programs are international in name only, so take a hard look. The global exposure and experience you'll get on an international MBA will be valuable, even if you plan to pursue a career at home. The key to internationalism is diversity. Seek out programs that offer a mix of student and faculty nationalities, backgrounds and cultures. Americans, in the main, tend to study in their own country. But perhaps more will be tempted to Europe as the new-economy wave heads across the Atlantic.

Some say the North American-style MBA, which is the global model, serves you better in the long run. Europeans and Asians often go to the US or Canada for new-world training, then return home to put it to work. It's also worth considering exchange programs. Many of the top schools have deals with their counterparts around the world. You can actually make global contacts at numerous schools around the world through their exchange programs. You needn't go abroad for it.

Chicago led the way among US schools, launching an Executive MBA in Barcelona, which is taught by the school's own faculty. It is one of the few US schools to take global-ization seriously. The school also has 20 partners, including the Chinese University of Hong Kong, Japan's Waseda University, Yonsei University in South Korea and Wirtschaftsuniver-sität-Wien in Vienna, Austria.

MBA students at the Wharton School in Pennsylvania can spend a semester at SDA Bocconi in Italy, the Keio University Graduate School of Business Administration in Japan, the Asian Institute of Management in Manila, and the Stockholm School of Economics in Sweden, among others.

Will you fit in?

This is an important – and sometimes neglected – point. Different business schools have different cultures. Go with your gut reaction – intuition is a much under-valued management competence. If you don't like the smell of the place now, it will stink to high heaven after six months.

It's important to determine what the daily study requirements for your MBA will be, as these vary from place to place. But the culture runs deeper than the class timetable. One obvious difference is student profile – the peer group you will be part of. Until relatively recently most US schools took a high proportion of students with minimal or no work experience. The average age of an MBA student at the bigger schools was about 25. That has now increased to around 27 or 28. At most European schools, students are older – typically in their early 30s.

One of the reasons for doing an MBA, of course, is to meet new and different people. A degree of discomfort is part of the experience. But you have to figure out whether you really want to hang out with 20-somethings or 30-somethings. The top European schools also offer much greater cultural diversity. At INSEAD, IMD and London Business School, for example, there is no dominant nationality among students. The US schools are becoming more international, but typically have around 70 per cent American students. Professor Leo Murray, dean of Cranfield School of Management, one of the UK's leading schools, agrees: 'Chemistry is very, very important. You can't beat campus visits for getting a feel for the place. Have a wander about and talk to people. Have a sniff around and see if you feel comfortable, because if something about the place annoys you now, it's going to be a lot worse when you're working 90 hours a week.'

Campus visits are the best way to find out what the school is really like. Do it. You'll be glad you did. MBA marketing brochures are like vacation brochures. They accentuate the positive and gloss over the fact that the hotel is ten miles from the beach, and still under construction. Go see for yourself. Some schools are prepared to pick up the tab for campus visits if they think you are a really strong candidate. It's worth a try.

Once you arrive, and have taken the mandatory tour laid on by the admissions office, insist on sitting in on some classes. Later, when you've shaken off the admissions minders, make a point of hanging out with the students. Bars are generally a good place to find them. If the bars are empty, that should tell you something. Talk to alumni, and recruiters as well.

'I would recommend visiting the school and talking to people … mention one or two (at most) names in your [admission form] essays of relevant things people said that impressed you,' says one Tuck MBA. 'Visit the school, and talk to alumni. That will enable you to choose the right schools to apply to and make your essays compelling.'

'Once you've decided what range of schools to target, speak to as many existing students as possible in those schools to make sure you understand whether or not the school has the right 'fit' for you,' an LBS student advises. 'Treat the decision-making process in the same manner that you would if you were interviewing candidates for a staff position – the person you are interviewing may be brilliant but if you don't get along, you will not get anything out of them.'

Class size and mix are also important. 'Find out how the school divides participants into study groups,' advises one student. 'This is where you'll learn to trust or reject others, and it's where your networking will be done. This aspect of your business-school education is one of the most crucial and far-reaching. Once out of school, your network contacts will serve you for the rest of your career.'

When choosing a school, too, you might also ask yourself a question: Do I want to be part of a big anonymous machine, where I can choose from 600 electives? Or do I want a more intimate environment, where I can walk in and see the dean if something's wrong? Bigger campuses usually have better resources and more extensive alumni networks. Teachers on smaller faculties will know what their colleagues are doing, which means they can plan courses and integrate lessons better, avoiding repetition. Smaller schools admit you'll have a more limited alumni list, but claim the quality of the contact is better. It depends whether you think size is – or might be – important.

Is the program up to speed?

The new economy presents b-schools with new challenges. They have to keep up with changes in business practice, but also build links with the new-economy companies leading the change. To date, the chief beneficiaries have been b-schools on America's West Coast, within networking distance of Palo Alto. These schools attract e-business luminaries and VCs to do presentations and give lectures. This works against schools that are a long way from the action. Asked whether he is worried about being so far from Silicon Valley, for example, INSEAD's Antonio Borges, was unequivocal: 'Yes. Silicon Valley deserves a great deal of attention. But while Stanford Business School is close geographically it is mentally distant. Stanford University has plenty of connections with Silicon Valley, but the business school is the most academic in the US. Nor is Harvard Business School close to what's happening in Silicon Valley.'

Big name schools such as Stanford, MIT Sloan and Harvard also act as magnets for venture capitalists. The business plan competitions run by schools are becoming more important for students as a way to attract funding for start-ups. At the same time, as b-schools vie with each other to convince students that they offer the most progressive curriculum in this exciting new area, the e-commerce content is being beefed up.

Content-wise, there are two basic approaches: bolt-on electives in specialist areas such as e-commerce and the internet; and the integration of on-line business practice into the core syllabus – for example, studying e-commerce business models as part of the strategy module. At present, most schools do a little of both. They are also ramping up opportunities for students to develop their own business plans, including business plan competitions.

In Europe, a similar scramble is now underway. The words internet and e-commerce are being hastily added to existing courses and new electives hurriedly assembled. While most schools are simply following fashion, a select few are making significant moves. Some b-schools clearly see an extended role for themselves, with moves to provide not just an educational experience but also an environment which supports entrepreneurial activity.

As we have seen, some schools have now established incubation units. The aim is to create a launch pad for internet businesses. These schools are responding to new student demands. But changes are also being driven by traditional recruiters. Companies such as General Electric and Ford are using new technology to integrate their operations with suppliers and retailers to improve communication, reduce costs and production time, as well as reach consumers. They will demand that MBA programs take account of the new requirements.

The dot-coms that survive will also be big recruiters in the next few years. 'I would say that the dot-com companies are arguably developing to the point where they need professionally trained managers and managerial skills just as much as the old economy companies. They will need exactly the same competencies,' says London's John Quelch.

The best b-schools are already responding to the challenge. 'We have ten new elective courses that didn't exist two years ago, mostly dealing with e-commerce and the new economy. For example our managing.com course is now well established and very popular.

It brings together four faculty members from different disciplines,' says Professor Quelch.

In the US, the Wharton School at the University of Pennsylvania has announced a new major in e-commerce for MBA students. More will follow. The Spanish business school, Instituto de Empresa, launched Europe's first complete degree in e-business in February 2000.

How good is the teaching?

The top schools tend to attract the best professors. The Graduate School of Business at the University of Chicago, for example, has a scholarly tradition. It was the first business school to boast a Nobel laureate among its faculty. In recent years, however, scholars have been overtaken to some extent by more media-friendly professors.

The presence of a 'guru in residence' can make a big difference to the choice of school. Everyone wants to go to a school with its own media or best-selling stars. Gurus add to any school's aura. Some institutions go out of their way to attract the top talent. In recent years, a number of academics from leading US b-schools have crossed the Atlantic to European schools.

However, many educators believe the guru-in-residence is unlikely to be the best professor. Great professors, their peers say, are either great classroom teachers or great researchers, but rarely both. Remember, too, that what you see isn't always what you get. Some top schools, both in Europe and the US, have seen on-campus rebellions by disappointed MBAs. Though the brochures promised celebrities, no well-known professors had ever taught them. This made the participants feel they weren't getting value for their money.

How approachable are faculty? Many schools have gurus in residence, but not all teach on their MBA programs. One or two still take the teaching role extremely seriously and are famously approachable. For example, co-author of *Competing for the Future,* C.K. Prahalad and his wife recently invited all the students from a strategy course that he was teaching to dinner at his home when the course was over. Other faculty stars are less approachable.

The teaching methodology is also important. Harvard is famous for its case study teaching method – using case studies of companies to educate students. Other schools have different approaches, and mix and match learning styles.

How much will it cost?

MBAs are not cheap. At the top US schools, for example, the cost of two years' tuition, plus living expenses and loss of salary can easily exceed $100,000, leaving many students with a financial millstone round their necks when they graduate. On the whole, European courses tend to be cheaper – not least because most full-time courses take only one year to complete instead of two. Most MBA students are still self-funded, but any chance of getting someone else to pay is well worth investigating, including company sponsorship, grants, scholarships, and bursaries for minority groups. Smart MBA applicants regard the funding question as their first assignment.

Tax concessions are also worth investigating. Some governments, in Germany and the Netherlands, for example, will refund part-time MBA grads 60 per cent of their tuition. This can include books, phone calls and other expenses. In the UK, government declarations have revealed that, contrary to expectations, the part-time MBA is not going to be tax-deductible. However, fees can be offset against tax if your program is less than one calendar year long, and if you are over 30 years old. This stands to make the full-time degree even more attractive in Britain than the part-time one – provided you can find one of 364 days' duration.

Will you get in?

Not everyone can go to Harvard. Not everyone wants to go to Harvard. Be realistic. Most quality MBA courses require a good first degree, but some schools will waive this requirement for special cases. This can have a bearing on which schools you apply to. Today, you generally need prior work experience to get into an MBA program. Some schools are less hung up about academic qualifications and more interested in career track record. But most schools also require applicants to take the Graduate Management Admissions (GMAT) scored out of 800.

Some b-schools don't insist on GMAT, but it is a standard part of the MBA admissions package at nearly 1,000 schools world-wide. A few years back, Harvard actually dropped the GMAT requirement but has since reinstated it. The GMAT is very US-oriented, both in style and content. For this reason some schools in Spain, Italy and elsewhere have their own tests, in their own languages.

Remember, too, that in your application package, the GMAT isn't the only item the admissions office will be looking it. There are letters of recommendation, your job track record, previous academic performance, special achievements and extra-curricular interests to take into consideration. Attitude also matters.

An applicant's GMAT score is a useful pointer, but it doesn't keep some schools that use it from proceeding with caution. Professor David Norburn, head of Imperial College Management School in London notes: 'If you get in the top percentile – roughly a 770 score – alarms ring in my head. Such a score correlates with insanity and poor social skills. I get worried. These people can do GMATs, and nothing else.' Norburn is quick to add that he hears alarms if he sees a score below 450, too, however.

Some schools say the GMAT is an accurate predictor of how you will do in your first months at business school. Yet Imperial, with 150 MBA students, as well as a few others, uses it as more of an indicator. 'We put more emphasis on the personal interview,' Norburn says. 'I want to see them, see if they fit and feel right here.' Such an approach would be nearly impossible for larger institutions, particularly in America, with thousands of applicants – though Kellogg interviews all applicants.

Attitude matters. Paris's École Nationale des Ponts et Chaussées lists its qualifications for the MBA as: 'Personality: initiative, values, open mindset, creativity, cultural respect. Those who are willing to think differently.' Karina Jensen, spokeswoman for international communications and development, adds, 'Our participants have something in common: global vision, innovation and collaboration.'

What happens when you graduate?

What you plan to do with your qualification should affect your choice of business school. The top investment banks and management consulting firms recruit from a select group of schools. Finding out which companies fish in which ponds is vital to land the job you've set your sights on. If you want to work for a new-economy leader, such as Dell or Yahoo, find out which schools they recruit from.

The famous Wall Street doyen Morgan Stanley Dean Witter recruits heavily from nearby Columbia Business School.

Many b-school graduates go into consulting. At INSEAD, the number is nearly half of all graduates. McKinsey & Company, the famous strategy consultancy, is developing close relations with the new Said Business School at Oxford University, for example, and is now the school's largest recruiter. Other schools such as IE in Madrid pride themselves on the number of graduates who go on to start their own businesses.

Finally, if you want to raise finance for that internet start-up, look closely at schools with good VC contacts.

chapter 3

getting in

One thing you should know – getting into an MBA program is the hardest part. Once in, no one really ever fails out of b-school unless he/she does absolutely nothing.

STERN STUDENT

What are b-schools looking for?

Getting into one of the top b-schools is tough. Intake in any given year is limited by the size of the program, so regardless of the quality of applicants it comes down to a straight fight for places. Harvard, for example, has an intake of about 900 MBA students each year. The school aims to ensure that those places go to the best 900 applicants. To do an MBA at HBS, you have to make sure you're one of the chosen few.

Stanford (leading school; wonderful climate; Silicon Valley), which may be the toughest school of all to get into, has consistently had an acceptance rate of around 7 per cent. To put that in context, in 1999/2000, Stanford received some 6,606 applications for 730 MBA places. The average GMAT score of successful applicants was 725 out of a maximum 800 score. That's pretty stiff. Elsewhere the competition is also intense. In 1999/2000, for example, Columbia received 6,406 applications for 1,250 places, with 11 per cent of candidates being offered a place. The average GMAT score was 700.

The top schools don't make it easy. They all want to be the number one choice. You have to humor them. The application process is designed to weed out the weaker candidates. It also seems to be designed to make the whole business of getting into a school as time-consuming and paperwork intensive as possible. At a time when many companies are trying to eliminate bureaucratic chores, most b-schools have stoutly resisted the trend. They demand the full attention of prospective students. They expect them to jump through hoops. It's their way of ensuring that only people who are serious about the MBA get in. B-schools want it all.

As one student observes: 'Getting into Chicago is a multi-faceted process, like every school. Clearly, you need top scores, good grades, and a strong work history. Other things that Chicago really favors are: active volunteer activity, a STRONG knowledge of the school, its programs, its offerings, and what is special to you about Chicago, a history of leadership in and outside of work, and an understanding of what you have done, what you want to do in school, and where you want the Chicago degree to take you. Advice I would offer to potential candidates is this: know yourself, know the school, and then be prepared to be grilled about both with your application and interview.'

The same is pretty much true for all the top schools. Our research did throw up a few people who seemed to have cruised effortlessly into the school of their choice. 'I applied online and, with the exception of the essays, I found the process fairly painless. The interview was low-stress and the day on campus clinched my decision,' says a student at Vanderbilt's Owen School. But these are the exceptions that prove the rule.

So what do schools look for? Basic selection criteria are pretty much what you'd expect from academic institutions. The top schools want:

- a solid academic record – a good first degree
- a good GMAT score (650 plus)
- work experience (always valued by European schools, in recent years this has become increasingly important at North American schools)

- leadership potential – as demonstrated through sports, club or work experience
- good interpersonal/social skills
- high motivation
- to believe they are your first choice of school (whether it's true or not).

Increasingly, too, schools are looking to increase the diversity of their student bodies in terms of:

- international experience – for US schools this usually means a foreign passport
- gender – the ratio of women to men has improved in recent years but is still on the low side
- ethnic minorities (WASPs are still over-represented)
- unusual career or life experiences
- languages spoken.

The top European schools, in particular INSEAD, LBS and IMD, place even more emphasis on international experience. 'They seem to be looking for international and "interesting" people more than straightforward overachievers as they might in the US. If you have several nationalities emphasize the rare one,' says one American at a European school.

Faced with such a stringent application process, it's easy to prevaricate. 'The application process was at first very intimidating,' one Columbia student admitted. 'I postponed applying for at least a year because, one, the course descriptions (i.e. Black Scholes and Capital Asset Pricing Model) are unintelligible to me; two, because I'd been out of school so long and never intended to attend graduate school; and three, I was continually told how unlikely admission would be.'

Some people find the application unnerving. They procrastinate and delay. Don't. It's just another game with a set of rules to be mastered. 'Just do it. As long as you have the requirements, you should be ok. Study for the GMAT. If your score isn't good enough, write it again,' advises a student at Western Ontario's Ivey.

And applying early gives you an advantage. The first or second round is the best time to get your application in. Obviously, you don't want to rush if that means you don't do yourself justice, but there are real benefits to getting in early. At Stanford, for example, the admissions office says the acceptance rate is around 10 or 11 per cent – compared to an average of 7 per cent. This is because the process is skewed towards filling the places – and early acceptance is more likely to secure a good student. By the time you get to the third round of applicants, most of the places will already have been allocated. So, if you're below the 7 per cent cut-off, the best you're going to get is an offer for the next intake.

Let's face it, too, if you're not going to get into the school of your choice, you might as well find out now. Then you can put it behind you and do something else. You won't know if you don't go for it. As one student at Michigan put it: 'Apply even if you think you won't get in because it doesn't cost you anything and you never know. If it's what you want to do you should do it. If you have good work experiences let the admissions people know, talk to counselors about what they are looking for, get your essays etc. read over by as many people as possible.'

The admissions office: your best friend and worst enemy

Getting past the admissions office is the first hurdle to getting your MBA. The admissions office at your target school or schools is your best friend and worst enemy. Handle with care. Despite the move to on-line applications, the admissions procedure seems to become more labyrinthine with each passing year.

Surveys among MBA applicants show that one of their biggest concerns is the admissions office (along with job placement and financial aid). Many MBA students say that their experience of the admissions office is a significant factor in choosing a particular school. In recent years, schools have taken this to heart, placing a lot more attention on the efficiency of the service provided by admissions staff. For this reason, in all likelihood you will be treated politely, greeted with smiles, and generally made to feel welcome. Most undertake to reply to queries within a specific time scale. They are generally helpful and aware of applicants' needs. This does not mean you will be accepted, of course.

Make no mistake, the admissions office will do everything within its powers to attract the best students. This includes a growing number of events designed to lure prospective students onto campus. Once they get you in their clutches expect a hard sell – friendly but unrelenting. Off-campus recruiting receptions and forums are also increasingly common. With the drive to attract more international students, admissions staff also scour the major cities of the world in their quest to find the best candidates. These events are well worth taking advantage of, especially if you're applying to a school on another continent.

As well as the usual sack of informational bumf and brochures, they give an insight into what the school is like. But campus visits are the best way to get the smell of the place. Does attending a roadshow event in Paris or Tokyo earn you brownie points? Probably not. The tracking processes most schools currently have do not measure interest in such a sophisticated way. But you may be able to make a connection with an individual member of the admissions staff which might be useful later. It can't hurt to address inquiries to someone you've met – and to remind them that your commitment to their school involved travelling 1,000 miles to attend.

The diversity imperative means that schools actively target women and ethnic minorities. With the number of women applying to the top US schools declining, they are trying to address the gender imbalance by hosting events aimed specifically at women. Ditto minorities. You might conclude that non-WASP women, in particular, are actually at an advantage in the application stakes, although most schools say they have the same high standards for all applicants.

The admissions office is also the door to financial help in the form of scholarships, bursaries and internships. Remember, they are trying to sell the school to you. It is their job to make it as attractive a package as they can. This changes once you have made an application. At this point, their job becomes screening out the weakest candidates. If they want you, they will be even more attentive. If they don't then their interest will tail off. Special pleading is worth a try, but rarely yields results.

The dreaded GMAT

For some, the dreaded GMAT test is just another hurdle to be cleared on the way to an MBA. 'Get a 700+ score on the GMAT and then forget about the test and the score,' says a Tuck student. But for others it is a nightmare. So what's the real deal? What's the truth behind the GMAT mythology?

Most b-schools require applicants to take the Graduate Management Admissions Test (GMAT). GMAT is owned by the Graduate Management Admissions Council (GMAC), which is made up of about 130 graduate schools of management. The test is administered by the Educational Testing Service at Princeton, and is scored out of 800. It is a general intelligence test, which evaluates comprehension and reasoning ability. It has a verbal and quantitative element.

There has been some controversy over whether the GMAT is culturally biased against non-American applicants, especially Japanese and other applicants from Asia. In recent years, the exam has been massaged in an attempt to counter these criticisms.

However, the fact that the GMAT is only available in English (American English, in fact) means that there is an inevitable bias against those with another mother tongue. You might as well get used to it if you're applying to an overseas school as most b-schools teach in English anyway. Interestingly, Dave Wilson, president of GMAT, has said that, on average, Asian candidates tend to score much higher on the quantitative side of the test than Americans.

Essay questions were added in 1994, but the GMAT is mainly multiple choice. GMAC claims that the essay questions are not intended to test applicants' writing skills, but their ability to think. It is difficult to prepare answers in advance, but practising with past GMAT exams can be highly beneficial, especially for students who are unused to the US format and approach.

Schools insist that the GMAT is not the be-all-and-end-all for evaluating applications. 'GMAT scores matter,' counters a student at MIT's Sloan school. 'The school is dominated by former engineers, but they are definitely on the look-out for strong liberal arts candidates who can prove that they have strong quant skills.'

It's possible to score 620 on your GMAT and still get into one of the top schools if the rest of your application package, especially the essays, are outstanding. But why make life difficult for yourself? Do your homework – practise with past GMAT questions – to get your score up as high as possible. You can also re-sit the test as many times as you like.

'I know many admissions people tend to downplay the GMAT. However, I would say that taking a prep course and spending a lot of time preparing for the GMAT is an important step that will improve your chances of getting in. The other things like work experience are tough to change as quickly as one can improve/prepare for the GMAT,' says a Michigan student.

Unless you are super-confident, super-bright or super-arrogant, it is advisable to practise with past GMAT exams to improve your chances – especially if you are not familiar with the US educational system. There are a number of books and websites to help. The *Official Guide to GMAT Review* contains more than 700 sample questions, one complete test and a useful guide to the different sections. In the US, it costs $19.95. Software that reproduces the CAT-experience is available for PCs. There are even GMAT tutoring services available at a price, although how helpful these are is a matter of opinion.

Work experience

In the past, many US schools took students with very limited or no work experience. This has changed dramatically over recent years. This is reflected in an older age profile for MBA students in the US. Most students now enter US programs with at least two years' work experience under their belts. Many have spent four or five years in the workplace. Some US schools think that the trend towards work experience is something that started in the US. But in Europe, where one-year programs predominate, schools have always recruited more mature students, with many insisting on a minimum number of years' work experience.

To some extent, then, the US schools are simply waking up to the fact that some first-hand knowledge of business adds a great deal to the MBA experience. In the past, schools were criticized for sending out classroom trained officers with little or no experience in the trenches. Schools now believe that some real-world savvy gives graduates a competitive advantage when they go for summer placements, and when they re-enter the job market. It makes them more self-reliant. The growing importance of work experience has a useful effect for less academically oriented applicants. It levels the playing field. To some extent, a strong business track record can help balance a less than perfect GMAT score. So what sort of experience do schools look for?

'We look for two things', says Ilsa Evans, executive director of MBA admissions and career services at the Haas School at Berkeley. 'Someone who has had an impact in their work world and someone who has explored beyond their immediate surroundings. The latter could have involved experience abroad or setting up a company in a widely different environment than they were in before. We're looking for someone who is entrepreneurial and willing to take risks and try something new. We have a strong sense of community at Haas, so we are also looking for someone who has made a contribution to the community.'

The GMAT test can be taken at locations throughout the world. It is administered as a computer-adaptive test (known as GMAT CAT). A paper-based version used to be offered twice a year in locations where the CAT test was not available but has now been withdrawn. According to Pam Rice, associate program director for GMAT, the test is given to approximately 200,000 people every year. In 1999, around 189,000 people took the GMAT world-wide.

To take the GMAT, you sit at a computer terminal and the screen displays one question at a time. The first question is always of medium difficulty. The selection of questions after that is dependent on the responses to previous questions. The idea is that in this way the test adapts to your level of ability. It means that you have to answer every question as it is displayed, and that you can't go back and change previous answers.

What's involved?

You have 75 minutes to complete 37 quantitative questions; 75 minutes to answer 41 verbal questions, and 30 minutes for each of the two analytical essay questions. The quantitative and verbal sections are computer adaptive; but the two analytical writing questions are not.

The GMAT CAT is offered three weeks a month, six days a week throughout the year at about 400 computer-based testing centers in North America and other major cities around the world. Unofficial verbal, quantitative and total scores are available at testing centers as soon as the test has been completed. Official confirmation, including essay scores, usually drop through the letter box about two weeks later. A registration form is available from the Educational Testing Service at Princeton: PO Box 6108, Princeton, NJ, 08541, USA. It costs $150 in the US and $195 outside.

ETS will also send students the *GMAT Bulletin of Information* which details test centers and gives some sample questions. The website www.gmat.org provides details of the test, sample questions and other useful information. Applicants can schedule or change a test appointment by telephone. Tests can be arranged with just a few days' notice. You can take the test as many times as you want – but only once in every calendar month. If you think you can improve on your GMAT score, take it again – and again. You can take the exam as many times as you like. ETS, the organization that administers it, only reports a student's last three scores to business schools.

Most schools that teach in English require evidence that non-native English speakers will be able to follow the course and participate in class discussions. TOEFL (pronounced toe-fell) is the Test of English as a Foreign Language and is widely accepted by b-schools as standard for foreign students. Like the GMAT, however, it has its critics. Details of the TOEFL are available from the Educational Testing Service at Princeton.

In 1999, the average GMAT scores for successful applicants at top schools were:

Stanford	717
Chicago	697
Kellogg	695
MIT Sloan	690
Darden	685
Wharton	684
Anderson (UCLA)	680
Columbia	680
Yale	680
INSEAD	676
Stern	675
Haas (Berkeley)	674
Michigan	672
Tuck (Dartmouth)	670
Fuqua (Duke)	662
Texas	660
Said (Oxford)	656
IMD	650
London	640
Australian Graduate School of Management	637
Cranfield	630
HEC (France)	630
Singapore (National University)	630
Judge (Cambridge)	622
Bocconi	620
IESE	620
Melbourne	610
Chinese University	604
Hong Kong UST	600

(Figures for Harvard are not available)

Source: Economist Intelligence Unit

Doing the paperwork

One look at a business school application form is enough to put you off doing an MBA. US schools in particular have elevated form-filling to new heights of bureaucratic tedium. The European schools, too, are becoming more officious with each passing year. 'I found the application process a complete pain, especially as an international student,' says one student at Kellogg. 'I didn't realize that the process would take so long, and I only had 24 hours to do my applications. Also the GMAT required some advance thought. On the up-side, at least you can apply and pay on line.'

MBA application forms seem to be designed to confuse. Those who hate such administrative chores will not enjoy the experience. For this reason alone, it is well worth doing your homework so that precious time is not wasted on applications for schools that you don't really want to go to. It is sensible to apply to more than just your number one school, but spreading your efforts too thinly is not recommended. We recommend applying to two or three schools – four as a maximum.

Many b-schools now offer electronic application forms. At least one school insists on it. But whether they are screen or paper, expect to spend many frustrating hours filling in these documents. When the temptation to tear up the paperwork – or delete the file – becomes unbearable, try to remember that getting the application right is the first step towards getting into the school of your choice. Treat the application form as an initiative test, and you will find the whole thing more tolerable. Think of it as a marketing document where the product being offered is you. It is a package. It should tell a story.

'I feel applicants who can weave their prior education, past work experience and future career path into a logical reason of why they choose Owen will have a better chance at admittance. Apply early. I believe that it helped in my case,' says an Owen student.

By the time they applied most of the students we encountered knew what to expect. 'It was no more burdensome than those of other schools and thus met with my level of expectation. The accessibility of the admissions staff made it particularly easy relative to other schools,' said a positive-minded London student.

Indeed, some people even appear to enjoy the process. 'Applications are certainly time-intensive, but I really enjoyed Harvard's application process,' one successful applicant told us with apparent sincerity. 'The questions were thought-provoking and enabled me to pull from a variety of experiences. The interview was fairly straightforward, though interesting, provocative questions were asked there, as well. I only applied to Harvard, so I don't have a lens for comparison between Harvard's application process and that of other business schools.'

Formats vary from school to school, but the basics are the same. Most schools ask for:

- personal details
- work experience (important for an MBA)
- academic record, including grades

- three or four short essays
- references from two or three people, bosses or former teachers and normally unseen by the applicant.

A tip from former students is pick the schools you are really serious about – your A-list – and invest time in their application process rather than dissipate energy by applying to B-list schools that you aren't really interested in. Remember, too, that different schools have different areas of interest. 'Ivey really focuses on leadership skills/leadership potential. A potential candidate should demonstrate the ability to work in teams quite clearly,' says an Ivey student. If you are applying to the fervently global Thunderbird school it is better to possess some degree of commitment to global business.

For the most part , b-schools want Renaissance men and women. Once students are accepted they quickly believe that they are interesting, intelligent and well-balanced. Take this Haas student: 'I believe that Haas tries to attract individuals who have a wealth of experiences. A prospective student must be an interesting person, with interests outside of their career. Haas also focuses on entrepreneurship, and this requires students to have a sense of initiative and a passion for life.'

Back down to earth, others suggest that a good tactic is to relieve the tedium of the admissions office. A student at North Carolina's Kenan-Flagler advises: 'MBA apps are really boring to read. Perform some *pro bono* work before you apply… have outside interests that you can talk about. The school looks for team players and go-getters so the best way to get into school is to highlight your team skills and the fact that you go out of your way to get things done. They look for people who go that extra mile to ensure success.'

You may have difficulty in transforming yourself into a philosophy-reading, spiritually aware, Renaissance man or woman with an impeccable sporting pedigree, experience of volunteer work in Somalia and a range of corporate jobs under your belt. Fear not. There is always Plan B. As a student at Cambridge University's Judge Institute suggests: 'To get in: Make sure you are real.'

Another Kenan-Flagler student summarizes:

To get in, I think our school really emphasizes well-rounded intelligent students. It is not enough just to have diverse experiences, I think one has to have demonstrated a strong academic background or a good GMAT score. Kenan-Flagler still insists that all applying interview – so those interpersonal skills are still very key. Finally, apply in the first or second round to maximize chances of being accepted. This year our applications were up more than 50 per cent so it can't hurt to get it in early.

The wow factor

Given the intensity of the competition for places, the difference between a successful and unsuccessful application is often marginal. The aim, as with job applications, is to cover all the bases and offer a little bit extra to make you stand out from the crowd – what some schools call the 'wow factor'. 'The MBA program tries to improve the intellectual capital of the participants – what they know; improve their social capital – who they know; and improve their emotional capital – their knowledge of themselves,' says Julia Tyler, MBA program director at the London Business School. 'So, we are looking for people who have a sense of themselves; who have demonstrated ability outside of the business frame; people who are confident in leadership situations; and who have a thoroughly international outlook.'

'We're always talking about rating applications – and applications which have the "wow factor",' says Marie Mookini, assistant dean and director of MBA admissions at Stanford. 'It's not one or two things in combination, it's the total package. It's going through a file and reading very sincere, well-thought-out essays, in combination with references that just glow. The references talk about the applicant's work performance, impact within an organization, emotional intelligence as well as interpersonal skills. All those things together add up to "wow".'[1]

'GMAT scores, university transcripts, essays and work experience are all very important but are not enough,' says Alberto Arribas, admissions director at the Spanish School, IESE. 'The wow candidates all have something different. As one of our interviewers once put it, "I would want this candidate in my classroom and on my team, whether at work, at IESE, or on the rugby pitch".'[2]

The first part of the application process consists of a number of hurdles designed to weed out the weaker candidates at an early stage. The object here is not to be eliminated. The second phase – especially the interview – is a more positive process, offering an opportunity to impress the admissions department. From start to finish, the application process is tortuous. Do not underestimate the commitment required.

'I found the application process for b-school in general to be very time-consuming. I had to start the process about one and a half years before I expected to begin b-school (this includes preparing for and taking the GMAT as well). While the process is tough, it really confirms your commitment to going. I see it as a part of the screening process. If your heart is not in it, you will never make it through the applications,' a Michigan student told us.

Essays

A key element of the application process, essays are designed to reveal the candidate. 'Be creative with your essays and make sure you have a good "story" on why you are pursuing an MBA. Make sure some of your essays talk about accomplishments or projects you worked on in teams,' says a Kellogg student. 'Know what your objectives are before you start writing essays. IMD, like other business schools, wants future leaders as MBA participants. Focus on your leadership experiences in your essays and on your future objectives and goals,' advises an IMD student.

Good advice, but many students say that the essays are the biggest challenge they faced in getting into b-school. 'Writing the essays was the hardest part. I come from a culture where you don't talk much about yourself, and writing pages about yourself was difficult. I had great relationships with my boss and a couple of other people, so getting recommendations was no problem. I prepared for about three weeks for the GMAT (no prep courses), and did fine,' a Tuck student told us.

There is no doubt that essays require deft handling. Most schools ask for a minimum of two short essays (some require more), usually as part of the application form. The aim from the school's perspective is to garner insights into the personality, motivation and attitude of the applicant. At Stanford, which doesn't interview applicants, the essays are seen as the candidate's opportunity to sell themselves. 'We encourage students to use the essays as their opportunity to tell their story,' says Marie Mookini, 'to talk to us about what's really important to them. That's essentially what one would be doing in an interview, talking about their accomplishments, things that are meaningful to them, people who are meaningful to them.'[3]

Essays are an excellent opportunity to reveal either too much or not enough about the inner workings of your mind. The going is personal. 'What struck me about Haas's application form was its focus not just on career-related questions, but also on personality-indicative questions that would filter out non-well-rounded individuals. As a result, the range of experiences and personality types of the students here at Haas has been so impressive,' says a Haas student. What schools want to see is that you are a balanced individual with an open and inquiring mind. They prefer their students sane. Then the Catch-22 of the b-school application kicks in. You also have to be fiercely ambitious, obsessed with achieving and possess an almost unnatural interest in business. This balance is not easy to achieve. A degree of Machiavellian cunning is required.

As one Stanford student observes: 'Writing the essays was a pain and required the positioning of yourself as a balanced, complete person, which, in fact, you're decidedly not if you've applied to HBS or Stanford. On the whole, though, I'd describe the process as healthy in that it forces you into brief moments of introspection.'

The attitude to take is that in every painful exercise there is an opportunity – at worst, you might find out something about yourself. Those who've been on the receiving end of applications, say essays are the chance to differentiate yourself. 'I can assert from reading applications as part of the Dean's Student Admissions Committee, take a mild chance on your essays,' advises a student. 'This is not to say that you need to be bold and completely different, but out of 100 essays, 80 of them will say essentially the same thing. Then, the only difference comes down to other admissions criteria. If you stand out in the essay (and don't wow the committee with big words and historical references) by being unique, interesting, and someone I genuinely want in my class with me, then I can assure you your application will stand out more than the person with the 720 GMAT and 3.6 from a good school, of which there are hundreds every year. There are plenty of those people, but all too few leaders and creative people.'

In the quest to be interesting and different it is easy to forget the basics. Common mistakes when writing essays include:

- not answering the question asked. This often results from cutting and pasting answers from one application form into another where the question is similar. This, the schools say, they can spot. 'Applicants should know that every school wants to feel as if they're the only one the student is applying to,' says Stanford's Mookini. 'We always ask applicants to indulge us in that fantasy and really tailor their essays to answer the questions we ask.'[3] So indulge them.
- writing what the applicant believes the admissions office wants to hear instead of what they really think. This is one of those areas where judgment is required. By all means offer some insights on the state of the economy or your view on social policy. Best not to get too deep into your politics or more exotic sexual pastimes. With this in mind, get someone you trust to read your essays before you submit them. They will be able to advise on how the message comes across – and whether it does you justice.

References

References are another integral part of the application merry-go-round. Some candidates see these as an exercise in name-dropping, submitting the details of people they hardly know. Impressive as this may be, if the person writing the reference doesn't really know you, chances are it will show. If you happen to play golf regularly with Jack Welch, then fine. But if you once spoke to him in the John at a conference, then Mr Welch probably isn't your man. Better a tub-thumping endorsement from a middle manager than a bland confirmation of employment from the CEO.

As one Harvard student suggests: 'Seek recommendations from individuals that know you well and can really offer informed opinions/assessment of your aptitude/potential. Quality of the recommendation was far more important to me than the title of the individual offering it.'

For students whose academic track record and GMAT are less than miraculous, references are the ideal counterbalance. Ask referees who believe in you – and your potential. People who will be prepared to stick their necks out for you. People who will write such glowing reports that even the most jaded admissions officer will be forced to sit up and take notice. Failing that, get someone with a vivid imagination who owes you a favor. (And if their imagination is really good and they owe you lots of favors let them advise on your essay!)

Sample essay questions from the 1999–2000 application round:

Columbia:

1   What are your career goals? How will an MBA help you achieve these goals? Why are you applying to Columbia Business School? (Maximum 1,000 words)

2   In reviewing the last five years, describe one or two accomplishments in which you demonstrated leadership. (Maximum 500 words)

3   Discuss a non-academic personal failure. In what ways were you disappointed in yourself? What did you learn from the experience? (Maximum 500 words).

Darden:

1   Specifically address your post-MBA short- and long-term professional goals. How will Darden assist you in attaining these goals?

2   The Darden School seeks a diverse and unique entering class of future managers. How will your distinctiveness enrich our learning environment and enhance your prospects for success as a manager?

3   Describe a significant leadership experience, decision-making challenge, or managerial accomplishment. How did this experience affect your professional/personal development?

Stanford:

1   What matters most to you and why?

2   Given your reasons for earning an MBA degree, what type of alternative preparation might you seek if formal MBA programs did not exist?

Interviews

Not all schools interview applicants. Those that do take it seriously. Some also use alumni or visiting faculty to interview students in more far-flung places. So don't be surprised if you are given the once over by someone from the Class of '83. They will try to sell the benefits of the school to you. But don't let your guard down. They will also report back to the admissions office on whether you are made of the 'right stuff'.

As with any job interview, your aim should be to make the interviewer realize that you have a great deal to offer the school and will 'make 'em proud some day'. A Kellogg student says: 'Don't try to be someone you are not during the interview. Kellogg really looks for outstanding all-round individuals. You might have won the Nobel Peace Prize, but if you are not a good person who gets along with others, Kellogg will likely turn you down.'

Actually, we doubt they would, but there aren't too many Nobel Peace Prize winners who apply to b-school so it's hard to tell. The general point, though, is well made. 'Emphasize the teamwork and the level of involvement you put into your activities/community,' suggests a Washington University student.

The bottom line on interviews is easy: be yourself. Try and impress; try to act like someone you think they'd like; and you will not get in. You don't have to be totally frank and upfront, but you must appear genuine. If they don't believe you, they're not going to welcome you into their fraternal bosom.

'The interview process is designed for the interviewer to get to know the prospective student, so be yourself during the conversation. It is not something about which you should worry or be nervous. Let your natural personality shine through the conversation,' says a Darden student.

If all else fails, you can always fall back on your sense of humor. This, however, is a desperate measure. Now is not the time for cracking jokes. A Stanford student recounts his more frivolous approach: 'For getting in: tell a joke. Never forget that the admissions committee sees perfect applications every day and you therefore need to appear with more humor. I remember describing playing Fifa2000 with interns as an example of how I was a motivational leader (there was more to it, but you get the idea).'

Probably you had to be there. We wouldn't recommend this strategy, unless you are universally recognized as a wit, or raconteur. It might work for Billy Crystal or Robin Williams, but the average MBA applicant may not be so entertaining.

A wise and accurate summary comes from a Kellogg student: 'I would say that the interview is extremely important at Kellogg. Candidates should really make sure they come prepared to tell a coherent, logical story. They need to be able to explain the gaps on their resumés (we all have them somewhere), explain why they want to go to business school (demonstrating that they've thought about why Kellogg might be an option for them), and explain what they want to do after business school and how business school will help them get there (I think this is where a lot of otherwise good candidates fail … they say something like they want to work for a dot-com … but they have no logical bridge connecting that to their previous work experience as a product design engineer … the stories have to make sense! … remember … the interviewer is sitting there thinking … "will this person have a reasonable chance of getting that job when they leave our school if they tell that same story to the job interviewer?").'

Dare to be different

Michael Porter's Five Forces framework has been standard MBA fare for 20 years. Every MBA student knows that differentiation is a source of competitive advantage. Use it. This applies especially to essays, but to all aspects of the application process as well. Admissions offices see thousands of applications every year. Most of them read like the diary of a clone. If you can manage to be memorable – to stand out as having something unique to offer – then do it. The one proviso is that you don't overstep the line between being a little eccentric into wacko territory. 'My advice to applying students is be interesting, take chances and be yourself! Don't worry about trying to fit anyone's sort of template. I don't think there is one, really. If you can manage all three at the same time, so much the better,' says a Columbia student.

And, when the offers start coming in, you can move from interesting, Renaissance man or woman mode into Machiavellian game player. There is an element of gamesmanship in managing offers. Play the game.

An early offer can provide a useful bargaining chip with other schools. The usual rules of brinkmanship and negotiation apply. Remember, though, that the top schools like to believe they are your first choice, so factor that into any gambits. 'I really want to come to Harvard, but I've got this offer from Wharton/Stanford/Chicago …' is the right approach, and can lever additional benefits from the admissions office. It won't get you an offer if you aren't up to scratch, but it might help you extract a bursary, or other financial aid, from target schools. If money is a big issue, and likely to prevent you doing the MBA, then you may need to play the offers game.

It can also backfire. That's why we'd recommend that if you get an offer from your first choice school, or even a close second – take it. Get on with the next challenge – reorganizing your life in preparation for b-school.

Endnotes

1 'Meet the Admissions Director', *Businessweek Online*, 20 December 1999.

2 'Meet the Admissions Director', *Businessweek Online*, 31 January 2000.

3 'Meet the Admissions Director', *Businessweek Online*, 20 December 1999.

packing your bag

Whether or not the MBA is worth the money depends on what you want to get out of the MBA. If you simply want to improve your salary position, then this question is quite easy to answer. If you want personal growth opportunities, career changes, exposure to new people, etc., then the question becomes more cumbersome and all the more personal. Evaluate your current position and what it is you want to achieve. Make sure the MBA program you choose will help you achieve this.

LONDON STUDENT

Getting organized

Once you've secured a place on an MBA program the fun really begins. The dislocation caused by going back to full-time study is immense. If you're lucky you have a few months to get yourself organized. In that time you have to accomplish a number of tasks. In particular, you have to:

- bid farewell to your current employer if you have one
- organize your finances: including putting loans in place, persuading your parents or other family members to help you, and/or sorting out applications for bursaries, scholarships and the like.
- find somewhere to live
- pack up your life and move it to b-school
- settle in your spouse or significant other.

There is also the pre-MBA preparation to think about. This is likely to include:

- getting stuck into the reading list
- attending pre-courses
- brushing up on those scholarly techniques you thought – perhaps hoped – you'd left behind.

Money matters

No one ever said it'd be easy. Listen to one Fuqua student. 'I'm a dual masters student (MBA/Public Policy), so I'm actually paying for three years of education. Luckily, I received scholarship assistance from both the public policy school and the business school. But my wife really wanted to be at home to raise our first daughter, who was four months old when I started graduate school. So we went from DINK (double income no kids) to NIOK (no income one kid). For us, it was simply a matter of borrowing enough funds to survive (still about $25,000 a year), generous assistance from both sets of parents, some sense of frugality, and being careful about comparing my situation to my peers, who often had supplemental income from a spouse or had saved up a considerable amount of money before returning to school. The simple fact of the matter is that I'll be able to pay off this investment just fine. The benefit of having an MBA makes the early sacrifices all worthwhile.'

As these comments suggest, the most important task in the run-up to starting your MBA is sorting out the finance. Costs vary between schools, but basically comprise of:

- tuition costs
- living costs, including accommodation
- foregone salary – generally the biggest cost.

Tuition fees at the top US schools vary from around $18,000 per year up to around $31,000 (cheaper if you're resident in the state). Harvard, for example, costs $27,250 per year, giving a total bill of $54,500 for the two-year program. Stanford is about the same ($27,243) for off-campus. Kellogg is $27,273 (for the six-quarter program). Wharton costs $31,279 per year. But tuition is only part of the story. To that you have to add rent, food etc. This will be substantially more in a big city than out in the sticks.

The bigger schools offer on-campus accommodation – which is generally a good option if you're single, but not if you're planning to take the family with you.

Living expenses obviously depend on the style to which you are accustomed. Room and board at Wharton will cost you around $11,500 per year. Ditto at Stern. Room and utilities, on-campus or off-campus, at Harvard is likely to cost around $8,500, while living across town at MIT will drain you of around $17,000. At Kellogg, annual on-campus or off-campus room, board and expenses will set you back around $19,000. The Haas School at Berkeley, on the other hand, estimates that living off campus in California will be a modest $5,000 to $8,000.

The cost of tuition in Europe tends to be cheaper because most MBAs take only one year to complete instead of two. But it still amounts to a tidy sum of money.

Tuition at INSEAD, for example, costs around $23,250 (€ 25,000). IMD costs around $24,500. But the cost of living in Europe is typically higher. General living expenses at INSEAD, for instance, are around $15,500.

Fees for two-year courses in Europe will obviously be more – and living expenses and foregone salary will be double. London Business School is one of the few two-year MBAs in Europe, along with IESE in Spain and the Italian school SDA Bocconi. Fees at LBS are $20,625 per annum, giving a total of $41,250 for the two years. LBS estimates an additional off-campus accommodation cost of between $12,000 and $15,000 per year.

The total bill for any MBA is substantial. 'The average loan we're arranging now for full-time students is between £60,000 ($90,000) and £80,000 ($120,000),' says Mike Jones of the UK's Association of MBAs. 'Go to LBS and you're looking to borrow £80,000 to see you through the two years. Add in the fact that you're not working and it adds up to a lot of money. On the other side, full-time MBAs tend to get better salaries at the end. It rams home the point that this is an investment in your career. Like any investment, the bigger the risk, the bigger the reward. People taking a full-time MBA put themselves in a more difficult position financially.'

This is borne out by students' comments. Says one LBS MBA: 'Financially, it's very tough, especially in London! After years of working and maintaining a certain lifestyle it is difficult to return to student life. But it is manageable and pretty much everyone around you is in the same situation.'

Tuition fees at Harvard Business School are just over $27,000 a year. To this you have to add living costs – another $12,750 plus miscellaneous expenses. The annual budget for a single Harvard student, the school reports, tends to be around $50,000. But for most of those in the MBA program, the opportunity cost of foregone salary is the biggest financial drain.

'The single biggest cost for most of our students, frankly, is the decision to leave their full-time employment. Many of our students are earning well in excess of $50,000 a year in their current jobs, and so to leave the workforce for two years and effectively pass up on $100,000 of opportunity is a much greater cost than either the tuition or living expenses that students tend to incur,' says Jamie Millar, director of MBA Admissions and Financial Aid at Harvard Business School.

A substantial part of the tuition and living costs can be covered by an assortment of financing options. HBS, for example, has an extensive, needs-based fellowship program that a significant number of students – both domestic and international – are eligible for. Most domestic students also qualify for federal aid. But the school expects students to be able to contribute at least a part of their funding out of their own personal savings. Assistantship and work-study positions don't exist. The school doesn't encourage MBA students to work while they're in the program.

HBS offers a small number of merit-based scholarships, but most of the aid provided is needs-based. In recent years the total amount of money available has increased significantly – up by 60 per cent between 1998 and 1999. Around 47 per cent of the total student body receives a needs-based fellowship – about 60 per cent of the people applying for aid. The awards can range from $1,000 over two years up to as high as $40,000 over two years. The level of need is evaluated using a formula. 'Essentially we calculate what the cost of an education is less the students' liquid and, to some extent, illiquid assets,' says Millar. 'As a rule, we don't touch an individual's retirement money unless it's a huge amount.'

'I used savings from my working career, and also traded shares on the internet, in order to afford this year,' says one enterprising student at the Italian school Bocconi. 'I also received some degree of loans and support from my family.'

The best way to fund your MBA is to try to get someone else to put their hand in their pocket. There is a range of financial aid options. The main ones are:

- scholarships, fellowships and grants: often allocated on a needs-basis, it is essential to apply early. Bursaries are also available from some schools. (There are also reputable websites that offer useful information – for example, fastWEB and Fund Finder.)

- teaching assistantships: many North American schools in particular have part-time teaching positions either within the b-school or sometimes in other academic departments such as economics. These are generally negotiated on an annual basis, and can provide a useful income.

- 'working your passage': more common in North America, is another possibility. A part-time job with a company to make ends meet.

- sponsorship: an employer may agree to sponsor you through your MBA. This may be the dream solution, but watch out for any strings attached.

If you need to borrow, check your eligibility for:

- 'soft' loans, which are common in Europe. In the UK, for example, two schemes offer favorable terms to MBA students: the Career Development Loan, and the scheme operated by the Association of MBAs. Both allow students to borrow against the cost of tuition and defer interest until after graduation. Other countries also have similar offerings.

- the Federal Loan Program in the US, which includes Stafford loans and Perkins loans. The ceiling for federal subsidized and unsubsidized loans for domestic students is up to $18,500 in assistance. Many US schools also operate their own loan schemes, which offer favorable, subsidized, rates to students. These include lender partnership programs which provide foreign-friendly schemes for international students which mean that a foreign national does not have to have a co-signer. (These are available at Harvard, Stanford, and Wharton, for example).

- tax concessions may be available in some countries.

Future income

Some idea of future income is useful, too. When you're doing the sums, it helps to have a rough idea what value employers place on the piece of paper you're buying. Students are often blinded by starting salary figures. More useful are comparisons three or four years after graduation. Be aware, though, that salary figures quoted by b-schools tend to be optimistic, although they do offer some idea. The *Financial Times* rankings for the Top 75 full-time international MBA programs, indicates that the top US schools still lead in the salary stakes. Three years after graduation, it indicates that a Harvard Business School MBA can expect an average salary in excess of $173,000, which is 221 per cent increase on pre-MBA salary. Next comes Wharton at $160,468 (up 227 per cent), followed by Stanford at $159, 227 (up 200 per cent).[1]

The same survey indicates that three years down the road a full-time MBA from the London Business School attracts an average salary of just over $113,000 (up 146 per cent). A single year spent at INSEAD produces $115,959 after three years, and IMD, the best

More prevalent at US schools, scholarships or fellowships and other forms of financial aid are now available at most schools around the world. The beauty is that you don't have to repay them. Typically they fall into one of three categories:

- Merit: a small number of students – regarded as having very high potential which will reflect glory on the school – receive these.
- Need: strong applicants who don't have enough money to pay all the costs. In the US, there's a federal methodology, which takes account of income and assets, and allows for expenses, including tax and retirement provision. Some schools use this as an initial evaluation, and then apply their own formula. In broad terms they evaluate the difference between what a student needs and what a student actually has.
- Specific groups: usually designed to attract ethnic minorities or women (still a minority at b-schools), but can also involve funding for a particular industry.

Needs-based aid is more common than you might imagine. Around 47 per cent of Harvard MBA students receive a needs-based fellowship; 22 per cent of students at MIT Sloan receive fellowship support; and 40 per cent at the Tuck School at Dartmouth.

Most scholarships don't cover all the costs of an MBA, but it's worth making a strong case that yours should. They can pay as much as $40,000. If you think you might qualify for a scholarship or any other form of aid, go for it. Remember schools use this pot of money to secure strong students they might otherwise lose. They are concerned with bolstering their GMAT average, or creating a better international mix. In other words, if the school wants you, then you have a strong bargaining position. Use it.

Contact the financial aid office, and apply as early as possible. Don't worry about prejudicing your chances of being offered a place as the admissions and aid applications go to separate offices. Some schools, such as MIT Sloan, automatically review successful applicants for fellowships. Others do not. People who wait until they are already in the program to apply for aid may find that the money allocated has dried up. If you've already been offered a place, though, you may qualify for money earmarked for a specific group. (If you are a US citizen, you may have to submit a Free Application for Federal Student Aid (FAFSA).)

In addition, some international bodies offer scholarships, for example, the European Commission, the World Bank, the Rotary Foundation (and local rotary clubs) and the Inter-American Development Bank through its Japan-IDB Scholarship Program.

M ost MBA students pay their way through a combination of savings, loans and parental support. Among students who are self-financed (i.e. don't get support from their school or employer) the money comes from the following sources:

	North America	Europe	Rest of the world
Savings	36	46	68
Bank loans	42	28	11
Parental help	15	19	11
Spouse support	7	2	1

Source: EIU

European performer in the salary stakes, comes in at $135,501. Other UK schools also offer good returns. Three years after graduation, a full-time MBA from Cranfield can expect to earn an average of $104,000; one from Manchester Business School $89,000. Ashridge Management College, although ranked lower than these schools overall, scores the highest in the UK salary ranking at $122,000.

For those paying their own way, of course, future earnings must be weighed against the cost of borrowing.

A roof over your head

Finding somewhere to live while you're at b-school is a task that requires thought and not a little patience. Sure, you're on a budget, but remember you – and possibly your loved ones – are going to spend a lot of time looking at and bouncing off the four walls you end up with. Investing time in finding the right place is worth while. 'If you need help its there, just ask for it, but remember that you have to be flexible too and you have to learn to budget your time well,' recommends a Michigan student. Forward planning is often necessary – a Kellogg students says: 'It is impossible if you want to live in a nice place if you are from overseas, because you need to be here three months early, but student housing is convenient (if overpriced).'

The easiest places are college towns where renting property to students is well-established – places like Ithaca, New York (home of Cornell's Johnson School), and Ann Arbor, Michigan. A Michigan student says: 'Accommodation here in Ann Arbor is relatively abundant. I live in university-run housing but I am the exception rather than the rule. Most students live in the community. The number and breadth of rental possibilities in Ann

Arbor is awesome. It is a very progressive Midwestern college town but it is not a cheap place to live.'

Many schools have limited on-campus accommodation – although those in major cities may not. Room and board can be a useful stop-gap in the first few months while you're finding your feet. But those with significant others have no real option but to look further afield. Schools are generally very helpful in this regard, although they are also trying to placate all the other students with similar requests. An MIT student reports: 'Accommodation was not too difficult. I worked through the MIT Off-Campus Housing Office and found a great place.'

The people you really want to target are students who are about to graduate. They may have done your work for you. But don't jump at the first place you see – unless it's absolutely perfect. Shop around a bit. Talk to students about the best neighborhoods to be in – and don't part with a deposit until you're certain that it will work. Different countries have different rules on renting accommodation. In Europe watch out for hidden costs. (In Europe also the rental costs are higher. 'It is simple enough to find accommodation in London but one must be prepared to pay a premium,' says a London student.)

On campus or close to the school is good, from the convenience point of view. But a little distance from the academic goldfish bowl can also be attractive. Most students say it's smart to get all the help you can. And just like college, the early bird tends to get the best nest.

Pre-school courses

And then the work begins – and often earlier than you ever thought possible. Most schools offer some pre-school classes to help students fill in gaps in their basic skills or get some help with areas where they think they may struggle. Pre-school courses in math, especially quantitative analysis, can be a very useful investment of time. Most pre-MBA courses run two or three weeks before term starts. Once the MBA program proper gets under way, it is very difficult to address specific weaknesses. It's very easy to simply get left behind. In subjects based on cumulative learning, like math, the consequences – poor marks and personal unhappiness – can sour the whole experience. If you're worried about math, sign up for a pre-course or get some tuition. The worst that can happen is you find out that you're not as bad as you feared. And if you are, you will be able to focus on pulling yourself up.

As one student at Haas explains: 'Tips on lightening the load include: preparing during the summer according to the guidelines Haas provides, (the summer time, Haas math camp is not really necessary except as a way to meet people and assuage any fears the more neurotic among us might have had). I'd also suggest taking a class in one or more of the areas that seem most daunting: finance, accounting, statistics. I wouldn't bother with econ since it's taught differently here.'

Pre-school also offers a valuable opportunity to polish up language skills – especially in European schools which have a language requirement. Enrol on one of the pre-course language courses at European schools. 'Do math class in advance; if weak at math get the languages under your belt before you come here', advises another student at IMD.

Those who fear that their number-crunching skills may not be up to scratch can now get help on line. This year (2000) the e-learning company Quisic (formerly University Access) announced a pre-MBA course that covers accounting, statistics, micro economics and business mathematics. The course, developed in conjunction with the University of Chicago and the Kenan-Flagler School at the University of North Carolina, is distributed to the top schools in the US by University Access, and internationally by FT Knowledge, part of the Pearson Group. The course allows those about to start their MBA to study at home.

www.quisic.com

www.ftknowledge.com

Then there are the books. Schools send out long reading lists – to intimidate you. It is up to you whether you react to them. Obviously, it helps to read a few books before you arrive. But then, you'll be doing plenty of reading once the course starts. It makes sense to read around the subjects that you think you might struggle in.

'Don't bother prepping over the summer – just come to pre-term and have a great time meeting people and brushing up on your accounting, economics and math,' advises one MIT Sloan student.

Trailing spouses

B-school is notoriously tough on relationships, especially marriages. The trailing spouse issue is one that multinationals sending ex-pats overseas have long recognized. Most pick up the tab for relocation and schooling, and even provide help with finding a local job for the trailing partner. B-schools are also trying harder to address this issue.

The obvious solution is to uproot the family and move to the school for the duration of the program. This causes some dislocation – especially if the partner has a job, or there are kids involved. On the whole, US schools tend to be more enlightened in this regard, making an effort to integrate partners into campus life. Some also go to some lengths to try to find part-time work for partners, and have clubs and other events designed to help the MBA widow or widower to feel part of the school. Michigan, for example, has a Significant Others and Spouses (SOS) Club. One student explains: 'It's a great network for spouses and significant others. They have social events almost once a week, they have job fairs, they help each other locate different types of employment in Ann Arbor. I have made lifelong friends here, and so has my husband. And if you ask me, he has got the better deal. While we're in study groups all night, SOS has Monday night football, Tuesday night movies, Wednesday night bike rides, etc.'

European schools lag behind. IMD in Switzerland is an exception. The school claims to be the only b-school with a kindergarten, and also offers a special program for partners.

More than half of the school's annual MBA intake of around 85 arrive with partners, who can feel isolated in an unfamiliar culture. The school offers events and organizes lectures and language courses to help them fit in. If required it also provides counseling.

'These services are expensive,' says Professor Domenique Turpin, director of the MBA program, 'but we provide them to help students and to differentiate ourselves from other business schools.'

Despite such efforts, however, many MBA students acknowledge that there is a clear division between those people with partners and the singles community. A worryingly high proportion of students admit that their marriages and long-standing relationships run into problems during the MBA program, sometimes leading to divorce. Long-distance relationships are especially vulnerable.

'It is very tough. The casualty rate in terms of outside relationships is a high 75 per cent,' says a student at AIM. 'On the plus side, a lot of the students end up meeting their eventual mates right here on campus. In my case I spend a lot making daily long-distance phone calls to my girlfriend. But it is well worth it – to hear her voice.'

Adds another AIM MBA: 'Some relationships survive, but most of them don't. I can't say that b-school destroys relationships because it all really depends on the couple. Usually it is the other party who has to adjust. Relationships that don't last are usually the ones that were not very stable to begin with. If you want to make it work, you can really make it work. There's no such thing as school getting in the way – it is really up to the person if he wants school to get in the way. In my case, I was very lucky to have a boyfriend who was willing to adjust to my hectic schedule. Although he was working, he made an effort to visit me in school. We've survived AIM and we're getting married.'

Forewarned is often forearmed. 'It can be tough on relationships because it is difficult to understand the time constraints and stress if you are not in the same situation,' says a student at the University of Texas. 'I think most people start the program with the idea they can treat the program like a 60-hour-a-week job and then have a relaxed, balanced life outside of that. Though UT stresses balance, it can still be challenging to obtain it.'

Those who prepare in advance seem to cope better. 'The impact of b-school on relationships is an overdone topic. I am married, and never feel that school is interfering with my relationship with my wife. It's a simple matter of prioritizing the things that are most important to you in life. If a spouse or family doesn't come near the top of the list, then one shouldn't be surprised if a relationship is strained or even fails,' says one Chicago student.

Those that manage the tensions well say it pays to support the integration of partners in social situations, but also to ring-fence their time with partners. 'Students make an effort to integrate spouses/significant others at social events, and there is a "joint ventures" group that organizes events for married/committed couples. The key is booking time in to your schedule, to protect your time together from work or extra-curricular commitments,' says a student at UCLA.

All agree that an understanding partner is vital. One Stern student says: 'I'm married, so it's a little different. He understands that this takes up a significant amount of my time, although he doesn't always like it. He takes it upon himself to "save" me from too much studying on occasion. It's really all about prioritizing. I can see how this would be murder on a casual relationship though – I hardly have time to keep up with my best girlfriends.'

'For once in my life I'm glad I'm not in a serious relationship', adds another Stern MBA. 'B-school is very taxing not only on my time but on my mental and emotional resources. I imagine that this could be difficult for any partner who is not exceedingly understanding.'

Friendships can also suffer. 'It can be tough,' says a Harvard student. 'Most of my close friends are in other cities – so there are time-zone issues – as well as the simple fact that it's less fun to talk to your close friends on the phone for two years than it is to go out and have dinner and drinks all the time. In terms of friendships – it's tough because you are in an environment where you are working hard to build new relationships with people at school. So, on the one hand you're trying to spend time with people to get to know them – while on the other you're trying to spend time with your friends outside of school so you can maintain your friendships beyond superficial conversations. That's especially tough when you have lots of different friends in different places. You just have to ask your friends outside of school to be patient and understanding – and hope that they just don't get too fed up with you.'

The name of the game with relationships is adjustment. Make time to discuss the issues and how you will handle them, and you can come out with your relationships intact. Ignore the tensions, and you're storing up trouble for later. The MBA is tough enough without a whole load of emotional trauma and recriminations. One Michigan student confident in his relationship told us: 'It wasn't bad for my marriage because I have a wonderful wife. My only relationship that suffered was my one with the basketball court as class often interfered with playing.' Michael Jordan never went to b-school.

Endnotes

1 Based on a weighted average of this year and last year's salary, three years after graduation. *Financial Times*, Monday, 24 January 2000.

the academic life

The greatest piece of advice I can give is to temper your expectations. Everyone who comes to Wharton, or any top business school for that matter, has been in the top 1 per cent of their company or field. When you get all those people together not everyone can be the star or the valedictorian.

WHARTON STUDENT

Welcome to b-school

So, you've made it. You've negotiated the hurdles to get a place at one of the world's top business schools. You've demonstrated your intellectual prowess in the GMAT arena – maybe even done it a few times. You've dazzled the admissions office with your unique and irresistible individuality. You've filled in countless boxes on application forms and been well and truly grilled by the powers that be and not been found wanting. You've packed up your possessions and kissed the job goodbye. You may have attended summer school – some schools expect it. You will certainly have done some preparation – background reading and the like. Now you are ready to take your place among the other intellectual giants in the MBA class of 2001 or 2000.

How does it feel? OK, so you're feeling pretty damn good. A bit apprehensive, maybe, but you know you're at the top of your academic game. You know you can do it. You're ready. You've prepared mentally and spiritually. Now what? Well, reality is about to kick in. It's not that you're out of your depth – the selection process means you wouldn't be here if you were. The problem is that you may not have prepared for how fast the current of learning will flow, especially in the first year of a two-year program. Don't get swept away in the flood. If you're taking a one-year MBA, then you have to pack it all into that one year – or 11 months.

Going back into education can be a shock to the brain and the central nervous system. A student from Italy's Bocconi says: 'After being out of a study environment for four years, it was a shock to get back into the rhythm of studying. Organizing your time is key to not letting the heavy workload build up over time. This takes practice and at times it can seem like a never-ending pile of paper is invading your apartment! There is no trick to managing this as it depends on the individual. For me, the first few weeks took some balancing between study (what you're here for) and social life (which is too much fun to miss). Now, I think the balance is no problem.'

Even if you're fresh from a degree the going is set to become tougher.

The general agreement is that for those with an artistic bent, life is especially tough. 'For me, without a quantitative background, it was a very heavy first year. I had to work pretty hard (like every weekend for the first semester). I struggled and worked more hours than a lot of people, though,' says a Haas student. 'The more preparation you have done in the 'hard' subjects, such as math and stats, the better.'

A London Business School student says: 'Workload depends on: a) your background, i.e. it will be harder for someone from a humanistic background to learn finance; b) how fast you accommodate to the teaching style. Coming from different countries which have different ways of teaching, this is a major issue at school; c) how well you work in groups. Group work is a key component for LBS and, thus, the better you do it, the lower the workload and the more you will learn from others.'

Says a Tuck student: 'It depends on your background – if you had some quant training, it's not so bad. I did, and the winter of my spring term was the hardest in terms of time commitment – but that was a function of the classes I chose.'

Time is the MBA student's number-one enemy. There are just 24 hours in the day – a fact that MBA program designers seem to overlook. The answer, of course, is that you have to learn to swim a bit faster. And you have to learn quickly. And then there's all those other things you wanted to do while you were here. Extra-curricular activities, partying, sports, sightseeing, meeting recruiters, partying, seeing your loved ones, keeping in touch with old friends, networking, partying.

The solution is time management and it is probably the biggest challenge of an MBA. Asked about the workload, an Ivey student says: '[It is] very heavy, at least for the first year. But it is due to lack of understanding about how to manage time. You can do three things at Ivey: socialize, play sports, or study. You only have time to really do two of them.' The choice is yours. Or, as one Stern student advises: 'If you don't know time management now, learn it!'

And you'd better learn it fast. Students report that a time management strategy makes the whole MBA experience more rewarding. 'Academically, I'm sorry that I don't have more time to learn. I'm so busy trying to keep up with the workload, I find myself cutting corners to get things done. As a result, much of the book learning is short term. Also, I was hoping to hear more of my fellow students' experiences in the work world. However, none of the class discussions have given these opportunities,' says another Stern student.

There are only 24 hours in a day. MBA-time, however, aims to utilize each and every one. 'The workload, particularly in the beginning, is intense,' says an IMD student. 'Anyone looking to attend IMD should be aware of that. In the first four months a typical day can last from 6.00 am to midnight – and maybe you still won't have read all the cases.'

It is all a question of balance says a Fuqua student: 'The workload is not as heavy as one may think, but it is largely dependent on what you want out of your MBA. If you are looking towards obtaining a comprehensive perspective of business, then your time will be limited. If on the other hand you are interested in only the bare necessities, then your life will be a bit less hectic. Remember, though, your first year and your second year are very different in terms of workload. I have personally ensured that I take a full load of classes all terms, and this is something that has greatly increased the workload and smoothed it out over the two years.'

Have no fear, there are some tips and tricks that can help you keep up with the torrent of work. But first take a big breath. Here are the simple facts of b-school life:

- You can't do everything you'd like to or thought you would – so you have to prioritize. 'My only tip on how to ease the burden is to prioritize. You are assigned nearly more work than you could possibly do, so you must choose what to do wisely,' says a Darden student. An MIT student concludes: 'There is so much going on that it's very hard to choose sometimes (which classes to take, which social and extra-curricular activities to join etc).'

- There will be people who are smarter than you, probably in every class you take – get used to it. Says a Wharton student: 'Many people, smart people, have trouble accepting that there are other people out there who could beat them like a drum in a given class.

What these people don't necessarily digest is that you can't expect to compete with a CPA in an advanced accounting class if you haven't had considerable work experience in the field. Unless you have perspective and humility you will fight this unsuccessfully your entire MBA career.'

- You are following in the footsteps of many others who came before you – try to learn from their experiences.

- 'You must be able to have fun,' advises an Ivey student. 'It is the best form of stress release. It does not help to be high strung and nervous – everyone goes through the same cycle.' Message: It may be costing you an arm and a leg, but don't take it too seriously – it's just a course. As one Michigan student says: 'My best piece of advice for most people entering UMBS is not to take yourself and school so seriously. B-school isn't the only thing going on in the world. If you don't have something truly interesting and insightful to say in class, keep it to yourself. Class time could be cut by 50 per cent if people took that advice. I'm off to a start-up company to pursue excitement and millions of dollars.'

  A Tuck student adds: 'I suppose this depends a lot on the school, but at Tuck I would say it's important to try not to take yourself too seriously. There are many smart people here so it's easy for some people to get discouraged during the first term and feel like they don't belong. As time goes on, this evens out and people realize what their strengths and weaknesses are. While it's tempting to compare yourself to others in such a competitive environment, it's helpful to always keep in mind what you're in business school for and what you're trying to learn.'

- Business school is not the real world; it's not even the real business world – it's an illusion caused by reading too many books and case studies.

- 'If you get in and work hard, you will not flunk out,' says a Stanford student. It is virtually impossible to fail an MBA – whatever b-schools say. An Ivey graduate says: 'I don't feel any different. I don't feel any more "managerial". I feel that all I needed to do was get in. Once I'm in, I'll graduate and have the "Ivey stamp of approval". You just have to get through that first year – it is a lot of work, not hard, just lots of volume.' A Stern student adds: 'No one fails really. Some part-timers may leave early but few full-timers do. Even those starting businesses typically suck it up (perform not as well academically) and get the degree.'

- It doesn't last. Pain is always easier to bear if you know when it will end. No matter how rough the road, the MBA is a journey that has an end. The workload doesn't go on for ever – that comes later when you join a consulting firm. Keeping that in mind can make the whole experience more enjoyable. 'Just do it,' says an Ivey student. 'You're in there together with the rest of your class. You're not alone. You're all experiencing the same thing, and have each other to support. It is possible to do. Everyone gets through it (the person who dropped out this year was because of an ill family member, nothing to do with the program). Talk to second-year students for advice, use them as a resource. Have fun. The first year is the worst. It's only eight months. You'll get through it.'

More reassurance comes from a Kenan-Flagler student: 'Oh, you'll survive. The atmosphere is such that few people are really disappointed. Of course you can never satisfy everyone. But I think our mix at KFBS is so well-balanced that people learn a lot and sincerely enjoy the experience. I know I have made at least 200 first-year friends that I will be able to call on throughout life (not to mention dozens in the class above me).'

- Most important of all, in five years' time none of the class work or deadlines will matter – all that you will have to take away is the people you got to know, a scattering of knowledge, and a piece of paper in a frame.

In the end, it's down to you how hard you work. You can make it as easy or as tough as you choose.

If you want it, the work is there. Peter Drucker has written a lot of books for starters. 'The workload is heavy, really heavy. And the more motivated you are, the heavier it is. It's not just the school work, it's all of the other things as well: job search, club activities, lectures, seminars. There's so much going on and all of it seems valuable, so you really have to know how to prioritize and how to manage your time,' says a Stern student.

'I have just become cynical and decided that you really don't come here to learn anything, but rather to get the rubber stamp and the nice piece of paper to hang on the wall, though I would be happier paying $100,000 to learn something,' says a Kellogg student.

Here endeth the first lesson. Survival lesson two is to pack some humility. As a Michigan student puts it: 'As far as surviving in school, I think the key is to leave your ego at the door and come prepared to learn your weaknesses and improve on them.' This is harder than it sounds. The entire b-school experience is based around MBAs being Masters of the Universe. Some intelligent people may begin to believe that this is actually the case.

The other key is to recognize that b-school is not the same as business. There are useful skills you can learn in an academic setting. But there are others you have to master in the real world. Knowing the difference is half the battle. 'I would advise students to push themselves as much as possible in an area where tangible business skills can be learned,' says one Wharton student. 'It is my belief that skills like accounting or finance are best learned in an academic environment while things like strategy development can be developed on the job if you're smart. While it doesn't necessarily make your life easy during your MBA years, you will be glad if you put yourself out there in these areas and test your limits. Finally, I would say roll with the punches, MBA programs can, at times, be a harsh environment in which to learn important lessons.'

The MBA offers a great opportunity to learn about business in a structured, vigorous and challenging way. But it won't turn you into Michael Dell overnight.

Faced with a notoriously heavy workload, many MBA students find it hard to pack all the studying, networking and extra-curricular activity in. Donald Martin, associate dean at the University of Chicago's Graduate School of Business, offers a ten-point MBA survival guide:

1 Determine your priorities and stick to them.

2 Involve yourself in life outside the classroom as well as inside.

3 Focus on friendships and relationships as well as networking for career purposes.

4 Remember that enjoying your job over the long haul is much more satisfying than earning top dollar.

5 Keep in mind that the acquisition and application of knowledge is important but that people skills are even more important.

6 Allow yourself to take a break, to make a mistake, to say, 'I'm sorry.'

7 To paraphrase Calvin Coolidge: education, talent and genius are helpful, but persistence and determination ultimately make the difference.

8 Learn to be content despite unanswered questions, unsettled situations, unresolved conflicts and unfinished business.

9 Remember that it's far easier to do your homework than not do it.

10 Operate on this principle: 'The measure of my character is what I do when no one else is watching.'

Teaching and workload

The way your workload breaks down will depend on the teaching style and philosophy at your school. There is a suspicion that some up and coming schools push their students harder in their quest for a higher ranking. A Stern student says: 'According to many MBA students, the level of workload is inversely proportional to the spot on the Top 20 list (i.e. the schools in slots 11–20 work students very hard so the school can achieve a Top 10 rating. Similarly, the Top 10 schools are less concerned about workload since they're already in the Top 10). For example, I hear that Darden is a killer, but friends at Columbia are sliding through.'

In addition, not all academics share the same desire to burden you with assignments and cases. 'The workload varies from professor to professor,' says a Chicago student. 'Students have the choice to work as much or as little as they choose, but one common theme that runs through all Chicago students is that they are intellectually curious and have a strong desire to excel. Because of these characteristics, Chicago MBAs take their course assignments and learning very seriously and consequently work very hard.'

In addition to lectures and the other traditional scholarly techniques, there are three main methods of teaching the MBA:

- case studies: a method developed at Harvard Business School which adopted and adapted the approach used by law schools
- project work: which looks outside the b-school to the real world of business
- group work: this involves working in study groups (typically of five to seven people) and relies on a collaborative approach.

Most schools use a combination. Kellogg, for instance, uses lectures, reading, case discussions, role plays, seminars, group projects, field studies, computer simulations and independent study. Schools employ different blends of the learning methods. Some, such as Harvard, have a heavy bias towards the case method, while others rely less on cases or don't use them at all. The mix affects workload. Schools which are heavily dependent on the case study approach involve a large degree of discretion over study time.

A Fuqua student recounts his day: 'We have an average of three one-hour-twenty-minute classes a day (usually a max of four classes and on very rare occasions only one class). An average case is about 20 to 23 pages long in the first three months, shortening to an average of 10 to 15 pages afterwards. Therefore, we are looking at about 30 to 60 pages of reading a day. I generally get to bed about 2–3 am, with classes starting at 9:30 am. After classes end, the afternoon to the evening would be a mix of hanging out with classmates, eating, and of course studying. You could actually keep a pretty normal sleep cycle if you studied right after class, taking very occasional breaks for meals and such. However, I would like to think that studying is only one aspect of the MBA experience and a good balance is always beneficial to go through the big picture. In addition, some classes require group work so meeting time would have to be allocated during the day.'

MBA student life requires constant juggling of academic demands, extra-curricular activities, and basic necessities. According to Stanford, a typical day could look like this:

7:00 am	Check your overnight e-mail on the computer in your room at the Schwab Residential Center while you have coffee. Walk to the Business School and check your mailbox for the student newspaper and a draft of the paper your group is working on for a class project.
7:30 am	Grab a muffin in the Arbuckle Student Lounge while you visit with friends you plan to go hiking with next weekend.
8:00 am	Uh-oh. The CEO is in class to hear a case discussion of his firm. Bet you're glad you studied last night.
10:00 am to noon	Study group meeting for a required field research project. Work on a group presentation for senior managers of the firm. Get lunch at the Thai Cafe and attend a presentation by the Career Management Center with executives of an international banking firm.
1:30 pm	You are cold-called in your finance class. Since your study group spent three hours in the computer lab yesterday analyzing the effects of various international currency changes, you successfully defend your point of view.
3:30 pm	Meet with the ninth-grader you tutor in East Palo Alto as part of the ongoing *I Have a Dream* project.
5:00 pm	Jog with the Hash House Harriers to the Dish on the hills overlooking the campus and San Francisco Bay.
6:30 pm	Dinner with the steering committee for the Entrepreneurship Conference. Download a finance class data set off the class web page, then submit your on-line bids for the CMC interviews you want to schedule next week.
8:00 to 11:00 pm	From your suite in the Schwab Center, do an on-line search of library materials about the firm in this week's human resources class case. Then complete the reading for tomorrow's class.

This is part of Stanford's publicity so it is a sanitized version of events. The hours, however, are authentic.

Coping with cases

'Once a month, we have to do what is called a WAC or a Written Analysis of Case. It is a case which is distributed on Friday afternoon at 5 pm. Submission is the next day at noon. The written analysis is usually completed and submitted by students at around 4 to 5 am Saturday. Some students finish at about 1 or 2 am, while the latest finish an hour before the deadline,' says a student at the Asian Institute of Management. Hundreds of thousands of MBA students have had similar experiences. Somewhere on planet MBA right now, a student is staring blankly at a lengthy case study.

Exported around the globe, the case study has been one of the educational building blocks of MBA programs throughout the world. The case study method was established as the primary method of teaching at Harvard Business School as long ago as 1924. It presents students with a corporate example. From the narrative, they are expected to reach conclusions about what was the right or wrong thing to do, identify best and worst practice, and learn something about managerial behavior.

Students are expected to read, digest and prepare a large number of cases every week – often tackling two or three a night. It is down to the student to decide how to allocate their time to these cases.

'You typically have three cases to read and analyze every night. Some people spend three hours on every case (me), other people just read the cases. I study quite hard, probably spend eight to nine hours every night studying, while others would put in as little as three hours. Ivey marks are based on participation and exams. Therefore the more you are prepared for class each day, the more you will be able to participate,' says a student at Western Ontario's Ivey.

The case method also has its critics. A particular problem at some schools is the level of class discussion. 'Class participation could be better (more diverse),' says a Tuck student. 'A lot of the same people are raising their hands and speaking, for the most part. Most professors have been great, but a couple have sucked. I found many of the HBS cases that we've used to be painful and meaningless.'

Some people divide their time equally between different classes, while others use greater discretion. If you want to have any life at all outside of study, then there have to be trade-offs. Most students concentrate on some cases and hope to slide through on others. The problem with this strategy is something called cold-calling. Professors pick unsuspecting students to discuss the cases in class, and evaluate them on their response. You don't know if you will be called upon until the class is underway.

Nightmare time. 'The real key is making yourself talk in class. The more you talk – the less you have to worry about getting cold-called,' advises a Harvard student. 'This doesn't mean you can just say anything – you have to have read the case and say something of quality if you want to get positive feedback. The real stress is in the beginning when you don't know what's coming – and when all the other people around you are getting you worked up because they're in the same situation – that's what really drives first-year stress. When you see the people who are relaxed – these are the ones who've figured it out early.'

As a student at AIM explains: 'The first three months are pretty bad. Since AIM is a case method school, and class participation (CP) is usually the main pass/fail driver for us, preparation is very important. A good bullshit artist may get away with making CPs without reading the case by drawing out inferences from what classmates say. This, however, can be quite a gamble, particularly if the professor starts asking for support through case facts. In short, to pass, students have to CP, and in order to CP, they would have to prepare.'

There are many different studying styles, and therefore tips, that can help cut the case study load. The way MBA classes are organized varies from school to school, but the general principles are the same. A student at the Asian Institute of Management suggests the following tips for coping with cases:

- Divide the work. Divide the cases between the four or five members of the CAN group (Case Analysis Group, study and support group, or whatever). Then meet up to talk about the cases assigned.

- Read only selected cases. Sometimes, it is impossible to read and analyze everything because of lack of time. This is when priorities kick in. For example, if you were cold-called in, let's say, the last finance session, and you have finance tomorrow but have to read three more 20-page cases in addition to the finance case, you may just forego reading finance. Of course, you would generally keep quiet and try to remain inconspicuous during the finance class the next day. Priorities are the key as well as trying to balance active participation in all classes (but not necessarily all sessions).

- Check out case styles. For example, in Harvard cases, sometimes people in a rush get away with reading only the first three pages (to determine the background and issue) and the last three pages (to determine alternatives, possible solutions, etc.) They then go to class and listen for the CP of classmates and rehash case facts to support their own position. Personally, I don't really do this because getting caught and looking like an idiot is worse than not participating.

- Use available technology. I don't understand why people try to do stuff manually when it would be a lot easier to do it on the computer (i.e., income statements, balance sheets, etc.). It saves a lot of time and is easier to make adjustments for errors.

Making the grade

Students say it's hard to fail an MBA. But most people who go to b-school are not inclined to simply sit back and enjoy the ride. Most are conspicuous over-achievers. They want to do well – they just can't help themselves. There are two basic strategies you can follow – depending on your temperament, work ethic and general attitude to life. You can either accept that you will get by, and try to get the most out of all aspects of b-school life. Or you can obsess about grades. Alternatively, you can try to do both – probably a speedy route to a breakdown. The strategy you choose inevitably has an impact on your workload.

H BS cases are first-hand accounts of actual management situations, taking as their subjects problems that stem from many interdependent factors. The business community and faculty research provide a continual source of new cases. Cases involve organizations ranging from manufacturing companies to government agencies, from non-profit organizations to major financial institutions. Problems span operating policies, accounting methods, marketing techniques, and management styles. Harvard Business School cases are distinguished by the fact that they are bound by the constraints and incomplete information available in a real business situation. Students are asked to place themselves in the positions of the managers described in the case and to perform analyses and recommend courses of action without benefit of prior knowledge of outcomes.

Students first analyze a case individually, identifying the problems, examining the contributing causes, considering alternative courses of action, and arriving at a set of recommendations. Students often meet in small groups before class to discuss their findings, to consider options, and to prepare to contribute to the section meeting. In class, under the questioning and guidance of the professor, students weigh factors, probe underlying issues, compare advantages and disadvantages of different alternatives, and suggest courses of action in light of the company's objectives. Students later reflect on the issues discussed in class to clarify and integrate them into their own conceptual framework. Students study and prepare more than 500 cases at HBS. Through this daily exposure, they learn to recognize the unique aspects of different situations, define problems, suggest further avenues of analysis, and devise and implement action plans.

Over time and in different contexts, however, a single subject may be dealt with through a variety of teaching methods and settings. The faculty work together to integrate concepts across courses to replicate interactions, decision-making processes, and the diversity of skills required in the business environment. Joint teaching and shared cases allow students to examine issues from a variety of perspectives. Classroom experiences are further augmented by experiential learning and participation in a broad range of activities throughout the curriculum.

Case studies generally eschew the intricate and complex human side of management. It is this fundamental shortcoming that is increasingly being exposed. Business schools, some say, have placed too much emphasis on teaching students analytical techniques and not enough on managing people. Whatever its current and historical limitations, the emphasis on the case study method has greatly aided the development of management theory. It freezes management in time. It espouses rational contemplation, analysis and decision making. In doing so, it makes management theory more understandable and accessible.

There are myriad cases to choose from, covering every business eventuality. With over 14,000 titles, the European Case Clearing House, based at the UK's Cranfield University, is the largest single source of management case studies. During a typical year it supplies nearly 300,000 cases in response to requests from throughout the world. Harvard alone has generated 5,310 cases – the most prolific case generator in Europe is Lausanne's IMD with 1,058.

The case study method remains a widely accepted and practised approach in the US and in many other parts of the world. Harvard alone continues to churn out 600 cases a year. Its example is followed in places far distant from Cambridge, Mass. Take the China Europe International Business School in Shanghai. 'Case writing on the development of selected enterprises in China is CEIBS's most important research activity,' its publicity material announces. 'These cases are not only used in the school's own programs, but also published to serve as teaching material at other institutions.'

Despite the profusion of cases and the wide usage of the case study method, doubt and invective has been aimed in its general direction. Peter Drucker surely had the case study in mind when he said: 'Classrooms construct wonderful models of a non-world.' Once again one of the most consistent critics has been Henry Mintzberg. 'Superficial and disconnected,' he says. 'It's somebody else's world. You read 20 pages the night before and pronounce the next morning. Business schools using cases, like Harvard, train managers to be glib, that's all.' Elsewhere, he has noted: 'Business schools train people to sit in their offices and look for case studies. The more Harvard succeeds, the more business fails.'

The HBS website provides a vigorous defence for the case study method. 'Managers learn from experience by doing, by observing [Classroom] and inter-acting with others, and by soliciting and absorbing feedback. They deepen their learning through analysis and reflection. As such, managers obtain and retain knowledge by actively participating in its construction and use. Based on these concepts, the HBS Learning Model requires students to practise and perfect a process of inductive learning. The educational process goes beyond facts and theories, as students learn not only how to manage organizations but how to take charge of their own learning and development. The HBS Learning Model provides a framework for the pursuit and creation of knowledge by simulating the managerial work experience as closely as possible. Through the case method and other learning techniques, students examine problem-focused situations in ways that are managerially relevant, intellectually and emotionally engaging, and highly interactive.'

'The case study was introduced to bring a level of reality to a student in a remote environment so that theoretical concepts could be brought to life,' says London Business School's Jeff Sampler. 'The case study is not dead. The issue is finding different ways of bringing the business world into the classroom in a dynamic, realistic and lively way. Today's case studies take that still further with video clips of chief executives talking with real feeling and passion, as well as simulations which show what happens if you do a or b.' In practice, Sampler argues that the case study's chief role should be to introduce and explain fundamental principles. He warns against over dependence on the case study: 'Doing everything by case study leads to paralysis by analysis, an unwillingness to do anything or decide on anything unless there is a supportive case.'

'Everyone at business school has different expectations. Some want to get top grades, others only care about finding a job, others are at b-school to find a wife, so it is up to you to define your priorities and the workload really depends on that,' says one student.

Adds a Stern MBA: 'Once in, no one really ever fails out of b-school unless he/she does absolutely nothing. And even then, I don't know if he/she fails out. Despite this fact, we all work our butts off to get the best grades we can. We try to convince ourselves that "grades don't really matter" (which they don't unless you want to work for Goldman Sachs or McKinsey), but it's difficult to keep such an excellent attitude in this culture of over-achievers and go-getters.'

Accepting your limitations and the limitation of your aspirations is part of the education process – or should be. 'Corporate Finance was an incredibly important class,' says one student. 'I knew I'd be lucky to get a pass. If I was so hung up on grades, I would have spent way too much time trying to excel in an area that's not a core strength. Or I might not have taken the class in the first place, afraid that my GPA would suffer. Foolish!'

Some students remain admirably philosophical. 'Grades don't matter,' says a Fuqua student. 'Admit to yourself that there will be some subjects that you just aren't passionate about – be it finance, accounting, operations, marketing, whatever. But take a class in it anyway, even if you know you'll barely pass. I'm not a finance person – but I knew that.'

Others lament the lack of support: 'I thought there would be more support for when a student was in trouble academically in a particular course. There is tutoring available (and you've got some free in your core courses, in addition to help from Teaching Assistants) but you need to make sure you get it early.'

Not surprisingly, schools expect students to take their studies seriously. Very seriously. Most have enshrined competition in their cultures in one way or another. Some programs are more team-oriented. Others less so. Although they assign students to study groups, certain schools place more emphasis on individual achievement. In practice, the underlying philosophy of the school has a significant impact on the attitude of students, with some schools encouraging a dog-eat-dog approach. The larger US MBA programs, in particular, typically sharpen the competitive instincts of students. Harvard, for example, is one of a number of schools that has a forced-curve grading system. At HBS, this means that the bottom 10 per cent of all classes must technically fail. The system encourages rivalry between students – and discourages slackers.

Chicago has a forced-curve grade in every class throughout the two-year program. The Stern School limits the number of top grades. This means that students are automatically in competition with each other. As one student explains: 'Stern has a "35 per cent" rule, where an assignment/test/project will yield only 35 per cent A-grades. The rest are B+, B, B-, and sometimes even C. In the mentality of a b-school student, a B or B- is pretty much a failing grade. Some of the faculty and students are fighting to change the 35 per cent rule, so that any student who deserves an A gets it. However, much of the administration believes that this will hurt Stern's placement in the b-school rankings.'

Other schools have a pass or fail approach. Yale, for example, does not use the typical A to F grading system: 80 per cent of the class receives a proficient; 10 per cent gets a distinction; and the rest get a pass or fail. This breeds a different attitude to workload. There is a debate at the school about this. As one student says: 'If I have been disappointed with anything, it has been the battle going on at SOM over whether to implement a grading system that will supposedly increase our competitiveness in the global MBA market. It was the philosophy behind SOM that drew me here, and I fervently hope that nothing will change that philosophy so that SOM becomes like all other business schools.

'Because of the grading system, people are able to work together and support one another during the overwhelming times, rather than increasing the already existing stress by elbowing one another and fighting for coveted A grades.'

MIT Sloan, too, tends to be a bit more laid-back about grades. 'Grades are just not considered important here. People want to perform well, but there are no rankings or anything like that,' says one student. 'Basically, 40 per cent of the class will get As and the rest will get Bs. Learning is more important than grades.'

First-semester hell

'Practically, Yale SOM, has no grades so it's really up to you to decide how much you want to put into each class. I found myself balancing the academic work against the opportunities for extra-curricular activities, taking more classes, various events in the bigger Yale and getting to know my amazing classmates. If you are more academically focused the load will be heavier – but it is each person's own choice. First semester, first year, seems to be the hardest for most students – but even that wasn't too bad,' says a Yale student. Her view is unusual. Believe us. The first semester can be hellish.

This is largely because you don't know the ground rules. Learn them quickly, and life gets marginally easier. B-schools also seem to delight in throwing as much as they can at you – just to let you know that they are serious academic places. For those whose grasp of calculus is tenuous, there is the challenge of quantitative classes in particular.

'The beginning of the first year is the worst it gets. It's very tough starting out because the only real guideline you have is professors telling you you should spend two to three hours a night per case – and you usually have three case days. That makes for an unbearable amount of work. Once you've figured out that you can easily do this much work – it becomes much more pleasant. The key to being here is reading the cases – and getting a good understanding of the subject matter – enough so that you can speak intelligently in class. As you get more experienced with the case method – you know what to focus on – and what you can let slide – it's like anything else in life,' says one student.

The first semester is just the start of a tough first year. The first year covers the core curriculum. The second year, which gives students the opportunity to follow their interests through electives, is generally lighter. Some schools offer the option of deferring some of your core classes to the second year, to even out the workload. 'Wharton's first year is front-loaded. However, you can choose to defer classes until your second year. You can average 4.5 classes a semester if you want, which isn't bad,' says one student.

For most, however, workload in the first year is famously excessive. A Kenan-Flagler student says: 'First year is a killer. Especially, if you are not someone with a business undergrad (like me). You can slide by looking for a passing grade at 50 hours a week, but high marks are difficult to obtain.' Students variously described their first-year experiences as: 'brutal', 'a boot-camp', 'hell', 'nightmarish', and 'all consuming'. The image painted by articles, books and schools is of students burning their scholarly candles at both ends and in the middle.

Some beg to differ. 'I don't find it that bad,' observes a Columbia student. 'But I'm very disciplined, so it seems to take me less time than some other people to get the work done (especially readings . . . luckily I read fast). I have a boyfriend who lives in Washington DC so I try to get all the work done during the week so I can spend weekends with him. I think I work less hard in b-school than I did in undergrad, actually.'

'The level of academic difficulty here is a joke, particularly for quantitative classes, and it has really made me question the quality of the American undergrad and high school education (e.g. in our statistics class, they spent two hours teaching us what a variance is), and I am not sure that I am getting value for money on the academic side,' says a defiant but anonymous student at Kellogg. 'I never thought the workload was that bad this year. Of course, coming from an investment banking background has probably warped my perspective.' (Almost certainly.)

Most students acknowledge that they have their hands and heads full, but some indicate that it isn't nearly as bad as they anticipated. Some students appear to have a higher pain threshold. Once again, it depends on you and your attitude. You can either make your life hellish by trying to absorb everything, or you can have an easier ride by being more selective.

Students had this to say about their initiation into the MBA fold:

'The workload is challenging in the fall of the first year, there is no question. But the work is purposeful, and the students learn a tremendous amount as a result of the comprehensive program. The students who develop good relationships with their learning teams have an easier time getting through the rigors of the first year. The learning teams are an important support mechanism and a big part of the first-year experience. My team mates taught me so much!' – Darden student

'The core workload (during the first semester) is heavier, as is probably the case at most b-schools. Handling it is not particularly difficult, so long as you understand that late nights are a part of business school. The most important lessons to learn regarding workload are time management and group management. Get to the point, divide the work and come together to polish off the finished product.' – Owen student

'There are so many interesting things happening around the school, you do not want to miss out. The important lesson I learned from the first semester is to maintain balances. As the first two weeks pass, you realize that you cannot read everything you are asked to read and you can definitely not participate in every single event that goes on around school. Also, you need to keep up with the work. The good old trick of revising the week before the exam, that I grew so fond of during my undergraduate days, does not apply in business school. You need to keep up with the workload, and the courses are designed to ensure that.' – Haas student

'Workload is VERY heavy. In fact, a number of our foreign exchange students were amazed by the amount of work that was given to us. We read three to four cases a day, and meet with our CAN groups for projects at least three times a week. Finance and statistics take up a lot of our time since we have to crunch the numbers. We also have our overnight WACS (written analysis of a case) that ruin our Friday evenings. Then there's the ever famous MRR (management research report) which takes up a lot of our time. It's a pretty heavy load but it's also manageable.' – Asian Institute of Management student

'The workload is fairly heavy, especially in the first semester. However, you soon learn what you have to really study hard, and what you can let the professor teach you. For example, some classes are mainly lecture-oriented, while others are based on the readings. As long as you learn what is what, you can make it. I think the workload is as hard as you make it. There's enough time to do most of the work if you allow it.' – Yale student

Core requirements

So what is filling those days and nights? All MBAs consist of a core curriculum. Although the names of courses vary, all schools cover the following basic areas:

- macroeconomics
- microeconomics
- finance
- financial and managerial accountancy
- quantitative analysis
- information management
- marketing
- organizational behavior
- strategy.

Together these subject areas make up the core of the MBA. At most schools they are compulsory, and make up the first year of a two-year program, or the first two semesters of a one-year program. School attitudes do vary, however, even towards the core curriculum. In some cases, if you can demonstrate competence in a particular subject you may be able to skip the more basic class and substitute an advanced course in the same area. Your school may expect you to sit an exam to demonstrate your grasp of the subject, however. But this means that if you have a professional qualification in accountancy, you may be able to miss out the rudimentary stuff and get your teeth into something more specialized.

The second year of the classic two-year MBA is your opportunity to specialize through electives. These are optional courses, requiring students to make their own choices depending on personal interests and future career plans. One-year MBAs typically squeeze the core courses into the first two semesters, leaving the third for students to focus on electives – although inevitably there is less time for specialization. In any case, remember that in the second year you will be busy with other issues, like finding a job, so be selective about electives.

'During the second year, the work is not nearly as heavy as the first year,' says one Haas student. 'Or let's put it this way: in the second year, you can choose to do the electives you want and so you can take as little as possible to allow you to graduate or as much as you can fit into your schedule. On average, people have a lot more free time, a lot of us are working part-time for future employers or spend time looking for a job.'

The range of electives at the top schools is wide and widening. As a general rule, the bigger the school the more electives on offer. Some courses are offered only if there is sufficient student interest. Others tend to be over-subscribed. So be warned: there is no guarantee that you will be able to take the electives that you want. A number of the top

US schools operate bidding systems for electives. In recent years, this has caused a good deal of student frustration. Those who don't get onto the courses they really want are often deeply unhappy.

'Due to the free market that determines class availability, I was shut out for three of my six quarters of bidding. In other words, I was unsuccessful in winning the classes that I wanted and had to scramble among left-over classes to get a schedule. Bidding impacted my ability to secure classes of interest,' says one Chicago student.

A Harvard student notes: 'I couldn't get into all the classes I wanted to take and couldn't get some of the professors I wanted to have. There's a lottery process for second-year classes. Those with the most popular professors are obviously the hardest to get into. You usually get into your top two and then have to work down from there: that is, you list your top 20 choices – then you may get one, two, five, six, seven etc. So you get a lot of what you want, but sometimes not the top five.'

Those who have some knowledge of bidding enjoy an advantage. There are alternative strategies for dealing with this. Some students say there is a perverse logic at work. If you go to a school which specializes in, say, finance, like Columbia, then you may struggle to get on certain finance-related electives, whereas if you go to a school that is not so well known for finance, say Kellogg, which is particularly strong in marketing, you may find it easier to get onto finance electives.

Lightening the load

We asked current students for their survival tips. Most of the comments fell into the following categories.

● Time management

It's really up to the person on how he wants to handle the workload and pressure in school. Frankly, it's all about time management. It's all about doing things early to avoid the rush. But then that all depends on the person since some people work better when they cram. From my point of view, it's all about time management and self-discipline.

ASIAN INSTITUTE OF MANAGEMENT STUDENT

The most difficult thing is balancing the different priorities and deliverables pulling you in multiple directions. There is a large amount of team work and while it is easy to say prioritize, your various teams may place what you consider your fifth priority as their first and you have a responsibility to help them obtain their goals as well. Don't procrastinate – you'll never catch up if you do.

MICHIGAN STUDENT

You need phenomenal time management, easy to tout, harder to do, is the key. My tip would be to pick what you want to focus most on, be sure and learn the rest, and do things as soon as you can so that things and same time frame deliverables don't pile up. Provide the level of work needed to the teams and classes that are your lesser priority in advance so that they can meet their goals while still allowing you the time to focus extra effort until the last day on the things that are most advantageous to yourself and your goals for the future.

TEXAS STUDENT

Once you've figured out the work thing – the tough part is just budgeting your time between work and all the other amazing things that are happening in this environment. CEO's, company presentations, political debates at the Kennedy School, etc – there is always something interesting happening. You have to choose well.

HARVARD STUDENT

The core workload is pretty heavy, because it is all about time management and group work. They throw everything at you and want to see how you can handle it. Case work was new to everyone so we spent a ridiculous amount of time on the first cases. You can lessen the load with time management and coming to group meetings prepared with your thoughts, then come up with a group objective or outline and divide up the workload, the rest of the editing can be done through e-mail until you meet again to go over the final draft. Finding a couple of hours to meet as a group was my biggest challenge. Yes, you do give up your weekends, completely at first!

OWEN STUDENT

First year is heavy. Time management is key. If you don't do extra-curriculars then the workload is easier, but what's the point of being at school and not doing extra-curriculars?

UCLA STUDENT

Frankly, the only tips to lessen the workload are to stay organized or cut corners.

COLUMBIA STUDENT

- Prioritize

My only tip on how to ease the burden is to prioritize. You are assigned more work than you could possibly do, so you must choose what to do wisely.

DARDEN STUDENT

The first year is the most intense one, the core course. Expect at least six hours of work every day. The worst time is when recruiting and study coincides during the first year. In order to survive at those times, you should focus on what you want to do for your internship and manage your time very efficiently since there are tons of companies that come to campus for interviews. There are a lot of second/third rounds out of campus that keep you very busy, sometimes in other cities that are not Ann Arbor. Therefore, my tip would be do your homework about your professional goals beforehand and interact with recruiters from the first day of the program in order to be more relaxed when actual recruitment begins.

MICHIGAN STUDENT

Focus on why you came to business school and don't get sucked into the herd mentality. By knowing what you plan to take out of the experience, you'll be able to get that rather than diluting yourself with all of the possible opportunities.

UCLA STUDENT

KFBS's workload is not trivial. We are expected to work hard and work with our groups. The key to keeping the load manageable is to really understand your group and how you can maximize your learning while distributing the work. At first, everyone wants to do every project. After a while, one realizes that is not sustainable and that is when the groups really start working well. Also, the 80–20 rule definitely applies – one has to figure out how to prioritize. And of course, virtually everyone is involved in outside activities, so it is a balancing act.

KENAN-FLAGLER STUDENT

- Teamwork

Some subjects will be easier for you than for other people, and some will be harder. Work together to counterbalance each other's strengths and weaknesses, and remember that at the end of the day, you're there to learn. Grades aren't necessarily a measure of your success in doing that. In your first semester, don't forget to breathe. Often. And even if you don't succeed in a particular subject, don't rule out the possibility of taking more courses if you're really interested.

You absolutely have to develop good relations with your assigned group first semester. My group was extremely diverse – I was the only domestic student – so be prepared to communicate ideas and goals clearly. I personally saw groups of very smart individuals get poor grades because they couldn't come together as a team. The good relations with your pre-assigned group the first semester and managing subsequent team projects are key. You have to prioritize and sometimes split up work that you would rather do/learn yourself to get it done on time.

OLIN STUDENT

Kellogg is more time-consuming than difficult. Working in teams is a great learning experience. However, it is brutal to your schedule. Some days, I gave group meetings for six or seven hours in a row. It seems that every class has a group component to it.

KELLOGG STUDENT

Not surprisingly, the workload is incredibly heavy; however, another of the things that attracted me to SOM is also its saving grace: teamwork. There have been times when I felt completely overwhelmed, and there have been times I've felt on top of things; I imagine this happens to most serious students at any highly ranked business school.

YALE STUDENT

- Keep up

The secret to not being overwhelmed is to be disciplined in time about assignments and readings and to make sure that you are abreast with what the class is doing. Also making use of the weekends to do the readings ensures that one is not overly busy during the week and helps to keep a balance between work and play throughout the week.

KENAN-FLAGLER STUDENT

Don't bother reading or especially buying the books. In most cases paying attention and participating in class is more than sufficient. I think I bought a total of three books during my time at UMBS, course packs are a different story.

MICHIGAN STUDENT

- Balance the books. The real secret of success is balance. Not just in managing the workload but also in balancing the academic against the social, and the myriad of other things going on. Above all, remember: it only lasts for two years (or one even). Student after student advocated a balanced lifestyle though most admitted that for them it largely remained an aspiration rather than a reality.

Don't take on too much. Seek balance in life – business schools have a way of keeping you incredibly busy, and you think it's normal because everyone is so frenetic. Relax. Remember that you only get as much out of something as you put into it. Take advantage of the amazing opportunities around you. Get involved in community and school activities.

FUQUA STUDENT

I would suggest planning your schedule to try and get a mix of different types of classes at the same time. For example, my worst module was when I took financial accounting, supply chain management, compensation, and corporate value management at the same time. They were all fairly analytical, which added to the workload troubles.

OWEN STUDENT

Business isn't everything. Take at least one class in a different school – law, public policy, language, the arts. Get off campus once in a while to regain perspective, a sense of self and well-being, and a much needed dose of reality. Get out of the MBA school bubble ... take a break, help build a house for Habitat, go camping.

FUQUA STUDENT

Take time out every week to do something you really love. If you spend a few less hours each week on cases, to make time for things that make you happy, your overall well-being (and performance) will benefit.

DARDEN STUDENT

chapter 6

social life

Networking is by far the most important aspect of business school. The classroom is a distant second. If you want to be an investment banker or a consultant, then you had better get a 4.0 GPA, but even those employers like to see that you are doing something outside of school.

UCCLA ANDERSON STUDENT

All work and no play

All work and no play sucks. Worse, it dulls the senses. There is more to b-school than studying. Networking, remember, is one of the main reasons for doing an MBA. Bonding with your fellow students is part of the experience. At Wharton, MBA students talk fondly of the 'Wharton Walk' a well-known drinking ritual – or bar crawl – that involves a large number of bars in one night. 'A great bonding experience,' says one student. This is what happens at business schools. While most students simply get drunk; MBA students bond and network.

Fortunately, b-schools offer a wide range of extra-curricular life. 'Socially there's a little bit of everything, from the weekly keg Happy Hour to wine tastings and ballroom-dancing club,' says a Columbia student, 'so it's easy to find a variety.'

The problem is resisting the urge to sign up for everything that looks vaguely interesting. 'The most tempting (as well as necessary) activity that can take a lot of your time is clubbing, i.e. managing student clubs or participating in the events organized by the various clubs,' observes an LBS student. 'Since most of the clubs are engaged in extremely interesting activities (from entrepreneurship and e-commerce to media and emerging markets), I felt keenly interested in several of them and over committed my resources. Thus, prioritizing is crucial. You have to learn to live with the fact that no matter how interesting and alluring you find most of the extra-curricular happenings, you can not be involved in all of them; something that I took a bit long to learn!'

'Don't take on too much,' advises a Fuqua student. 'Seek balance in life. Business schools have a way of keeping you incredibly busy, and you think it's normal because everyone is so frenetic. Relax. Remember that you only get as much out of something as you put into it. Take advantage of the amazing opportunities around you. Get involved in community and school activities.'

The question is which schools offer the extra-curricular activities to suit your tastes? A peek at the social life at the top schools reveals that although the basics – sports, student clubs and partying – are present at all, different schools suit different people. Campus cultures differ, too. Some US schools offer a four-day work week, which comes as a big surprise to anyone visiting on an exchange program from overseas.

The biggest complaint from MBA students isn't the lack of social life, but a dearth of time to enjoy it. As one student says: 'The worst thing about the social life at Kellogg? Too many people wanting social time. I never try to forget that I'm at business school for a purpose, but there are definitely temptations to think that I'm a freshman in college again. I found that I know too many people to hang out with all of them … so I've made an effort to make sure to have some close friends whom I see on a regular basis. I've told non-business school friends that being at Kellogg is just like being at my own wedding … there are so many people I would love to spend more time with talking to … but I only have fifteen minutes to spend with each of them.'

Perhaps the biggest social risk is that MBA students are a little too anxious to practise what they have learned in their process management elective. 'When you and your MBA friends start to analyze the operational efficiency of the service at a restaurant, you know you're in trouble,' warns a student at Texas.

Students are full of wise words. No one advised studying harder, but some regretted not spending more time socializing. 'The worst thing about my social life is that I had a hard time socializing with non-graduate students,' admits a student at the Owen School at Vanderbilt University. 'My life was consumed by school and that is all I could talk about. It was also hard to relax knowing you always had something that had to be done or read, but hey that's normal.'

It is, and it is also manageable. Keeping your feet grounded in reality is difficult but essential. The sort of social life you'll have at b-school depends on a number of factors, chiefly:

- what's on offer
- peer group
- location
- size of school/class
- your attitude.

What's on offer?

Your school's location plays a big part in any social life you'll have during your MBA months. Students often choose out-of-the-way schools because they feel they'll have a chance to really knuckle down without distractions. But on out-of-town campuses, where diversion is scarce, students can sometimes forget there's a real world outside. Participants on intense programs in leafy retreats can tend to go over the top, living an overly insulated life, never even setting foot in the local community for everyday activities like shopping. Your MBA will be intense enough; make sure there are opportunities to get away and let off steam. Gyms, nearby beaches or mountains help. The International University of Japan is located in a ski resort. The Tuck School in New Hampshire is great if you enjoy a close-knit community, skiing and ice hockey. (The Dartmouth College campus, by the way, is said to have been the model for the frat film *Animal House* starring the late John Belushi.)

Elsewhere, other schools have their own recreational advantages. Stanford boasts the best that California has to offer – with mountains and beaches in easy reach. Big city schools have more to offer by way of cultural interest, too. Schools based in capital cities tend to be more cramped for space, but more than make up for it with access to museums and art galleries. Columbia and Stern offer the buzz of New York City. 'The best things about the social life is that you don't have to go looking for it. This is Manhattan, social life surrounds you 24 hours a day. The worst thing about the social life is making the time for it. It's incredibly difficult to forego some social events because of school commitments,' comments one student at Stern.

'New York is great and there are tons of things to do. The theater, shopping and restaurants are amazing. The downside is that b-school social life is very much centered around drinking, and I got over that in college. I have a better time when a smaller group of us go out to dinner or something (we do that a lot). Also, it's expensive, especially if you live on the Upper West Side and have to cab home. But overall, I can't complain – it's great!' adds a student from Columbia.

Similarly, London Business School is in the middle of one of Europe's hippest cities; the Spanish school IESE offers two-years in another European gem, Barcelona. But city life presents problems, with students sprawled across the metropolis, with little or no campus life to speak of. This can result is a highly fragmented existence. Basically, people come together at the school and then scatter to the four winds. It's one thing to meet up at the school bar if you live five minutes away, but another if it involves a ride across town. For all your good intentions, you may not actually get around to doing stuff. As one Stern student explains: 'The best thing is the opportunities to do cool things in NYC. The worst thing is that no one actually does them. NYU is not "campusy". So, at the end of the day, many students go home to Brooklyn, New Jersey, etc. The physical gaps between where students live make it harder to be social.'

European schools boast added historical interest. Students at the University of Bath School of Management in the UK, for instance, can take tea in the magnificent Pump Room, immerse themselves in the famous Roman Baths, and enjoy the arthouse cinema, the Little Theatre.

On more isolated campuses, there will tend to be tight-knit interdependence among the students. This is especially true if the program is small. Big cities have their attractions, but glorious isolation often means being closer to the great outdoors. Those who enjoy skiing, hiking, and more tranquil pursuits will have a better time away from the noise and pollution of major metropolitan areas. On the other hand, the more provincial you get the less there can be to do off campus especially for ex-city dwellers.

An MBA at Kenan-Flagler, at the University of North Carolina says: 'Chapel Hill. What more needs to be said? Arguably one of the best atmospheres for learning and relaxing in the US. Along Franklin Street one finds a full range of college-type eating places and bars. Also, being a major university, there are many arts available. Additionally, sports at UNC are exciting. For personal sporting, it is hard to find better golf courses concentrated within 45 minutes of the university. Also, the university offers a full range of intramural sports. By the way, I golfed every month of the year and played ultimate frisbee throughout the year. The weather in Chapel Hill is great. The worst thing is without a doubt the restaurants. The school does have every kind of college eating imaginable. But coming from [Washington] DC before school, I am hard pressed to find good foods from other places.'

Nearby Fuqua students also gravitate to Chapel Hill. 'Durham does not really have much social feeling to it,' explains one student, 'but if you go down the road to Chapel Hill, this changes. In fact I think the Orange County Police make a living off rich Duke students going home in the evenings (speeding tickets galore for even seven miles over the speed limit).'

The risk of insularity is a real one for MBA students with massive workloads locked in the rarified world of b-school. It depends, too, on what you're used to. Everything is relative. For a native New Yorker, Boston can seem like a backwater. 'The best thing about the social life is that you can have one on a more consistent basis than when you are working,' says one Harvard student. 'The worst is that Boston is not really that much fun – and Cambridge in particular is less so. There's enough to do – restaurants, theater, etc. But it's not New York or London. Bars and clubs close early (2 am) – and there's not that many that are interesting anyway. Things are better in the fall and spring when you can be outside. During the week it's sometimes hard to motivate people to go out.'

For others, there is a novelty factor: 'Many people probably wonder about life in Nashville,' says a student at Owen. 'For two years, it's a blast! For a west-coaster like me, heading down to the honky-tonk bars after a tough week of studying is a great time. Don't worry, there are plenty of non-country activities around Nashville as well.'

Some schools seem to offer the best of all worlds. Bocconi, for example, is in Milan, Italy. 'Milan is great as a winter/summer base being within easy reach of the Alps for skiing and the Italian Riviera for beach weekends,' says one student. 'It's also near the fabulous cities of Verona, Florence, Venice and the wine regions of Tuscany and Piedmont. Excellent transport links support Italy and Europe.'

Schools on America's West Coast also offer a rich diversity. Stanford, Haas, and Anderson, for example, combine the benefits of being close to the action in Silicon Valley, with the bustle of major cities. There's skiing at Lake Tahoe, and plenty of beaches. Las Vegas and Reno are within reach for those who want to practise the finer points of game theory, and for those with a yen for the outdoors, there's hiking in the National Parks.

Peer group

Another major factor affecting your social life is the peer group. One of the great things about going to b-school is that you will be surrounded by kindred spirits. In fact, many students say that they get as much out of mingling with peers as they do from the formal education. 'Everyone is cool and friendly. They realize that everyone is in the same boat and are quite open in helping each other out. A big part of the MBA experience is the networking. Everyone realizes this as well so a lot of time is spent getting to know class-mates,' says a student at AIM.

'The people you meet in this environment are great friends (networking buddies) for the rest of life! Limited for those who do not drink,' notes an Ivey student. A Kellogg student adds: 'The best thing about the social life at Kellogg? Everyone is social. It seems that there weren't many people who slipped through the admissions committee with less than strong interpersonal skills and a desire to meet new people.'

But don't expect everyone to see the world in the same way you do. Some schools offer a richer diversity than others. The leading European schools, for example, pride themselves on their international mix of students. Among the MBA class of 2000 at the Swiss school

IMD for example, out of a total of 84 students, there were no fewer than 38 different nationalities, with no one nationality making a majority. 'This is truly the best, not only are you at IMD to learn, but the cultural exposure you get by working 18 hours+ per day with such a diverse group is a learning experience all on its own,' says one student.

Most students enjoy the diversity. North American schools talk about being international but are still dominated by American nationals. A Columbia student cites mixing with foreign students as a highlight of her MBA experience. 'There's an incredibly diverse student body, people with all kinds of backgrounds, very individualistic, and a large component of foreign students. That translates into a great experience and a really amazing network of peers.'

A few of the students we talked to complained about undesirable elements, but most said b-school was surprisingly progressive. 'Socially, I have had no bad encounters with the "old-boys' network", said one woman student. 'It's a watered-down phenomenon that is completely un-PC. In one instance, I was conversing with two bankers when one censored the other by saying, "Dude, you're being a tool. That's completely rude".'

Living in a goldfish bowl

The downside of all this camaraderie is that it can also be intrusive. You can't switch it off. One student laments: 'One of the best things is that you do pretty much know everyone. But one of the worst things is that everyone pretty much knows you. It's a fish bowl – i.e. romantic relationships. Many people are afraid to go out with other people for fear of being judged by their taste, or failure in snagging who they're after.'

Small may be beautiful, but it can also be oppressive. 'It can get a little claustrophobic at times due to the size, but that same characteristic gives Anderson a VERY tight bond among students. Most of the school-organized social life involves supporting a charity. There are a million things to do in LA, and Anderson students seem to take advantage of most of them … albeit in a spontaneous way,' says a student at Anderson.

Small classes allow better interaction and a sense of community. 'The best things about the social life is related to the small size,' says a Darden student. 'You get the opportunity to get to know nearly everyone in your class and that leads to a wide array of social events. Every weekend there are great parties and social events to partake in. Also, there is a great golf course very nearby and we play a ton of golf in the second year.'

'The best thing about the social life is the ability to have a lot of friends rather quickly,' adds a Yale student. 'You're all thrown into a difficult situation together, so it's equivalent to boot camp in that respect. Yale is a small school, so it's easy to know (and feel friendly towards) a majority of your classmates, plus the class above you. On the downside, a school as small as Yale doesn't allow for much privacy. Everyone knows everyone's business. Kind of like a small town.'

A Haas student adds: 'It can be a little bit college-like, especially first semester. Big groups, bars, etc. for those people who were a bit older than the average age, or with significant others, or who lived in [San Francisco] before school and so had another life outside of school; sometimes it felt a little overwhelming.'

Big schools, on the other hand, can be a bit too big. Big programs may mean that you can't get to know as many people as you would like to. 'Since Michigan is a big program it is difficult to know everybody. During the first year you spend most of your classes with a section. Therefore, you get to know them pretty well but you spend only a little time with other people. It would be great if the school can smooth these differences even though I realize it is difficult because of the size of the program,' says a Michigan student.

A Stern student observes: 'Socially, I wish it were a closer-knit school. Although I'm meeting great people and making great contacts, I don't know if I've had the opportunity to develop deep friendships.'

Tempers can also become frayed. 'Worst things are if you have a problem with other students,' says a student at AIM. 'The idea here is that a good manager is a good communicator and has the necessary interpersonal skills to fix problems and patch things up. There have been a few fights recently but they are very, very rare and are generally resolved (these usually start because of disagreements exacerbated by school pressure and such). One bad thing also is if things start to get really competitive. Sometimes the students' drive to be number one is to the detriment of relationships with classmates. In general, though, this isn't really a big issue.'

Clubbing

B-school offer numerous opportunities for getting involved. In particular most have any number of clubs and associations. Many of these would sound good to round out a CV. And that's probably the best way to view them. But you have to be selective. Extra-curricular life can easily take over. The real trick is to only sign up for the ones that either you are passionate about or will help your career. To paraphrase William Morris, the famous designer: 'Have nothing in your life that is not either beautiful or functional.' Ideally they should be both.

Extra-curricular activities are also the antidote to academic overload. 'It's the same adage from college … sign up for ones that you're really interested in … not just because you want it on your resume. That way, your day will be full, but full of things YOU have put on your schedule. My calendar was extremely full during the year, but most of the things on it were things I was really looking forward to … that makes any workload seem reasonable,' says one student.

Associations and clubs abound. Students at Columbia, for example, can sign up for any of the following:

American Finance Association
American Marketing Association
Asian Business Association
Australasian Club
Biotechnology Club
Black Business Students Association
The Bottom Line
Boxing Club
CBS Cycling Club
CBS Party for Kids
Central and Eastern European Business Club
The Christian Business Fellowship
The Class Committee (promotes the Fall and Spring Balls among other things)
Columbia Basketball Association
Columbia Gaming Society
Columbia Women in Business
The CORPS Fellowship (Columbia Outreach Programs)
Distinguished Leaders Lecture Series
Electronic Bulletin Board System
Emerging Markets Club
Entrepreneurial and Innovation Management Association
European Society
'Follies'
Gay and Lesbian Business Association
Golf Club
Gourmet Club
Harlem Tutorial Program
(The Columbia Harlem Tutorial Program, begun in 1982, is a joint project
   between the Business School and the Law School)
Health Care Management Association
Hedge Fund Club
High Technology Group
Hispanic Business Association
The Hispanic Business Association (HBA) Hockey Team
Human Resource Management Association

Ice Hockey Club
International Business Society
International Development Association
Internet Business Group
Investment Banking Club
Investment Management Club
Japan Business Association
Jewish Business Students Association
'The Journal' (Business School Yearbook)
Karate
Latin-American Business Association
Management Consulting Association
Media Management Association
Micro-Brew Society
Middle-East Business Forum
Military in Business Association
Operations Management Association
Public and Nonprofit Management Association
Real Estate Association
Rowing Crew Club
Rugby Football Club
Running Club
Ski Club
Soccer Club
South Asian Business Association
Speakers' Corner – 'All members speak for at least two minutes on an unrehearsed topic. Students also have the opportunity to: present a prepared speech; serve as the toastmaster; assume the role of topic master (write the speech topics); or serve as the jester (tell a joke).'
Squash Club
The Student Faculty Academic Affairs Committee. (SFAAC allows students to address their concerns about the academic program.)
Students for Responsible Business
Tennis Club
Venture Capital Club
Volleyball Club
Wine Society of CBS
The Wine Society

Party people

No campus would be complete, of course, without copious amounts of drinking. B-schools are no exception. Consumption functions are a part of the MBA lifestyle.

Thursday night is often party night. At the Owen school, it's kegs in the lobby. 'Owen sponsors kegs every Thursday after class,' a student explains. 'This is a great way to relax and get to know your professors and peers.' At LBS, weekly Sundowners are a tradition. Every Thursday evening throughout the year some company or other sponsors drinks for the MBA community at the School. 'There may be nothing like a "free lunch" but I bet that an LBS MBA certainly gets used to the idea of "free drinks" by the time they graduate!' a student observes.

All schools have their own special events. For reasons not entirely clear, Darden students like to dress up as Vikings and drink large quantities of Absolut vodka on the top of a mountain. 'Beer trucks are rolled up, salmon steaks are grilled, there's a big bonfire and lots of dancing,' explains one student. 'It's better than something from a movie.' At London Business School, students enjoy cultural diversity. 'One week you have the Indian Diwali Night with Bhangra Music and the other week you are dancing Salsa at the Latin American Party,' says a keen LBS socialite. 'And then there's the Chinese New Year Party, the St Patrick's Day Party, the International Week and so on and so forth.'

In California, too, they like a bit of diversity. Haas has its bar of the week events and regular consumption functions. 'The most famous consumption functions are the European and Latin American,' says one student. 'The European is famous for its food, there are tables with traditional food from different European countries. The Latin American consumption function is famous for its music and party atmosphere. In my time at Haas, I cannot recall one Latin American consumption function where I left without being drunk on tequila and exhausted from dancing to samba rhythms.'

At Ivey, there's a designated party house, known as 'the 70s house' or 'the Party House'. 'There is a house right near the campus that five people from Ivey have rented out for over five years,' a student explains. 'The tenants of this house graciously host most of the major parties for the full two years. A great time is usually had by all.' Remember the alternative to all this is a night alone with an accounting textbook.

Not for profit

B-schools are also hotbeds of philanthropy. This serves a dual purpose. No CV is complete without a scattering of good works and noble sentiments. Since supporting worthy causes can often be combined with networking and partying, they are popular with MBA students.

As a Haas student explains: 'C4C (Challenge for Charity) organizes a variety of events and all money collected goes to charity. The most famous C4C events are: The hoedown

(Texan cowboy bar night with appropriate dances, everybody dances!), the ski weekend (a weekend of skiing and games in Lake Tahoe), the C4C sports weekend (a weekend of athletics organized at Stanford with six participating business schools from California), the C4C auction (gifts from the business community and Haas are auctioned to raise money for charity; this year's top item was a lunch with the founder of Netscape Communications that went for close to $2,000) and the talent show (a show that demonstrates the non-business talents of students at Haas).' Such activities are an essential part of the MBA experience.

Romance

'Business school is not the ideal place to meet a mate, but many people do,' says a Yale student yet to come to grips with the rigor of logical analysis. Romances do blossom at b-school. But the odds if you are male and straight are not great. The ratio of men to women is about 3:1. If that's your aim, try a dating agency or a singles bar. 'The MBA is 70 per cent male ... if you are not dating someone before you enter MBA, good luck!' says a Kenan-Flagler student.

The male–female imbalance has other implications. 'The worst things about the social life stem from the poor male/female ratio (70/30). Doesn't matter much for me since I'm married, but many of my single guy friends are bummin'! Thank God for the close proximity of the law school!' says a Darden student (married we presume to a lawyer).

Romance is possible but not to be relied upon. A shared elective or mutual agreement on the merits of Igor Ansoff's earlier work are probably not the best grounds for a relationship. A Tuck student's comment is typical: 'I was hoping that b-school might be a reasonable place to meet a life mate, better than bars because you get to know people. But I think what happens is you end up knowing people so well on such narrow dimensions (business) that you become overcritical. Also the ratio, while no worse than other schools, doesn't help guys ... came single, leaving single.'

job search

If you are a dean's list student, you are basically guaranteed a job in investment banking or consulting – and this is what most students want.

IVEY STUDENT

Seller's market

Academic achievement is fine, but it won't pay the bills. And the bills are likely to mount once the student loans kick in. That's why the biggest issue facing MBA students is finding a job. Not just any job, obviously: the right job. There was a time when most students left this activity until the second half of their course – either the second year of a two-year program, or the final semester of a one-year. These days most start earlier.

The good news is there's plenty of jobs out there at present. A Haas student says: 'The career center at Haas has done an excellent job this year, organizing numerous info sessions, company presentations, career panels, and much more. A lot of companies have come to recruit on campus from all areas (consulting, banking, S&P 500, etc.). We also have internet and high tech companies in every stage (start-up, pre-IPO or post-IPO) on campus doing presentations, recruiting and career fares. There are many more opportunities than you can take.'

Confidence and expectations are high. 'People have higher expectations of earlier wealth (although recent market corrections have diminished that somewhat),' says a Columbia student. 'There's still a huge influx of people going into the more traditional post-b-school jobs (banking, consulting) but the demand for consultants exceeds the supply and people who might have felt the traditional options were their only options before now have a lot more opportunities in the dot-com world as well.'

And, after a lean spell in the early 1990s, signing bonuses are back and fatter than ever. In fact, there has probably never been a better time to take an MBA into the labor market. If you are at a top school you can pick and choose. 'The quality of leads at Wharton and HBS are without peer. People come here to hire as many good people as they can get and then go to other schools to round out their recruiting needs or regional offices. Sometimes I would see stuff that would require a double take it was so amazing,' says a Wharton student.

The story is not exactly the same elsewhere. The size of a school clearly also plays a role. A Tuck student says: 'The only downside, which affects some people, is that Tuck doesn't get as wide an array of recruiters as other schools because of its size. In other words, if recruiters have previously gone back empty-handed (with no one taking their offers), they are less likely to invest in recruiting the following year. So a small student body means fewer overall offers accepted.'

In recent months the business press has been full of stories about the executive talent shortage, and the problems recruiters are having filling their MBA quotas. No wonder then that recruiters are becoming more and more aggressive. It's a seller's market right now – and looks likely to stay that way for the foreseeable future. In the big scheme of things this is obviously good news for MBAs, but it can also be disruptive. 'You could end up with a nightmare scenario where Goldman Sachs takes options on babies before they're born based on their genetic profile,' quips John Quelch, dean of London Business School. 'It could become that farcical. Obviously, if recruiters are doing presentations aimed at second-year students then the first-year MBAs will be tempted to go along. But MBA students are mature enough to make their own decisions.'

'We ask students a question: how many interviews did you take this year? When I came to Duke in 1994, the average student had 15 interviews. This year, the average student will have four or five interviews on campus because they have an offer in their hip pocket,' says Dan Nagy, director of career management of the Fuqua School, Duke University.

How early should you start job-hunting?

Preparation for life after b-school starts on day one. Students report that job-hunting starts the minute they step onto campus – and sometimes before. In some ways this is a shame. For most people who take an MBA, it represents the last opportunity to be a student – to forget about the world of work for a while and to concentrate on their personal development. To hang out. To let their hair down. In fact, many students say they would prefer to leave job-hunting until later, but that they feel under pressure from day one to meet recruiters who come on campus. Trouble is, it's a competitive world and few feel they can afford the luxury of letting opportunities slide by.

'The students have a huge challenge when they come on campus, which is that there are all kinds of demands on their time in terms of juggling the academic requirements, the work that they're involved with, extra-curricular activities, and the career search. People who are the most successful in business school are those who can say that all of it is a major priority, and then figure out day-by-day how they can manage their time,' admits Martha Patton, director of career counseling services at Stern.

The new economy has, to a large extent, focused MBA students on the job opportunities back in the real world. Silicon Valley is a magnet for business talent. The current crop of MBAs clearly think so. The new generation of MBAs want to get out and go their own way, often toward the internet, shunning traditional careers with corporations. Where once they couldn't wait to sign up for a job with a Wall Street star like Goldman Sachs or a place among the consulting élite of McKinsey or Bain, many now prefer to join small start-ups or do their own thing.

In the 1970s, MBAs wanted to work for a major blue-chip corporation like GE, GM or IBM. In the 1980s interest switched towards investment banking. By the end of the 1980s and for much of the 1990s the consulting firms were where aspiring MBAs sought to work. Now, a growing number want to pack their bags and head for Silicon Valley. There is something of a herd mentality to this. 'The interesting jobs are usually discovered by a lot of MBAs at once,' says Ilse Evans, executive director of MBA admissions and career services at the Haas School at Berkeley. 'It's so competitive that positioning has become important. It was always important in consulting and investment banking, but it's becoming more important in smaller high tech firms.'

A Chicago student offers a critical perspective on the job market: 'Bozos are getting into consulting because the dot-coms are haemorrhaging talent, which is headed to start-ups. I question the calibre of consulting services delivered by the incoming class the same way that I questioned the technology in mid-80s American cars. Consulting firms have updated pitch materials to sell graduates on the notion that, by accepting consulting offers, they won't be missing the dot-com revolution because dot-com practices are rapidly expanding. However, incoming consulting classes will still be responsible for rust-belt work.'

Clearly, West Coast companies are in a great geographical position to cash in. 'Anderson is going through a big change because of the dot-com revolution,' says a student at UCLA's Anderson School. 'Big corporations are getting frustrated at spending money to recruit here when many if not most of the students don't want to leave California and want to work for smaller or high tech companies. Because of its location in LA, we get a tremendous number of job positions coming across e-mail. I think the dream job is more related to how hard you look for it than luck. Most of these small companies will talk to you if you are aggressive and show an interest.'

One impact of the rush to high tech companies is that forward planning may be less relevant. 'The success of many high-profile internet companies has had an affect on all major business schools. From a recruiting perspective it is most apparent in the number of students who are graduating without jobs,' says a student at Wharton. A Stern student reports: 'Students aren't as worried about landing jobs in the fall. There are many who still don't have jobs and that is on purpose because the opportunities at small start-ups are real-time and many students can't even start looking yet. So there is no longer the expectation that you have to get a job by December.'

For those taking the traditional long-term planning route, a useful means of positioning yourself is through a summer internship. Summer internships involve a couple of months work with a real company, and are a key component of the two-year MBA experience. Students regard these placements as their opportunity to test drive an employer, and earn some much needed cash. Naturally, the company will also be giving you the once-over, kicking your tires and having a quick look under the cranium.

The key to getting the placement of your choice is to get on the case early. The recruitment process for summer internships begins in January. Most schools have a list of companies that offer regular internships. Usually, it's an impressive list. But if your company of choice isn't on it then you may have to make the running. The placement or careers office is there to help. The sooner you enlist its help, the more helpful it's likely to be. There is nothing wrong either with showing some personal initiative. You can write to, telephone, and generally petition the company in any way you can think of. If you or someone in your network knows the CEO, all the better.

Drop-outs

Imagine this. You are half way through a two-year MBA program. It is hard work, very hard work. You work late into the night finishing assignments. Money is tight and already you

There are already signs of talent shortages at the top of US companies. One major US public company anticipates that it will lose 60 per cent of its executives within the next three years. Another talks of 40 to 50 per cent walking through the door. These companies only hint at a crisis facing corporate America. Forecasts show that a dearth of executive talent could be a serious problem not just for the next few years, but for the first few decades of the new millennium.

'Demographics mean that there are a lot of people nearing retirement age. Downsizing has meant that companies no longer tend to have developmental roles, like assistant or deputy jobs, from which people were traditionally promoted,' says William C. Byham, president and CEO of Development Dimensions International, a Bridgeville, Pennsylvania, firm that specializes in HR issues. 'At the same time, the experience, qualifications and skills needed to become a senior executive have increased.'

A number of trends suggest that the talent shortfall may be no mere blip on the radar screen; the problem could be with us for decades to come. Three factors, in particular, threaten to exacerbate the situation in the next few years.

First, and in many ways most seriously, the demand for executives appears to be moving in the opposite direction of supply. Remember the demographic time bomb that everyone was talking about back in the 1980s? It didn't go away when the magazine articles halted, and now it may be ready to detonate. Demographic predictions suggest that in the US the number of 35- to 44-year-olds – the traditional executive talent pool – will fall by 15 per cent between 2000 and 2015, while the number of 45- to 54-year-olds – the current senior executive population – will rise.

The demographic alarm bells date back to the post-World War II baby boom. The baby boomers created a surplus of middle managers in the late 1980s. Now they are creating an aging workforce – and an aging executive population. By 2002 there will be more US workers in their late 40s than in their late 20s. The number of 40 to 59-year-olds in the US, which stood at 53 million in 1990, reached 73 million in 2000 and 83 million by 2010. Add in factors like the long stock market boom of the 1990s, which boosted retirement nest eggs, and there are an awful lot of people eyeing condos in Florida.

'The American labor force will shrink in the middle,' says Paul Wallace, author of *Agequake*, which examines demographic trends. 'The baby-boom echo and immigration mean that the US does not face youth deficits. Even so, the bulging portion of the labor force will consist of people over 50. If companies are increasingly looking to younger executives, there will be a problem.'

▷

Broad demographic statistics are backed by the findings of surveys. A 1998 study by McKinsey & Company, covering nearly 6,000 managers in 77 companies, cautioned that the battle to recruit talented people was already intensifying. The McKinsey report, appropriately entitled *The War for Talent*, concluded: 'Many American companies are already suffering a shortage of executive talent.' The research found that 'three-quarters of corporate officers surveyed said their companies had "insufficient talent sometimes" or were "chronically talent-short across the board."'

Aside from demographics, the second factor in the escalating talent shortage is that companies expect more from their executives these days. Complex global markets require more sophisticated management skills, including international sensitivity, cultural fluency, technological literacy, entrepreneurial flair and, most critically, leadership. The proliferation of business-school-educated managers, especially MBAs, suggests that executives are better trained than ever before. The trouble is that business schools are good at turning out business analysts but have a more questionable record in producing leaders.

For large companies, the third factor fueling an executive dearth is the rise of many high-potential small and mid-size companies. For the first time, big companies have to compete with – and provide career opportunities and earnings on a par with – their smaller brethren. A host of high tech start-ups, especially internet-based businesses, are likely to draw off a growing proportion of high-fliers who might otherwise have joined the blue chips. Who wants to work for a faceless corporation when you can make more money and have more fun working for an exciting upstart?

The final ingredient in this is the simple fact that a growing number of MBAs simply do not see their futures within large organizations. Period. All of these factors point to an escalation of the recruitment war. There appears little doubt that attracting the best and brightest will become much harder for established companies. 'There will continue to be, for the foreseeable future, greater demand than supply of the best people – the most knowledgeable, skilled, innovative, experienced, entrepreneurial, creative, risk-taking supertalent,' says Bruce Tulgan, founder of Rainmaker Thinking. 'Every business leader and manager in every organization I talk with says that they are spending more time, energy and money on recruiting at all levels.'

have built up a veritable mountain of debt awaiting that golden day when you return to the world of work, wiser if not necessarily richer. One day the telephone rings. It is someone from a dot-com business offering you a job. You can start immediately on an attractive salary, be at the cutting edge of the new economy, potentially receive a healthy batch of shares when the company is floated and stop worrying about that thorny marketing assignment. Tempted?

Such scenarios are likely to become ever more common as new economy companies seek out the professional management expertise they require to cement their place in the marketplace. As we have seen, research repeatedly suggests that there is a genuine shortage of executive talent – despite the increasing numbers of MBA graduates produced every year. In addition, with their analytical skills MBA students are well placed to come up with the bright ideas to create tomorrow's dot-com wonders. 'As the e-commerce revolution gathers pace, we will see MBAs looking to hone their entrepreneurial skills in high tech and other start-up ventures,' predicts Mike Jones, director general of the Association of MBAs.

Even skeptics are gaining the skills they need to board the bandwagon. 'Even the traditional students all want to take at least one or two courses in e-commerce etc. so that they can see how it will affect their job too. Many more students are pursuing their own businesses while in school as well. Dozens of teams are looking for funding and many more are looking to join the early stage companies,' says a Stern student.

Some big name US institutions have seen blocks of students drop out of school to work for new-economy start-ups. At Wharton, for example, 25 students failed to return after their 1999 summer placements – five times the normal drop-out rate. Most saw a window of opportunity and dived through it. They include Jonathan Hogan who, having got a summer internship with Towers-Perrin, then got a better offer. Some friends asked him to help them draw up a business plan for an on-line automotive lending company. He liked what he saw and jumped.

So far, there is no evidence to suggest that the new economy is making significant inroads into the MBA population. Drop-out rates reported from European schools are small. Typically, the UK's Imperial College Management School reports a 'negligible drop-out rate' from its one-year program and that students generally wait to achieve their qualification before setting up their dot-com. Some are less patient, but stick with it. Strathclyde Graduate School of Business has a number of students studying for an MBA while running their own dot-coms. To help them on their way, Strathclyde is introducing four new e-commerce-related classes in June, including one on setting up an e-business.

Elsewhere, the Spanish school IESE reports there were seven drop-outs in 1999, which actually represents about 3 per cent, given that the admissions is set at 210 students a year. Five of those who left did so because they could not keep up with the academic demands of the program and the other two left for personal reasons. 'For the moment, there is only one case of an MBA student dropping out for a start-up,' says Alberto Arribas, IESE's MBA admissions director.

Jonathan Slack, chief executive of the UK's Association of Business Schools, believes that the potential drop-out problem is exaggerated. 'There is no hard evidence of this – either in Europe or North America. Indeed, given the recent fall-out from the new economy it can be argued that actually having an MBA is even more important. The MBA is about being able to generate powerful long-term strategies for businesses. If these new ventures are going to get off the ground then MBA programs can provide the strategic oversight required. Knowledge of issues such as finance, marketing and strategy are increasingly important.'

Some schools are taking a proactive approach to any talk of student drop-out from MBA programs. Julia Tyler, MBA program director at London Business School, argues that it is up to business schools to create vibrant cultures which are in touch with the new economy so that temptation is easily dismissed. 'People are being approached,' she admits. 'But my experience is that students are aware that finishing their MBA will make them more marketable. They know it is an investment they need to follow through on. After all, the new economy isn't going to go away.'

The message from the London Business School is that business schools need to be attractive places where students feel better off. 'There are ten faculty teaching on new-economy-related subjects and 90 per cent of our MBA students take an entrepreneurial elective. The atmosphere is similar to that of an incubator. People believe that being here is valuable,' says Julia Tyler. The success of companies like Iglu.com, started by a London Business School MBA student, adds power to the argument that students are better off finishing their MBA and then moving on to their start-up with the school's backing and the benefit of completing the full program.

There is also a compromise solution. Rather than tempting students away from MBA programs, another strategy is to build ties with them early in their studies. This old-economy strategy is now being adopted by new-economy companies anxious to create bonds with the brightest graduates of tomorrow. The on-line venture capital company Garage.com now has a summer internship program – JumpStart 2000 – which is designed to provide first-year MBA students with experience of working in start-ups. Garage.com places ten students with companies in its portfolio for an intensive 12-week internship. 'We want to provide a unique opportunity for MBA students to contribute to exciting high tech start-ups. JumpStart 2000 is a great way for our portfolio companies to find smart, entrepreneurial business school students who want to gain start-up experience while learning about the world of high tech business,' says Garage.com's Amy Vernetti. Business schools participating include INSEAD and the London Business School as well as leading American schools.

The recruitment frenzy

'There are two processes on campus and off campus. The split is about 50/50 for placement of students,' explains one student at UCLA. 'On campus: the company book is distributed to students with listings and job descriptions. Students send resumés/cover letters and hope to get on closed lists. Students are selected for closed lists and then will go through first interview on campus. Some companies will have open lists so that students can bid to get on them. After the first round, a second/third etc. round is usually held at the company. This is a pretty typical process for b-school. Off campus: our office of career development will offer many workshops to help you network through getting a job on your own. Plus there are job postings and e-mails sent out daily from companies looking for students but can't afford to (or don't for another reason) come to campus.'

On-campus recruitment events have always been a big part of the MBA experience. The top companies send recruiters to the top b-schools to sign up the cream of the MBA crop. The investment banks, consulting firms and blue chips continue to flock to the top schools. It's a rich diet of schmoozing and high-level salesmanship. The product is the company, and the customer is you. They come loaded with enticing brochures, invites to cocktails and dinner – and fat check-books. Some, like the leading consulting firms, prefer a more élitist approach. They'll try to convince you that you're lucky they even want to talk to you. Either way, conversation is likely to take a tour of corporate values, career development opportunities, and the prestige of a job with their employer, and be accompanied by a fascination with understanding what your career aspirations are. Think of Tom Cruise being wined and dined by the top law firms in *The Firm,* and you'll get the picture. At least, that's the traditional recruitment process.

The great benefit to students is that they get to meet a lot of recruiters without going very far off campus. Recruiters like to fish in well-stocked ponds, which makes schools with big MBA programs like Harvard, Chicago, Kellogg and Wharton popular. For this reason, the bigger schools tend to attract more companies, as do those that are in major commercial centers. Schools that are out in the sticks face more of a struggle to lure recruiters onto their campuses.

The traditional recruitment cycle is changing. New-economy firms in particular don't hire only at particular times of the year – they are looking for people year-round. In the old days, students would complete a summer internship, be interviewed for jobs in November and December, and make a decision by February of the next year. (Most schools have a rule about how quickly a decision about an offer has to be made). But start-ups don't tend to form an orderly line before Christmas. They practise something called just-in-time hiring. This is forcing traditional companies to change their recruiting habits, too.

The new-economy companies are also changing the rules of employment. As Bob Bonner, Wharton's director of career management, observes:

There's a lot of chaos out there. A lot of these new opportunities are new and exciting. But, at the same time, job descriptions change fairly dramatically. The companies also flip their business model to meet the market. Employees have to be agile to meet those changes. Some graduates are faring well. They had their minds set on this chaotic nature. Others weren't necessarily prepared for all that comes with the dot-com world. For instance, there isn't one corporate culture, or a corporate ladder.

The new-economy recruiters are also forcing b-schools to change the way they approach job placement. Ilse Evans at the Haas School believes that the needs of smaller high tech, high-growth companies will mean that, in the future, formal recruiting will play a less prominent role.

Since the market is fragmented, it doesn't operate through centralized recruiting. The high tech firms don't have an investment in a recruiting staff. And if they do, they focus on technical recruiting and not the MBA world. So we have to deal with gazillions of hiring managers instead. These companies have to market themselves more because they don't have mature recruiting activities. Haas is experimenting with many different models and giving students a lot of access to companies. There is an advantage to that. Students and recruiters discuss the real-world work from day one. They're in touch with a manager who has hiring needs and are talking about the content of the work instead of all the preliminary pre-screening things that are discussed in more formal recruiting.

The alternative to all of this is to step outside the system and do it yourself. This is not entirely foolhardy – especially if you have a clear idea of what you're looking for. In the era of free agency we suspect that more students will seek their own ways forward in the future. They remain, for the moment, in the minority. It can work. A Fuqua student says:

I never took advantage of the Fuqua recruiting process – not once. No interviews. Not for an internship, not for a full-time job. I worked the entrepreneurial environment in North Carolina from day one, since I was 99 per cent sure that I was going to work for a local start-up. So I schmoozed with a number of class speakers that addressed entrepreneurship – getting their business card, asking for their input and advice. And my role as Entrepreneurship Club co-president gave me great exposure to the local start-up scene. All in all, I was incredibly narrow in my job hunt – I interviewed with a total of three companies for my summer internship, and six for my full-time job.

Treks

There are also some new innovations in the recruitment process. Start-up career fairs are making an appearance at the major schools. These aim to bring start-up companies onto campus, or some other convenient location. Start-ups rarely follow the traditional recruitment season. They tend to recruit according to need. Some schools also include more established new-economy players. Amazon.com and FreeMarkets, for example, are candidates for these events. Students like having the high tech, high-growth companies as part of the regular recruiting fest. The new on-line divisions of some large companies also attend, like E-General Motors, and E-Bank of America.

A growing number of schools, though, now accept that they have to go to where the recruitment action is, rather than expect the companies to come to them. Over 100 MIT-Sloan students visited Silicon Valley in January 2000. (The most popular management track at Sloan is the New Product and Venture development track.)

'Go West young MBA' is advice that b-schools now practise. The 'trek' is the latest technique to become fashionable with North American schools. The phrase on the lips of b-school career officers is 'mobile recruiting'. 'The new model is mobile recruiting,' says Wharton's Bob Bonner. 'In 1999, we did ten treks to high-growth regions to help Wharton students connect with dot-coms, because a lot of dot-coms don't visit campuses; they don't have human resources departments with recruiting groups. That has turned the tables on the recruiting process.'

Recognizing that many of the companies graduates want to work for are located in Silicon Valley and don't actively recruit on campus, schools are now organizing tours for MBAs. These give the graduating MBAs the opportunity to see the new economy at work first hand – and to meet recruiters and interview for jobs. The trek made its debut in 1996 when Harvard Business School's career services department helped students organize a series of information sessions with about 40 Silicon Valley companies over the Christmas break. Around 75 students paid their own expenses to attend. This has now grown. In 1999, around 500 of the school's 1800 MBA students took the opportunity to meet more than 200 firms as part of 'West Trek'. The school now has similar smaller treks to other cities including London.

Other schools including Michigan and Yale have cottoned on and now offer similar opportunities. In 1999, for example, Michigan organized its own 'West Trek' after graduation. In May 2000, it took a group of MBAs to Palo Alto – the capital of the New Economy. Some 270 Chicago students went on the school's West Quest.

At Stern, students have organized their own trips to the West Coast. (Treks can also involve heading East. West Coast schools such as Haas at Berkeley organize student trips to Wall Street.)

Wharton has now taken treks a step further. It has hired a full-time person to work with students to organize visits to nine different cities. The leading technology companies are now making sure that they feature on such trips, often making senior managers available to talk to MBAs. Wharton students report that on one recent trip no lesser personage than Charles Schwab, co-CEO of the eponymous brokerage firm, greeted students personally.

Increasingly the business plans and bright ideas studied by business school students are picked up by venture capitalists. It used to be management consultants who hovered over the best brains in business schools. Now it is venture capitalists with their bulging wallets.

One expanding hunting ground is the business plan competitions run at many business schools. These have become an industry in themselves – MIT's Entrepreneurship Competition has a $50,000 prize. Zefer, an internet consulting firm, won the business plan competition at Harvard Business School and went on to attract funding of $100 million. Akami, a loser in MIT's competition, brought in $43 million. The 1998 winner of the MIT competition, Direct Hit, was so flush with cash that it returned the prize money.

While internet start-ups are fashionable (accounting for 38 out of 68 teams entering Stanford's 1999 competition), MBA programs have provided the impetus to more traditional business ideas. Among INSEAD's entrepreneurial alumni is Paul Chantler, managing director of the Paris Real Ale Brewery. Chantler's inspiration came through INSEAD's new ventures elective. This led to a business plan for a micro-brewery and the creation, with a fellow MBA graduate, of an English-style pub and micro-brewery in Paris.

Among those taking the new ventures elective as we undertook our research was Adam Norwitt. He was dissecting the potential of an internet-related start-up in a group made up of himself, an American, an Irishman and a Mexican. 'We each bring knowledge that's very useful. The Mexican guy knows the internet. The Irishman is a former software engineer. You might not be able to bring such a group together anywhere else,' said the former lawyer.

Other schools point to their track records with enthusiasm. Spain's Instituto de Empresa in Madrid strongly emphasizes entrepreneurialism. The subject is part of the compulsory MBA curriculum and is also offered as an elective. In the last ten years, more than 350 companies have been set up by Instituto students – each employing an average of ten employees.

In the UK, Cranfield School of Management points to the success of Robert Wright, a 1982 graduate, as an example of what can be done. Wright took the entrepreneurship and planning your own business electives on Cranfield's MBA program and went on to launch his own airline, eventually sold for £6.25 million. His current venture is CityFlyer Express which has a turnover of over £89 million.

Given such figures it is little wonder that business schools and their students are anxious to board the entrepreneurial bandwagon. With growing student demand for entrepreneurial skills, business schools have moved quickly to add new elements to their programs and to expand their services and facilities. For example, London Business School dean, John Welch, has identified entrepreneurship as one of the school's main priorities. It has £4 million ($6m) available to fund student start-ups through a venture capital fund.

The entrepreneurial trend means that schools are sometimes to be found taking the leap themselves. Cambridge University's Judge Institute of Management Studies has announced plans for the Cambridge Entrepreneurship Centre. Most notably, Imperial College has established a number of spin-off companies and estimates that around 750 people are now employed in 37 companies which originated from technologies developed at the College. Imperial's MBA program includes a 120-hour specialization in entrepreneurship and innovation. This is run by Professor Sue Birley who regards the entrepreneurial spirit as being intrinsic to Imperial's role. 'I believe the creation and sharing of intellectual property to be the core role of a university – its prime asset. Managing it for commercial profit is a serious future challenge,' she says.

One problem facing schools is that the world is hardly awash with academics with specialist entrepreneurial knowledge. 'There is new emphasis on entrepreneurship though there is shortage of faculty in that area,' admits former INSEAD dean Antonio Borges. 'We are responding to a perceived need for the future. The fast-growing, very innovative high-risk companies pose questions as to how they should best be managed. We must help answer those questions as those companies will be one of the main drivers of the world of management in ten years' time.'

Finding your dream job

Students offer their advice on making all that work pay off:

- Adapt your approach

    If [your dream job is] investment banking at Goldman Sachs or consulting at McKinsey, it can certainly happen, just keep those grades high and practise for interviews. If it's something internet, join the internet business group, read the Standard.com every day, choose companies from the industry to do your class projects on.

    COLUMBIA STUDENT

- Do the ground work

    [There are] many workshops and mock interviews offering advice to land your dream job. It depends on industry, but in general: network, know the company

inside and out, PREPARE PREPARE for the type of interview you will have and FOLLOW UP FOLLOW UP.

STERN STUDENT

The best tips are to be aggressive and to learn about each targeted employer.

LONDON STUDENT

- Take the initiative

Go after what you want (many people were under the mistaken impression that career services is there to get them a job). Career services facilitates the process, and has lots of info and advice, but it is up to you to get that job.

IVEY STUDENT

- Be realistic

The expectations for salary are going down slightly, but the expectations for early retirement and huge stock option packages are on the rise. Everyone thinks they'll be the next millionaire.

STERN STUDENT

- Compete with yourself

Overall, don't be so overwhelmed and threatened by the recruiting process that you ever forget who you are. The most competition I saw at Columbia was during recruiting (academically people are very collaborative).

COLUMBIA STUDENT

- Find the right job for your skills

I think there are quite a few people who are looking at working at a dot-com because of the potential upside who really don't fit in that environment. It really is a start-up and some people aren't that comfortable with the ambiguity and lack of direction that are present at start-ups, yet they are looking at going there because of the potential for the big payoff. Many students may also feel that they deserve a higher position in the company coming right out of business school than they really do. In that sense, I think it has changed expectations.

UCLA-ANDERSON STUDENT

afterlife

Many people say that business school is really about networking (I, personally, believe this). With that in mind, a strong alumni program is critical. Many schools lack the alumni support that would make it an even stronger school.

STERN STUDENT

The network

Cold-calling on anybody and mentioning Yale is the best door opener. As a friend told me before I applied – once you are a Yallie, you always have a place to crash anyplace in the world. Alumni have struck me as very loyal and helpful. Several alumni have come to speak in classes and for presentations, and I contacted some people for advice and contacts in marketing for my summer internship. I was interviewed by returning alumni for my first-choice internship, which I eventually took. I imagine this is a self-perpetuating cycle; I have deepened my business school experience by frequently interacting with alumni; so, when I become one, I will return the favor.

YALE STUDENT

Networking has always been important in business. The traditional power networks have often been education-based – Ivy League, Oxbridge, Grand Écoles, take your pick. More global in their reach, the top business schools are power networks without parallel.

The fact is that people don't go to the top business schools just for the learning; they go, in part, to join an exclusive club – the alumni association. They span the globe, and their influence extends far beyond the world of business. Forget the freemasons, rotary club and other traditional business networks, the business school alumni associations are the new networks of power, influence and affluence.

We all use contacts and networks. It is just that some networks open more doors. Part – some would say a big part – of the reason for going to business school is to make the right contacts. Belonging to a powerful professional network can be very advantageous to someone looking for a fast route to the executive suite. Along with the promise of a big salary at the end of it, graduates of the world's top business schools also get another benefit. The cherry on top of the business school cake is access to their school's alumni network. This is a network to die for.

According to the *Financial Times*, no fewer than a quarter of the directors of the Fortune 500 companies are Harvard alumni. That's a lot of doors. Companies can come to resemble alumni outposts. Morgan Stanley Dean Witter recruits heavily from nearby Columbia Business School. At the last count, Morgan Stanley Dean Witter had no fewer than 100 Columbia graduates at senior management levels – including 50 vice-presidents, 30 principals and 20 managing directors.

And the networks of power are continually expanding as business school graduates move out of their corporate offices into other spheres. A number of leading politicians have MBAs and other business school qualifications tucked in their back pockets. Among them are INSEAD alumnus and ex-McKinsey man William Hague, now leader of the UK's Conservative party. Archie Norman, chairman of the supermarket chain Asda and deputy chairman of the Tory party got his MBA from Harvard. On the other side of the British political divide is another INSEAD old-boy David Simon – now Lord Simon – the former chairman of BP who cashed in his shares in the company to become a leading light in Tony Blair's Labour government.

The b-schools' alumni clubs help graduates develop their careers, update skills, make new contacts – and generally open doors in the world of business, politics and beyond. At the bigger and better known schools, the alumni networks are world-wide fellowships. From Boston to Beijing, and most cities in between, there will be a member of the alumni network who is only too pleased to make you feel at home. A couple of phone calls, and a graduate of Harvard Business School or one of the other top tier schools can be sure of a friendly reception in most parts of the world. This makes life a lot easier than scrabbling around desperately for contacts.

The power networks are not only restricted to the big, best-known schools. An Owen student says: 'I think the alumni network is extremely important, especially for a small school like Owen. Being small, everyone appreciates having someone else out there familiar with Owen. Also, Owen is not a competitive place to study, and the students are usually very friendly with each other, which I think carries over to the alumni connections. I feel completely comfortable contacting any alumi now that I am one.

'I've found that many of the recent graduates are very enthusiastic about the school and assisting fellow Owen students in finding jobs, giving tips on interview tactics or general advice. I used the alumni network to make a contact with a (non-Owen recruiting) company and was able to schedule an interview, and called another recent graduate for advice on how to prepare for a difficult interview process. He not only gave me some great advice on how to prepare for the interview and gave me insight on his internship, but also offered the opportunity to be considered for opportunities within his company. In addition, I called a local alumnus from my city for housing advice for moving to Nashville.'

Consider the French school INSEAD, among the best in the world. The influence of INSEAD's alumni association is legendary. In the beautiful forest of Fontainebleau, the former hunting ground of French kings, alumni meet at the famous châteaux. (Not one château, but five châteaux – although the school insists they are 'small ones.') Introductions are made. Doors are opened. Deals are done. It is civilized, urbane and integral to possessing an INSEAD MBA.

With 18,000 members, the INSEAD Alumni Association wields great power. Its members are drawn from the MBA program (9,700) and from executive programs (8,300). More than 12,900 of INSEAD's alumni are based in Europe, making the European network twice as large as that of any other business school. INSEAD's alumni live in 120 countries throughout the world.

The INSEAD Alumni Reunion Survey shows that 20 years after graduating, 36 per cent of MBA alumni are company chairmen or CEOs. International mobility and an entrepreneurial outlook are also highlighted, with alumni spending around 30 to 65 per cent of their careers abroad, and 42 per cent of alumni running their own businesses 20 years after graduation. These are successful people, and successful people who keep religiously in touch with INSEAD. Indeed, alumni make up 30 per cent of INSEAD's International Council, and hold 10 of the 23 seats on the Board of Directors.

INSEAD alumni take their affiliation seriously. To celebrate the Alumni Association's 35th anniversary, over 1,000 alumni and partners returned for reunions on campus in France from as far away as Buenos Aires, São Paulo, Santiago, Cape Town, Abidjan, Seoul, Ho Chi Minh City and Suzhou. The MBA classes of 1966, 1976, 1986 and 1991 achieved 55 to 65 per cent attendance. The geographic distribution of alumni present was nearly as broad and global as that of the classes themselves: 25 per cent France; 20 per cent UK; 10 per cent Germany and Austria; 8 per cent North America; 8 per cent Southern Europe; 8 per cent Benelux; 6 per cent Switzerland; 5 per cent Scandinavia; 3 per cent Australia/Asia; and 2 per cent South America.

Eight hundred alumni volunteers world-wide serve in various capacities on national alumni association committees, and help to organize reunions and international speaking events as well as interviewing MBA candidates in their home countries.

In 1997, a new alumni association was established in Argentina and the founding of further associations is underway in Ireland, Brazil, Indonesia, and Mexico, which will bring the total number of IAA national associations to 34 world-wide. Alumni contact networks are also present in another 13 countries. Management Update events have been co-organized with alumni in London, Vienna, New York and Utrecht. They attract 100 to 200 alumni, drawing 25 per cent of them from INSEAD's world-wide population, to hear faculty speak and to have opportunities to network.

Other major schools are similarly well organized, with connections stretching throughout the world like tentacles. Switzerland's IMD has 25,000 alumni in 140 countries, including Peter Wallenberg, head of the famous Swedish industrial empire, and the CEOs of Lego and Nestlé. Members of London Business School's alumni association number more than 12,000, of which some 5,000 are MBA graduates (some schools count only graduates, others include anyone who has taken an executive program).

But when it comes to power networks, the Americans make their European cousins look like amateurs. True, they've been at the business school game longer. Their alumni networks span the globe like empires. Armed with their MBAs they march into overseas territories with the school badge as a standard. J.L. Kellogg holds alumni events all over the world. Its network extends to over 80 countries around the globe. Wharton's alumni network amounts to over 69,000 alumni in more than 130 countries – making it the largest business school network in the world, so the school says. Wharton alumni have organized 76 US and international clubs and regional representatives.

The Graduate School of Business at the University of Chicago counts some 30,000 alumni, including the CEOs of RJR Nabisco, Harley-Davidson, and Revlon. Columbia has 20,000 – with 11,000 based in New York, New Jersey and Connecticut and another 9,000 scattered around the globe, including one well-known citizen of Omaha – the sage himself Warren Buffett.

But with more than 60,000 active alumni world-wide, in terms of pure networking muscle Harvard Business School is in a class of its own. Take its 1997 Global Alumni Conference held in Hong Kong. The organizers reported that more than 800 alumni, and guests from over 45 countries gathered in the former British colony on the eve of the handover of power to China. 'A once-in-a-lifetime opportunity' is how one HBS alumnus described the event. 'Three days of lively discussions among alumni, 12 HBS professors, and a distinguished group of Asian business and government officials, focused on the June 30 transfer of Hong Kong to the People's Republic of China and the expected impact of business in the region.'

That's some serious networking. It's Harvard's calling card. As HBS dean Kim Clark observed in his address to those present: 'It is important to recognize that what we are doing here in Hong Kong is a hallmark of the school. We bring together important people to work on important problems. This is an opportunity to build relationships.'

Tours to Shanghai and Beijing gave participating alumni plenty of opportunity to make contacts. In China, they also had a chance to visit a number of joint ventures between Western companies and their Chinese partners, and to learn how those relationships were developing in the climate surrounding the handover of Hong Kong. The changeover from one regime to another seemed to strike a chord with the HBS dean, who talked of a three-pronged defense of the school's empire.

'We're really at a turning point,' dean Clark told a gathering convened on the Sunday afternoon. 'To stay ahead in an increasingly competitive, global economy, the business school has to continue its tradition of excellence. That means ensuring that the faculty are close to practise, the school cultivates its powerful alumni network, and new technologies are incorporated into teaching and student life.'

Those new technologies also play an increasing role in the activities of the alumni networks. In recent years, the leading business schools have been investing in more and more sophisticated IT infrastructures which enable members to leverage even more from the already powerful alumni associations. For example, e-mail addresses were integrated in the 1997 INSEAD Address Book, now in its 30th year of publication. A designated alumni area has grown up and has now merged with the INSEAD website.

But alumni networks aren't just about business. They also give business school graduates a helping hand with their other interests. The program for a Harvard alumni event in Chicago, boasted: 'Private visits with senior management at some of the top venture capital companies in the city. And, depending on playoff dates, a behind the scenes tour of the United Center (home of the Chicago Bulls and Blackhawks) and a certain well-known locker room, led by Blackhawks owner Bill Wirtz.' Sports and business. Who could ask for more? And there's always that $100,000 plus starting salary to get you on your feet, of course. It all makes perfect sense. After all, what's the point in going to Harvard Business School unless you can leverage the hell out of the brand?

Career elevators

Alumni networking has become something of an industry. Alumni make use of the networks by reading the school newsletters and directories, which contain up-to-date information on ex-students. Schools also operate their own databases which, like exclusive dating agencies, can help put former students in touch with other old boys and girls around the world. So, if your company wants you to drum up some business in Miami or Malaysia, the database will help you find out who on the ground might help you.

Whether it's making the odd introduction to government ministers or other dignitaries or recommending suppliers, alumni are usually only too pleased to help. As management commentator Joshua Jampol notes: 'If the firm wants you to open a market in India, the database will tell you who on the ground can help you meet ministers and other heavy-weights. Calls between graduates almost always get results. They share a bond and enjoy lending each other a hand.'

The power of networking is a fail safe. But the system rarely fails – for every MBA who is a bankrupt there are a lot of millionaires. While others use the career ladder, business school graduates go by the career elevator.

Business schools themselves like to put an educational spin on the activities of alumni associations. They talk about 'lifetime learning' and 'top up skills' – and the alumni associations can help members take advantage of both. Access to new research and the latest management thinking, say the schools, is another benefit to be gained from an ongoing association with your alma mater.

Alumni are also used by business schools to market their courses to potential students. Many use former students based in other countries as their ambassadors in new markets, or as their eyes and ears to spot new opportunities. Schools use graduates to talk to and persuade applicants who have been made an offer that theirs is the 'best' school. In some cases, especially where distance is a problem, they will even ask alumni based near to the applicant to carry out an interview and report back prior to making an offer.

An MBA from Harvard, Wharton, Kellogg or another top school is an élite qualification. And herein lies the opportunity for business schools: their alumni rely on the high standing of the school to bolster their own career and are, as a result, prepared to help in maintaining the high standing of the business school's brand. It is win–win. The business school gets money and support; the alumni maintain the kudos of their qualification and have access to a powerful network.

Names on plates

Why do alumni give so generously? After all, many who study for an MBA are paying out of their own pocket. They are buying a product and a hefty endowment appears an overly generous tip.

First, there is a degree of snobbery. Alumni appear more willing to give donations to business schools – commercial ventures – than to universities, which are usually more needy. There appears more cachet in giving a donation to Harvard Business School than to Boston University even if the experiences that shaped your personality were at the latter.

Second, there is a self-perpetuating element to the matter of alumni fundraising. Alumni are almost obliged to continue to support their school. Inverse blackmail is at work.

The number of ways to leave your lover are more than matched by the number of ways you can give money to Harvard Business School. The HBS Fund raked in gifts and pledges in excess of $28 million in 1996–97. Its tactic is simply to give the donor as many possible ways to give money. So many that the major decision is not how much, but how? They include:

Outright gift

Tax efficient. 'You may give cash, securities, closely held stock, real estate, and tangible personal property such as art.' Monets welcomed.

Life income gifts

The Harvard Management Company manages the assets (minimum $10,000) and the donor receives an income. The Pooled Income Funds include the Harvard Balanced Fund, Harvard Growth Fund, International Bond Fund, etc..)

Charitable remainder trusts

For $100,000 plus the donor can set up an individually managed trust.

Retained life estates

For those who are extremely grateful indeed for their education. 'With this plan, you can give your principal residence to HBS while retaining the right to live in it for the rest of your life.' As an extra attraction 'a class gift credit is available for alumni who graduated 50 or more years ago.'

The Cornerstone Society

More appropriately the Tombstone Society. Membership is restricted to 'all deferred-gift donors and those who notify the school that Harvard Business School is included in their estate plans.'

After all, the value of an MBA lies in where you took it rather than whether you covered global marketing in the second semester. By giving to your alma mater you are seeking to ensure that its standards remain high and that, as a result, your CV resounds with intellectual gravitas. If your CV boasts an MBA from a school that has since collapsed through lack of funds, its impact is lessened.

More cynically, some make donations as a statement of how wealthy they are and how seriously they take the education of the next generation. Having a successful business

The list of those who have reached prominent positions in their industries grows longer each year. High profile MBAs, for example, include Harvard graduates Scott Cook, founder of Intuit Corp; Michael Bloomberg, the business news/technology tycoon; IBM CEO Louis Gerstner and former Northwest Airlines CEO Al Cecchi. Peter Lynch, the renowned stock fund manager, and American Airlines CEO Robert Crandall, both earned their MBAs at Wharton, and David Johnson, CEO of Campbell Soup Co., went to the University of Chicago. Investment sage Warren Buffett is an alumnus of Columbia. While Alan Greenspan is a Stern alumnus.

Famous European MBAs, include Simon Critchell, president and CEO of Cartier; Ronaldo Schmitz, a member of the board of Deutsche bank; Helmut Maucher, chairman of the board and CEO of Nestlé; Barbara Kux-Parein, vice president of Nestlé; Lindsay Owen-Jones, president, director general of L'Oreal; Robin Field, CEO of Filofax. The list goes on.

Martin Sorell, founder of the advertising agency WPP has an MBA from Harvard and is a big noise at the London Business School where he is governor. He is also on the advisory board of the Judge Institute, the business school at Cambridge University, and IESE, the famous Spanish business school based in Barcelona.

Sir Paul Judge, whose name adorns the Judge Institute at Cambridge University received his own MBA from Wharton. Another influential Wharton MBA graduate is Richard Koch, the consultant turned would-be management guru, and a non-executive director at Filofax. John Neill, CEO of Unipart, got his MBA from Strathclyde. Greg Hutchings, chairman of the conglomerate Tomkins picked his up from Aston. David Sainsbury, now Lord Sainsbury, who recently stepped down from the helm of the family supermarket chain J. Sainsbury, is chairman of the governing body of LBS, but received his MBA from Columbia.

person's name attached to a building/room/chair/program provides a constant message: join this program and you may end up as rich and as wise as the man who endowed it. But of all the needy causes in the world, a business school is not one whose need would place it high on the list.

For some, donations are memorials. For example, Michael Bloomberg, founder and president of Bloomberg Financial Markets and a member of the HBS class of 1966, gave the university a $3 million gift to establish the William Henry Bloomberg Professorship in honor of his late father.

The ultimate is to have an entire school named after you. This demands a great deal of money and an ego the size of a continent. There are no recorded examples of individuals endowing schools anonymously. There are a growing number of business schools with names attached. Cornell has its Johnson School of Management; Atlanta's Emory University boasts the Roberto C. Goizueta Business School named after the late Coca-Cola chief. In 1979 the John L. and Helen Kellogg Foundation gave Northwestern University's School of Commerce a gift of $10 million. Mrs Kellogg was curiously overlooked and the school was renamed the J.L. Kellogg Graduate School of Management. (Women are notable by their absence in the names of business school patrons.)

the planet

inside 20 of the planets leading b-schools

Asian Institute of Management

Address	Joseph R McMicking Campus 123 Paseo de Roxas 1260 Makati City Philippines Tel: + 63 2 893 7631 Fax: +63 2 893 4595 E-mail: admissions@aim.edu Website: www.aim.edu.ph
Teaching staff	Full-time 62 Others 10
Student intake	140 average
No of applicants	n/a
Average age	26
Estimated annual cost *(tuition fees) – 1999–2000*	Tuition $12,000
Median base salary (1999)	n/a
Student profile (1999)	EU and North America 3%

Why AIM?

The Asian Institute of Management in the Philippines is one of the most respected b-schools in Asia. AIM offers a two-year Master of Business Management (MBM), rather than an MBA degree. Less well-known in the US and Europe, the program is nevertheless equivalent to a traditional MBA. AIM also offers a one-year Master in Management (MM) program. The course is work-intensive.

Founded in 1968, the school was one of the first to bring Western-style management education to the region. It was influenced by Harvard, and adopted the case method, the teaching style that remains to this day. Located in the business district of Makati City, and with good links with the local business community, the MBM places special emphasis on Asian management styles and strategies. It also has an excellent network of student exchange connections with schools in other parts of the world. Tuition fees are high compared to other local schools, although not relative to US and European MBAs. Students say the AIM program is a cut above other Asian universities.

'AIM is the best school in the Philippines and one of the best business schools in Asia. It is definitely better compared to the local universities, however the high tuition fees is a big consideration in going to this school. But, given the number of job offers I am getting from very reputable companies – I know I definitely made the right choice,' says one student.

Says another: 'I actually intended to apply to a US or UK business school to do my Masters. Specifically, I was looking at the LBS Masters in Finance Program. But my boss convinced me that even if the two-year MBM is considerably longer than the nine-month MiF, the extra value I can gain from the full program would be more beneficial. I chose AIM primarily because of cost. Studying abroad costs an arm and a leg and the economics played a major role in the decision. On the plus side, though, AIM has a very good reputation both in the Philippines as well as around Asia. My bosses took their Masters at MBM and I was quite impressed with them at work. An uncle of mine likewise took an AIM MBA and is currently the CEO of a very large corporation here. I also know a lot of AIM graduates that did very well in their respective fields. Since I will probably be working in the Philippines or around Asia later on, AIM seemed the place to be.'

Average student age is 26, younger than Western MBA programs, with some students joining the program at 22. Although the school is international in outlook, and boasts 33 per cent foreign students, most are from other Asian countries, with a high proportion from India. US and EU students make up only about 3 per cent of the total. The percentage of women on the program is actually quite high at about 35 per cent.

For Westerners with a yen to work in Asian markets, the school offers a good grounding in Asian business practices and cultural nuances. For local managers who intend to stay in the region, the school has a very strong brand presence. The Action Consultancy strand of the MBM, which actively involves companies in the region, is highly regarded and provides a good way to meet local business people and prospective employers.

Getting in

The school requires a first degree, at least two years' work experience, proficiency in written and spoken English, and GMAT. There are about 140 places on the MBM program and about 25 per cent of applicants are accepted. Applications have to be submitted by mid-May.

Academic life

The two-year MBM program is largely case-based, with students covering around 700 cases during the program. CP (class participation) is an important component of student assessment. Once a month, too, students are given WACs (written analysis of cases) which they receive on a Friday at 5.00pm and have to submit by noon the next day.

Core courses are covered in the first year and the first term of the second year. The second and third terms of year two are given over to elective courses. During the summer between the first and second year, students carry out the Action Consultancy assignment

– an in-company project and work on the Management Research Report (thesis), which is a major part of the MBM.

'Workload is VERY heavy,' a student observes. We read three to four cases a day, and meet with our CA (case analysis) groups for projects at least three times a week. Finance and statistics take up a lot of our time since we have to crunch the numbers. We also have our overnight WACS (written analysis of a case) that ruin our Friday evenings. Then there's the famous MRR (management research report) which takes up a lot of our time. It's a pretty heavy load but it's also manageable.'

Another adds: 'We have an average of three one-hour-twenty-minute classes a day (usually a max of four classes and on very rare occasions only one class). An average case is about 20 to 23 pages long in the first three months, shortening to an average of 10 to 15 pages afterwards. Therefore, we are looking at about 30 to 60 pages of reading a day.'

The heavy reading burden means that diligent students can end up losing out on some sleep. One says: 'I generally get to bed about 2 to 3 am, with classes starting at 9:30.

Best teachers: Distinctions go to: Professors Morato and Mendoza (because they scare the hell out of everyone); and Professors Gavino, Bernardo and Herrera ('She's like my second mother in this institution,' says one student).

Social life

The school is located in the middle of the main commercial and business center in the Philippines. The best nightspots, restaurants, coffee shops and bars are just a stone's throw away.

'In general, the students here are party people so there is rarely a lack of people to go out with for drinks, or whatever. Since the campus is so small, everyone generally knows everybody and there is this big sense of community over here,' says one AIM student. 'The name of the game here is adjustment. The first three months are the most difficult particularly since there is really not enough time. A few relationships with outsiders have been broken and new ones made with a number of them being both students. In general, though, if both parties understand what happens during the MBA and both agree to work things out and adjust, everything can work out fine.'

'The best things are that everyone is cool and friendly,' says another student. 'They realize that everyone is in the same boat and are quite open in helping each other out. A big part of the MBA experience is the networking. Everyone realizes this as well so a lot of time is spent getting to know classmates.

'The best thing about school is that you get to meet new people – local and foreigners alike. It's also a good time to establish your network with people of different countries. It was definitely a good break for me – going back to school, hanging out with people your own age. It was a lot of fun!

'Social life with friends isn't really a problem. It's family time that suffers with the hectic schedule in business school. Most of us (especially those who stay in the dorm or live within the school area) get to see our parents only during weekends. It was a big change for most of us. My family had to adjust to my new schedule as well. It was difficult at first, considering that they are used to seeing me everyday but they eventually also got used to it.'

Social highlights: International Day, in March. This is the time when students get to dress up in their national costumes and show off their respective countries. This is also the time when the school's board of governors visits the institution. The students make a presentation to the visitors.

Other highlights include school-wide parties: the Cubs Night (a party for incoming students), the Deepavali Celebration (an Indian holiday party – the majority of foreign students at the school are Indian), the Christmas Party, and the Tiger's Night (a send-off party for graduating students). These parties are attended by about 200 to 300 people (the population of the school), and beer consumption is about six to seven kegs per party. 'The parties serve as a jumping-off point for a lot of the students who transfer to bars outside after,' says one student.

Cool places to hang out: The school is opposite a mall so there is a diverse selection of food places. For those with a better meal in mind, restaurants are all around for virtually any taste and budget. The Venecia bar is the most popular bar in Makati – as the place to be seen. But most of the students hang out in Bistro because it's cheaper and is nearer the school. They also hang out in Cable Car (it's open 24 hours and has billiard tables). Chili's is a favorite because it's near the school. There is a bar next door in a building owned by AIM, which students say is a good place to hang out if you don't want to go far. The real party places in Manila are between 10 to 15 minutes' drive away.

The Anderson School – UCLA

Address	110 Westwood Plaza Los Angeles, CA 90095 US Tel: +1 (310) 825 4321 E-mail: mba.admissions@anderson.ucla.edu Website: www.anderson.ucla.edu
Teaching staff	Full-time 134 Others n/a
Student intake (Class of 2001)	330
No of applicants	4,926
Average age	27
Estimated annual cost (tuition fees) – 1999–2000	Single student $40,989 ($20,756)
Average GMAT (1999)	Mean – 690 Mid 80% range – 630–730 Average GPA – 3.6
Median base salary (1999)	$75,000
Student profile (Class of 2001)	Women 28% Minorities 23% International 24%
Notes	The number of applicants for the class of 2001 was the highest in the school's history.

Why Anderson?

Considering it is part of UCLA, Anderson is a largely unsung part of the b-school world. It exists quietly, rarely attracting attention. This is strange. Based in Los Angeles, Anderson is brilliantly placed, well funded and its students say nice things about it. Part of the problem is marketing – a bit ironic for a b-school. 'I would like to see Anderson's program marketed better. We have all of the programs that are touted by other schools in publications yet get no recognition for them,' says one Anderson student. Clearly, an MBA from a slightly uncelebrated school lacks the kudos of one whose merits are sung from a million rooftops.

If Anderson gets its marketing act together under new dean Bruce Willison, its competitive advantages are manifest. First, location. Los Angeles is attractively warm and happening. The media and entertainment industries are within reach. 'Having lived and worked on both the East Coast and in the Midwest, I know the place just feels different – you can literally see the pulse of the new economy. Further east, the vibe just isn't the same,' says one student with a colorful turn of phrase.

Second, Anderson excels at entrepreneurialism, perhaps the subject of the moment. (The only other school on a par is Babson College which has a long-established bent towards matters entrepreneurial.) Virtually all of the Anderson students we spoke to mentioned the school's entrepreneurial culture and outlook as a positive force. 'The focus of the students and school [is on] entrepreneurship,' says one. 'People here live, eat, and breathe it, and there are classes to support that. It's a very different atmosphere when such a high percentage of the student body are thinking this way – the speakers attracted, the projects you choose for your classes, the jobs you take – all make it very different from a more traditional school.'

Not all students are so positive. 'The core curriculum at Anderson is weak and needs significant improvement,' observes one. 'As a state institution, the school has a hard time keeping the best professors because of the budget and many of the core classes are taught by first-time teachers.' This is a recurring criticism.

Getting in

Increasing applications and Anderson's location and expertise suggest that competition for MBA places will become fiercer.

Academic life

'I expected more from my fellow students – to be more aggressive in pushing the envelope in class discussions. On the flip side, I learned more from my professors than I expected to – largely due to their personal experience, and the high number of opportunities to interact outside the classroom on projects and in extra-curricular activities. Socially – it has been great. An outstanding community,' concludes one student.

Anderson gains plaudits for its finance and entertainment programs. 'The entertainment and entrepreneurial program are unparalleled. The finance program is strong with many leading academics,' says a student. Anderson makes the most of its location through an impressive entertainment, media and communications speakers program. Typical speakers include the likes of Frank Biondi and Ted Harbert.

Best teachers: Teachers on the entrepreneurial program gain top marks from virtually all students we talked to. Outstanding are Bill Cockrum, who teaches entrepreneurial finance, and ethics. 'Very tough, with cold calls that keep you in a sweat, [but] I learned a lot.' Honorable mentions go to Al Osborne (new venture initiation), Alan Carsrud (business plan writing), and Eric Sussman (accounting). Others rate Randy Bucklin on pricing and distribution; Vic Tabbush's economics class, and Matthias Kahl's takeover and restructuring and governance class. The core class in marketing was picked out as the worst class. (This may explain the school's low profile).

Social life

Anderson students tend to live in four main suburbs: Westwood, home of the campus; Brentwood, one suburb to the west; Santa Monica, on the beach west of Brentwood; and Manhattan Beach, about 40 minutes drive to the south. Second-year students tend to live on the beach. There are worse places.

Anderson is highly social. 'The worst [thing is that] it can get a little claustrophobic at times due to the size, but that same characteristic gives Anderson a VERY tight bond among students. 'There are a million things to do in LA' says one student.

Weekly events include Lit Club, held in a different bar with a different 'literary' reader every Wednesday, and a 'Sundowners' on Friday afternoon in a bar near the beach. The biggest one-off event is probably the Palm Springs weekend, where the bulk of the student body decamps to Palm Springs every March. One student says: 'We take over a hotel, and rent sports facilities from the town to practise for the upcoming Challenge for Charity, an annual competition among West Coast business schools that involves raising money for charity, volunteer hours, and a sporting event at Stanford in April. It is a great time to spend the day playing all kinds of serious and not-so-serious sports, followed by one of the best parties of the year – and all the money and volunteer hours support the Special Olympics and Planet Hope.'

The highly active Anderson Student Association organizes a host of clubs – everything from DooWopoly (a cappella singing group) to a Salsa Club.

Cool places to hang out: 'It's LA. There's a million wonderful restaurants,' a student explains. For Westwood, tops go to Westwood Brewing Company, whose slightly upscale prices tend to keep most of the undergrads out, and whose microbrews and cider improve the atmosphere, as does the good food. In Manhattan Beach, Sharkeez has great nightlife and wonderful fish tacos. Ques in Santa Monica is also a favorite.

Social highlights: The annual Challenge for Charity and the suitably theatrical Cabaret, a spoof of Anderson life featuring students, faculty and staff.

PS

Anderson is a recruiter's paradise. Students tend to eye Silicon Valley expectantly.

Chicago Graduate School of Business – Chicago University

Address	1101 East 58th Street Chicago IL 60637 US Tel: +1 (773) 702 7743 Fax: +1 (773) 702 9085 E-mail: admissions@gsb.chicago.edu Website: http://.gsb.chicago.edu
Teaching staff	Full-time 107 Others 64
Student intake (Class of 2001)	1,009
No of applicants	n/a
Average age	28
Estimated annual cost *(tuition fees) – 1999 – 2000*	$47,930 ($28,020) including computer allowance ($3,000) and health ins ($900)
Average GMAT (Class of 2001)	Mean – 690 Mid 80% range – 630–750 Mean GPA – 3.43
Median base salary (1999)	$75,800
Student profile (Class of 2001)	Women n/a Minorities 5% International 31%
Notes	Chicago has had five Nobel Prize winners on its faculty. Discipline-based approach, not case-based.

Why Chicago?

Chicago is a big school in the classic US tradition. It has a reputation for academic excellence. 'It has more Nobel laureates on its faculty than some business schools have professors,' one noted commentator observed. This reflects the school's strong commitment to research. It is also one of the most flexible programs. As one student put it: 'There's no required "track" of classes to follow. No majors are required. I wanted flexibility and control over my studies. As a 28-year-old, who wanted to go to school before the baby clock started ticking, a school that would accommodate my timing needs was also important.'

Another adds: 'Chicago has one of the most flexible and academically rigorous programs among all of the top business schools. The program was well suited to complement my undergraduate degree in business (from Babson College) and prior work experience in investment banking. In addition, there is a noticeable absence of arrogance at Chicago; the students here are down-to-earth and very hard-working. Finally, the caliber of the faculty and strength of the finance program, made Chicago and easy decision for me and my top choice.'

The b-school is about a 20-minute drive from downtown Chicago, giving easy access to the bustle and buzz of the Windy City. The atmosphere on campus is scholarly. Students breathe the rarefied air of academia, reflecting the school's close links with the rest of the university and an emphasis on post-graduate programs. The architecture is early twentieth century – although the school has recently invested $5 million on refurbishing the MBA classrooms and career services suite (which is one of the most impressive anywhere). The administrative block is a 10-minute walk from where most of the full-time teaching takes place.

Students confirm that Chicago is strong in finance, as the school has long claimed. More surprisingly, they say it's fast acquiring depth in people management and negotiation. 'Traditionally, Chicago MBAs hit the promotion ceiling after five years because they were excellent 'doers', but deficient people managers,' notes one. 'The school is trying to train better leaders and the faculty is quite passionate in their mission to make graduates more competitive and people savvy.'

'I came to Chicago to get the financial grounding that I so desperately needed and wanted,' adds another student. 'I am concentrating in finance and accounting and have been amazed at the applicability of many of the concepts I've learned to what I wished I would have done three years ago. The finance program at Chicago is clearly among the best in the country, and I have not been disappointed in any way by the faculty, the classes, or my classmates. I also chose Chicago because it was the one school that totally left the direction of the classes you take up to you. I have had no class forced upon me (save an introductory, soft skills class called LEAD) and I have totally controlled the direction of my studies. Finally, I wanted a school that encouraged students to work in teams, yet rewarded them for individual skills and effort on exams and projects. In the real world, although you will always be needed in teams, it is your individual contributions to the team environment that determine your worth. If I was led to believe that in researching a case or deriving the Black-Scholes equation that I would always have someone sitting next to me when I start my post-graduate career, I would be mistaken. Chicago offers students the ability to learn in groups, but demands them to be able to deliver individually.'

Getting in

'Chicago has a reputation for being the easiest Top Five school to get into,' one student told us. Despite its reputation for academic excellence, a number of students said that Chicago was, in fact, their back-up choice. 'It was not the 'right' school, rather, the school that accepted me,' commented a student. 'A remarkable number of students tell a 'back-up school' story when asked 'why UoC?'

Chicago is undeniably one of the élite US MBA programs. An average GMAT of 690 is lower than Stanford, but pretty much on a par with Harvard, Wharton and Columbia. It might be worth applying even if you'd rather go to one of the other top schools. No doubt, the school does not see itself this way. In fact, students suggest that Chicago expects to be reassured that it is the first choice.

'Getting into Chicago is a multi-faceted process, like every school,' one student told us. 'Clearly, you need top scores, good grades, and a strong work history. Other things that Chicago really favors are: active volunteer activity, a STRONG knowledge of the school, its programs, its offerings, and what is special to you about Chicago, a history of leadership in and outside of work, and an understanding of what you have done, what you want to do in school, and where you want the Chicago degree to take you.

'Advice I would offer to potential candidates is this: know yourself, know the school, and then be prepared to be grilled about both with your application and interview. Further, I can assert from reading applications as part of the Deans Student Admissions Committee, take a mild chance on your essays … If you stand out in the essay (and don't wow the committee with your use of big words and historical references) by being unique, interesting, and someone I genuinely want in my class with me, then I can assure you your application will stand out more than the person with the 720 GMAT and 3.6 from a good school.'

Academic life

As noted, the Chicago course is highly flexible. The only required course is the LEAD (Leadership, Exploration and Development) program in the first year. Students are the architects of their own curriculum. Core courses can be waived and replaced with electives where students can demonstrate they are already proficient. Students select 11 electives from a smorgasbord of courses. Classes are bought and traded in a free-market system, and up to six electives can be taken at other schools in the university. Altogether, students must complete at least 21 courses. There are also good opportunities to do 'laboratory' work with real companies. The bidding system, though, is a cause of some frustration.

'Due to the free market that determines class availability, I was "shut out" for three of my six quarters of bidding. In other words, I was unsuccessful in winning the classes that I wanted and I had to scramble among left-over classes to get a schedule. Bidding impacted my ability to secure classes of interest,' says one student.

Flexible as it may be, Chicago is an academic place, and students are a competitive bunch. 'One common theme that runs through all Chicago students is that they are intel-lectually curious and have a strong desire to excel. Because of these characteristics, Chicago MBAs take their course assignments and learning very seriously and consequently work very hard,' says one.

Chicago also offers one of the best international MBA programs in North America. Aimed at those with global career ambitions, this requires them to take four international courses among their 21, plus some history, politics and social classes on another country to round them out. These can be taken at Chicago or abroad. Students spend three months in another country and complete an overseas internship.

Degrees are awarded on the basis of grades achieved in each course.

Best teachers: Professor Sanjay Dhar (marketing management) and Professor Robert Vishny (cases in financial management) got good reviews.

Social life

Most first-year students live in the rather cramped school accommodation, (although there are plans afoot to build a new campus center, and a 400-bed apartment building for MBA students). The high concentration of students makes for a vibrant if rather claustrophobic social scene. But downtown Chicago offers everything a young MBA student might want to let off some steam. A car is useful. 'I have no complaints of any nature, except if you want to count the bus system here in Hyde Park, which definitely needs some work,' said one student.

'The social life at Chicago is what you make of it,' another told us. 'The city is unbelievable and there is so much to offer. There are social clubs on campus, there are weekly "brats-n-brew's", there is a singles and a married scene, and in the Chicago fashion, there is no peer pressure to do anything you don't want to do,' one student enthused. Adding: 'The school could organize and subsidize more group functions as they do at other schools, but I think that is against the school's overall vision.'

'The best thing about social life at Chicago is the variety of opportunities to meet people through activities at the business school, the university, and in the city of Chicago. Students at the b-school have very diverse interests and talents and are eager to get involved in social activities/events. I developed many relationships that will last a life time,' said another.

Others complained about the cramped conditions. 'The worst part is being watched,' a student said. 'The conservative student-body of twenty-somethings is starved for gossip.'

Added another: 'About 60 per cent of the first-years live in the same building and watch each other. Students do stay home to polish financial models on Friday nights. Available single women are under 10 per cent of the student body. As a result, potential gossip curbs public behavior. Regardless of my three-year relationship with my boyfriend, I've been reported as having sex with classmates and my current male roommate.'

Cool places to hang out: 'The Chicago Chop House has the best steaks/prime rib in Chicago (and perhaps even the country). It's a bit pricey but a necessary stop for all steak lovers. For live music fans, Andy's Jazz Club and Buddy Guy's Legends consistently have outstanding jazz and blues acts.'

Social highlights: The winter formal in January and the Spring Boat Cruise.

Columbia Business School

Address	Uris Hall 116th St and Broadway New York, NY 10027 US Tel: +1 (212) 854 5553 Fax: +1 (212) 662 6754 E-mail: apply@claven.gsb.columbia.edu Website: www.columbia.edu/cu/business/home/index-js.html
Teaching staff	Full-time 100 Others 85+
Student intake *(Class of 2001)*	485
No of applicants	n/a
Average age	27
Estimated annual cost *(tuition fees) – 1999–2000*	Single student $20 881 ($13,890) excluding health fees ($683 per term)
Average GMAT (1999)	Mid 80% range – 650–750
Median base salary	n/a
Student profile (1999)	Women 35% Minorities 19% International 28%
Notes	Columbia has a strong international business reputation with students from over 68 countries speaking 35 languages. It is also strong in finance and communications and media.

Why Columbia?

For most MBA students Columbia means just one thing – New York City. Its location in the Upper West Side means that countless US and international firms are a short subway or cab ride away. This means that top executives drop in regularly as guest speakers ('I can't tell you how many CEOs come to campus – WEEKLY – one of the best parts of my experience,' says one student). They also act as adjunct faculty (about half of the electives offered are taught by practising managers) as well as acting as a source of internships and in-company projects. Most of the top NYC firms such as Goldman Sachs and Morgan Stanley Dean Witter employ Columbia alumni and some retired senior executives act as executives in residence on campus, counseling and teaching students.

Long-standing dean Meyer Feldberg, originally from South Africa, has done much to boost Columbia's reputation (and finances) during his 11-year stint at the helm. He put Columbia among the vanguard of US schools updating their staid curricula in the early 1990s and has been an early and constant advocate of the importance of internationalism. As a result, Columbia is now one of the most international of US schools, with much of its global activity, including exchanges, organized through the Jerome A Chazen Institute, set up 1991.

Columbia is also keen to be in the lead in new initiatives. Despite its international bent, it has, for example, added another US school, Haas at the University of Berkeley in California, to its exchange scheme. The idea is that students at Columbia interested in Silicon Valley can spend a semester there while Haas students interested in a finance job can spend a semester in New York.

More controversially, Columbia has also jumped firmly on the on-line learning bandwagon. The school has signed up to provide UNext, a web-based business education provider, with three courses in managerial accounting, management organization and marketing written by its faculty. The deal is reportedly worth $20 million to Columbia over five to eight years.

Finance is a key strength at the school as is entrepreneurship, international business, and a strong media/entertainment stream – helped by the university's well-known film school.

Two years studying in NYC isn't for the faint-hearted and Columbia tends to attract the type of students who like big city life, unlike, say, the quieter delights of Cornell and Tuck, both of which have fairly remote rural campuses. The student body is also extremely diverse – a direct result of another Feldberg initiative. Nearly a third of students come from outside the US and many of the American students have international backgrounds or experience. The school is also adept at recruiting minorities and women. At 35 per cent the numbers of women are relatively high for a top school. 'Columbia is the best school for women – with the highest percentage of women, great women's organizations, and a terrific network within the city,' says one student.

International students attending Columbia can now access loans on the same terms as US students, though they are not eligible for needs-based scholarship grants or federal loans. They may, though, be considered for academic fellowships. About two-thirds of students receive some form of financial aid from the school.

The school is based in Uris Hall in the center of the university campus. This houses classrooms, library, faculty and student lounges, offices, and a delicatessen, and has been recently renovated. All students must have a laptop and there are over 300 network data jacks throughout its premises, including study areas, conference rooms, classrooms, the library and even the delicatessen. The jacks provide access to the school's LAN, printing and university-based resources as well as external databases. A new eight-story building, which is shared with the School of Law and provides state-of-the-art classroom facilities, has been built just around the corner from Uris.

Getting in

As a top 10 school, getting into Columbia is not easy and there are at least 12 applicants for every available place. 'My advice to applying students is be interesting, take chances and be yourself! Don't worry about trying to fit anyone's sort of template. I don't think there is one, really,' says one Columbia student. It does help, though, if you have some idea what Black-Scholes and the Capital Asset Pricing Model are.

Academic life

The Columbia MBA is a fairly standard mix of a functional core studied over the first two terms followed by electives. These may be grouped into pre-designed areas of concentration or students may design their own, but concentrations are not a requirement. Some electives can be taken in other graduate schools of the university. A variety of teaching methods are used and the mathematics can be demanding. A requirement for at least one term of college-level calculus has been dropped but students are encouraged to attend a pre-program Math Camp. There are three terms a year, starting in September or January. September entrants complete the program in 20 months. An accelerated track, beginning in January and omitting a summer internship, can be completed in 16 months. The school has set up a center for education technology to help improve teaching quality.

Best teachers: The accounting class taught by Alan Brott – 'a very funny true blue New Yorker' – and operations taught by Fangruo Chen – 'awesome' – are popular with students.

Social life

There is an on-campus 'happy hour' every Thursday night (the end of Columbia's week) that most students seem to enjoy. But, hey, this is New York. Listing the numbers of bars, restaurants, clubs, art galleries, theaters etc. etc. is just not practicable. The main advice is don't just hang out around Morningside Heights (the campus location). There's a lot more to New York than the Upper West Side.

Social highlights: The Follies – an annual end-of-classes musical revue that pokes fun at MBA students, administrators and, not least, faculty.

Cool places to hang out: apart from the whole of NYC, students recommend The West End – 'good beers, munchies and reasonable prices'.

PS

Columbia is international, diverse, and very New York. Strong on entrepreneurship but not overlooking those old stalwarts of management consultants and investment banks. Booz-Allen, McKinsey, Chase, Goldman Sachs, and Lehman Brothers are all regular recruiters. If that's what you're looking for, 'just keep those grades high and practise for interviews,' says one student.

Darden School of Business – University of Virginia

Address	100 Darden Boulevard P.O. Box 6550 Charlottesville, VA 22906-6550 US Tel: +1 (804) 924 7281 E-mail: darden@virginia.edu Website: www.darden.virginia.edu
Teaching staff	Full-time 85+
Student intake (Class of 2001)	237
No of applicants	n/a
Average age	28
Estimated annual cost (tuition fees) – 2000–2001	Single student $37,208 ($24,208 non-state residents)
Average GMAT (1998)	Mean – 685 Mid 80% range – n/a Average GPA – 3.36
Median base salary (1998)	$77,750
Student profile (Class of 2001)	Women 29% Minorities 11% International n/a
Notes	Tuition based on case method. Scholarship aid 1999–2000 – Year 1 141 applied, 97 awards = 69%, Year 2 142 applied, 119 awards = 84%

Why Darden?

Although Darden is generally ranked just outside the top 10 US b-schools, it is nevertheless one of the best MBA programs in the world. It adheres to the case method – modeled on the Harvard approach – and has a reputation for working students hard, especially in the first year. With an intake of around 240, the school has the benefits of a close-knit community and the voracious academic appetite of one of the bigger schools. Students are exhorted to think like a CEO from day one.

The University of Virginia has a long and distinguished provenance. It was founded in 1819 by Thomas Jefferson, and is scattered all over the historical town of Charlottesville. It enjoys one of the most attractive and traditional university atmospheres in North

America. Jefferson's original vision of an 'academical village' – known as The Lawn – is an important American architectural site and provides a focus for university life. 'This area of campus (called "grounds" at UVa) is beautiful, with Jefferson's Rotunda sitting gracefully at the head of the lawn,' a student rhapsodizes. Darden is closely connected with the rest of the university.

Another student explains his reasons for choosing Darden: 'I was convinced that Darden was the right school for three primary reasons: the size, the culture, and the case method. First of all, the smaller size of Darden (240/class) was a big attraction for me – I wanted the close attention of the faculty and fellow students – I didn't want to feel like I was a faceless person in an MBA factory. Second, the culture here is one that is very supportive of fellow students. Though students have a competitive drive, nearly everyone is very willing to help others learn. For example, students who are CPAs led accounting review sessions for their fellow students before the exams. This happens for nearly every course of the First Year. I can't say enough about the fantastic culture here. Thirdly, the case method approach is much better for a person like me. The last thing I wanted was to listen to lectures, take notes and read text books. The case approach is entirely interactive and in my opinion, a better way to learn.'

Another says: 'Although meeting the dynamic students, seeing the beautiful grounds, learning about the traditions, and speaking with enthusiastic alums were all great sellers, attending a Darden class was what really convinced me that Darden was the right school for me. The case method style of teaching is terrific! Students engage in learning and actively contribute to the in-class debate. One by one they build on each other's comments and/or challenge points with which they disagree. It is a very active type of learning – after seeing that, I knew I wouldn't attend a lecture-based school.'

The five-building complex which houses the school was built in 1996, and offers good facilities. The school has plans to expand in the future, and has benefited in the past from generous benefactors. Accommodation is available on and off campus but the latter tends to be pricey.

Students say the school's strengths lie in general management and finance. It also has a good reputation for entrepreneurship and ethics.

Getting in

Average GMAT of 685 means Darden sets a high academic standard. There are around 13 applicants for every place. The school is careful to select students who fit with its culture, and interviews are seen as a way of screening for community spirit as well as academic prowess.

'The interview process is designed for the interviewer to get to know the prospective student, so be yourself during the conversation,' advises a student. 'It is not something about which you should worry or be nervous. Let your natural personality shine through the conversation.'

Academic life

As mentioned above, Darden has a fearsome reputation for hard work. Virtually all of the teaching involves cases. Case preparation – up to 14 a week – means studying long into the evening. Class participation is an important element of assessment. The school also emphasizes working in small groups. The first-year core is an integrated curriculum, with courses designed to build on what is being learnt in other classes. In year two, students combine electives with two required courses – one on leadership and the other an in-company project.

'The workload here is rather heavy compared to other MBA schools (so it seems in comparisons that I've made with folks in other programs). However, the workload was lessened for the class of 2001 – they have much more free time than we had,' says one student.

His colleagues concur: 'The workload is challenging in the fall of the first year, there is no question. But the work is purposeful, and the students learn a tremendous amount as a result of the comprehensive program. The students who develop good relationships with their learning teams have an easier time getting through the rigors of the first year. The learning teams are an important support mechanism and a big part of the first year experience. My team mates taught me so much!'

Despite the pressure of academic life, the atmosphere is generally not as competitive as the big schools. 'I thought students would be more selfish and competitive, but people are very friendly and they are here both to learn and have fun,' a student notes.

Best teachers: Plaudits go to Paul Farris and Ervin Shames (consumer marketing); Sherwood Frey (bargaining and negotiating); Bob Bruner, Susan Chaplinksky and Ken Eades (finance).

Social life

For those who like a bit of history Charlottesville offers a great deal. It also benefits from a surprisingly wide range of restaurants and bars. It has its own unique buzz, which emanates from a sense of continuity with scholars past, present and future. Hard to describe. The fact that the MBA program is compact also means that unlike bigger schools, students get to know most of their peers.

'The best thing about the social life is related to the small size,' a student observes. 'You get the opportunity to get to know nearly everyone in your class and that leads to a wide array of social events. Every weekend there are great parties and social events to partake in. Also, there is a great golf course very nearby and we play a ton of golf in the second year.'

Social highlights: The Viking Party. Students dress up as Vikings and climb to the top of a mountain. Spirits flow, beer trucks are rolled up, salmon steaks are grilled, and there's a big bonfire, and lots of dancing.

Cool places to hang out: There are many good restaurants in Charlottesville. Among them Tokyo Rose ('great sushi that even the Japanese students rave about' one student says) and Continental Divide ('an eclectic Southwestern mix').

MBA students like to hang out at the Buddhist Biker Bar, Biltmore, O'Neil's and South Street Brewery – a local microbrewery. Students also convene at 'the corner' which is close to main grounds and The Lawn.

PS

While most students say that the size of the program brings benefits, some also point out the downside. 'The disadvantages include getting to know fewer people while you are there and having a smaller alumni base. Sometimes I wish Darden were a bit bigger – I am glad it has decided to add another section.'

Fuqua School of Business – Duke University

Address	Towerview Road A-08 Academic Center Durham, NC 27708-0104 US Tel: +1 (919) 660 7705 Fax: +1 (919) 681 8026 E-mail: admissions-info@fuqua.duke.edu Website: www.fuqua.duke.edu
Teaching staff	Full-time 85 Others 10
Student intake (Class of 2001)	332
No of applicants	3,555
Average age	28
Estimated annual cost *(tuition fees) – 2000-2001*	$42,395 ($28,910) ex-health insurance and laptop/computer expenses
Average GMAT (Class of 2001)	Mean – 677 Mid 80% range – 610–740 Mean GPA – 3.35
Median base salary (1999)	$81 017
Student profile (Class of 2001)	Women 35% Minorities 23% International 20%

Why Duke?

The reputation of the Fuqua school has been growing in recent years, and is now widely acknowledged to be among the top schools in North America. In the 2000 *Business Week* rankings it jumped from seventh to fifth (although it slipped a couple of places in the 2000 *Financial Times* global rankings). It is also one of the most innovative. It has embraced on-line learning – especially on the executive education side (non-degree) – with an enthusiasm that is unusual among traditional b-schools. In its MBA program, too, Fuqua school has shown itself to be responsive to the changing business environment.

The school's philosophy emphasizes collaboration and team work. MBA students, it believes, should be effective managers who are able to contribute as part of a team from the moment they set foot outside the classroom. Functional skills are highlighted. There is a lot of focus, too, on developing the personal effectiveness of individuals. This is reflected in so-called Integrative Learning Experiences, that extend beyond normal classroom learning. These can be rapidly re-oriented to reflect new imperatives in the real world of business. This is reflected in the comments of students. 'Fuqua is a team-oriented school where the students want to learn and have fun doing so. This is the right school for you if you are interested in leadership, teamwork and being very involved in the school and the community. If you thrive in cut-throat competition, this may not be the best place for you. You don't want to be miserable for two years,' says one.

Another adds: 'I thought and still think that Duke is a school that is the best school in the top 10 in terms of down-to-earth faculty and students. The school provides for easy networking and/or access to the faculty. The student body is consistently open and friendly, and there is undoubtedly a high level of team spirit.'

Says a third: 'I wanted high standards in a collaborative atmosphere. Fuqua fit the bill. Also, during my visit, I was impressed with the students that I met and the culture.'

The area in North Carolina between Durham, Raleigh and Chapel Hill is highly regarded for research, and the school benefits from its links with the rest of Duke University. Although the main building is modern and well-equipped, Fuqua nestles in a wooded region on the periphery of the main Duke campus, which is neo-Gothic is style. Facilities at the b-school and the executive education center are among the best in the US. The MBA program is integrative. The school sees management as a pragmatic rather than purely academic discipline. The school boasts a strong student exchange program.

Students say the school is strong in finance, marketing and teamwork. It is also gaining a reputation for entrepreneurship, which some say is representative of the school itself. 'I think overall the school has an incredible ability to rally around an idea or need, accomplishing great things at a lightning pace. Perhaps this is attributed to the school's relatively small size, allowing the administration, faculty and students to be nimble and quick to improve. Perhaps it's a bit of the entrepreneurial bent of the school, where innovation isn't just lectured on, but put into practice,'one student told us.

Some would like to see that extend into the not-for-profit and public sectors. 'I'm currently working with the Fuqua administration to help them improve their focus on the intersection of business and society, specifically the topic of social entrepreneurship. I'd like to see the school realize that true leaders are not just the heads of businesses, but leaders of their community, active on nonprofits, cognizant of environmental and social issues. Fuqua is a top business school, and as such, we're not destined for middle-management. A number of us will be in high-profile positions – and such leadership requires that we are aware of the double bottom line.'

Getting in

Competition for places is stiff – with around 9 per cent of applicants being accepted (an average GMAT of 677 isn't far behind the biggest name US schools).

Academic life

The seven-week terms make for an intensive learning experience. The two-year program starts with a one-week workshop designed to help students bond (the first of four Integrative Learning Experiences which are spread throughout the MBA). Students are divided into sections of about 65, with lots of work carried out in small groups.

Most of the core is covered in year one, along with a couple of electives. Year two includes Competitive Advantage Through People and Processes, and the bulk of the electives. Students do not have to take an elective concentration and most opt for a mix. Some core courses can be waived – although the Individual Effectiveness course which runs throughout the first year is compulsory. The degree is awarded on the basis of grades achieved in each course.

In general, and despite its growing reputation, Fuqua students do not seem as obsessed about the academic side as their peers at some other schools. This seems to confirm the view that the culture leans towards collaboration rather than cut-throat competition. 'Grades don't matter,' one student told us.

'The workload is not as heavy as one may think, but it is largely dependent on what you want out of your MBA,' said another. 'If you are looking towards obtaining a comprehensive perspective of business, then your time will be limited. If on the other hand you are interested in only the bare necessities, then your life will be a bit less hectic. Remember, though, your first year and your second year are very different in terms of workload. I have personally ensured that I take a full load of classes all terms, and this is something that has greatly increased the workload and smoothed it out over the two years.'

Best teachers: None were singled out although students said standards were high.

Social life

MBA students live off campus and good accommodation is fairly plentiful. But social life centers on the b-school and wider university. Durham itself is a fairly uninspiring place. 'The social life of Durham and its surrounding environs are similar to any American college set up,' says a student. 'Lots of little bars and restaurants that serve mediocre food at best.'

Social highlights: Celebrate Fuqua.

Cool places to hang out: Fuqua's resident bon viveur advises: 'Best places to hang out, if you have a car, is in Chapel Hill, a place known as 'Top of the Hill' (good bar) or George's Garage (Durham). Good restaurants? None that I would really write home about. They seem to go on decor here (you know the better the place looks, the perception is the better the food will be). Nearly all food is either Italian-based or grill-based, in terms of filets and so forth. Not too much sophistication in terms of palate choices here. Anyway, my choices would be Magnolia Grill (Durham), Four Square (Durham), Four Eleven (Chapel Hill) and George's Garage (Durham).'

PS

Students report a growing interest in start-ups, and entrepreneurship and e-commerce classes. 'Unlike Stanford, however, we still have a large number of students who are seeking more traditional careers in consulting, finance or marketing with large companies,' says one.

On the whole, Duke MBAs tend not to grumble. As one explains: 'The place has high regard for its Honour Code, and because of this, things are kept relatively quiet. You don't hear banter about bad things, you just don't. I think we all respect each other too much.'

But one opined: 'Too many people (faculty and students) believe that there is a quantifiable answer to everything – that all subjects are either black or white ... or perhaps black and red, if you know what I mean. I expected a more healthy discussion of the gray issues, a sort of a liberal arts school environment where groups of students debate issues of interest. Whether it's that we're too busy or the mindset of students is more analytical than philosophic, I don't know. I had just hoped for more enlightened, thoughtful – and even perhaps contentious – discussions about the real issues facing our world.

Another mused that his only complaint was that he found himself among very academically oriented people who do not really have raw business sense. But both criticisms probably apply equally to most b-schools.

Haas School of Business – University of California at Berkeley

Address	440 Student Services Building Berkeley CA 94720-1902 US Tel: +1 (510) 642 1405 E-mail: mbaadms@haas.berkeley.edu Website: www.haas.berkeley.edu
Teaching staff	Full-time 141
Student intake (Class of 2000)	240
No of applicants (Class of 2000)	4,162
Average age	28
Estimated annual cost (tuition fees) – 1999–2000	$34,676 ($20 262)
Average GMAT (1999)	Mean – 674 Mid 80% range – 620–730 Mean GPA – 3.4
Median base salary (1999)	$78,000
Student profile (Class of 2000)	Women 38% Minorities 27% International 34%

Why Haas?

Location, location, location. With Berkeley Hills on one side and San Francisco Bay on the other, Haas has a lot going for it. Throw in Silicon Valley and you have a fairly persuasive argument to spend two years of your life there. At least, that's what its students say. 'I chose Haas primarily because of its reputation and location – right smack at the center of the new economy,' says one. 'UC Berkeley is recognized around the world, and international job opportunities would be much more available to me with the school's name. Haas has also consistently ranked high.'

Haas is seen by its students as more personable than Stanford with all the location advantages. Students typically mention its 'friendly and co-operative environment'. Other advantages most commonly cited are the small class size with only 240 people in one year; Haas's exchange program with other business schools and it being part of Berkeley. More unusually for an American school Haas has a reputation for attracting a highly diverse mix of students.

Haas has embraced the new economy with enthusiasm. It runs an annual business plan competition. Some students have a part-time job in dot-coms while studying in the second year. Many of the class projects are made on dot-com companies which provide the companies with cheap labor and the MBAs with exposure to start-ups. Haas also now has an incubator (two in fact) which helps students that are considering a start-up.

Getting in

Haas is highly rated, brilliantly located and popular. 'What struck me about Haas's application form was its focus not just on career-related questions, but also on personality-indicative questions that would filter out non-well-rounded individuals. As a result, the range of experiences and personality types of the students here at Haas has been so impressive,' says one student. 'I believe that Haas tries to attract individuals who have a wealth of experience. A prospective student must be an interesting person, with interests outside of their career.'

Academic life

As you would expect, big on entrepreneurship, and the management of technology.

Best teachers: Andrew Rose (macroeconomics), Rich Lyons (international finance) and Severin Borenstein (energy markets). The new venture finance class includes top speakers. Poor marks for organizational behavior – 'I am still wondering what they would do if they were ever forced to leave the artificial world of academia and enforce what they preached in the real world of business.'

Social life

Haas gains points for the copious information provided to new students and the housing office of UC Berkeley is highly rated. The only drawback of living in the San Francisco Bay Area in general is the very high cost of living. Apartment sharing is a good alternative. Haas provides an easy-to-use web-based system for getting in touch with admitted students to make arrangements.

Haas has been traditionally a student-run school. This means that students run almost everything outside the class. The Haas social calendar is seen by some as too 'youthful' in nature, a throwback to undergrad days of beer and excess. '[It is] a little bit college like especially in the first semester with big groups, bars, etc.,' says one student. 'For those people who were a bit older than the average age, or with significant others, or who lived in SF before school and so had another life outside of school, sometimes it felt a little overwhelming.'

Activities are many and varied. Every second Friday, there is a party at school, with free drinks, music and food. These 'consumption functions' each have a different theme and are organized by a different club. The best are said to be the European and Latin American events – 'In my time at Haas, I cannot recall one Latin American consumption function where I left without being drunk with tequila and exhausted from dancing to samba rhythms,' says one unrepentant student. For those who still have a thirst, there is also a Bar of the Week.

There are few limits to social activities outside the school. Haas is 3.5 hrs from the Lake Tahoe ski slopes, 3.5 hrs from Yosemite. You can always surf at the Berkeley Marina.

Social highlights: Haas's Challenge for Charity involves a variety of fundraising events including the hoedown (Texan cowboy bar night with appropriate dances), a ski weekend in Lake Tahoe, a sports weekend, auction and a talent show.

Cool places to hang out: If you haven't eaten and drunk to excess already, try the Albatross pub in Berkeley which has a range of beers, free pop corn all night and, the clincher, darts. Other bars include Henry's, on Durant Avenue, a couple of blocks from the school; Jupiter on Shattuck Avenue, which has a nice back yard with heaters so you can sit out in the winter; and, more soberly, Cafe Strata on Bancroft, a ready source of coffee and pastries.

Recommended restaurants in Berkeley include Thai House – very reasonable prices ($5–6), stone fireplace for the winter, nice dining veranda with flowers for the summer; Streets on Channing Way, only ten minutes' walk; Juan's Place (Carleton and 9th Street) – great original Mexican food at very good prices ($6–10), huge portions, free fresh and warm tortilla chips and salsa; Zachary's Pizza, fantastic stuffed pizza, two restaurants in Berkeley, one on Solano and one on College.

PS

The Haas career center organizes numerous info sessions, company presentations, career panels, and much more. As well as the usual suspects, Haas has a healthy proportion of internet and high tech companies in every stage (start-up, pre-IPO or post-IPO) on campus doing presentations, recruiting and career fairs.

Harvard Business School

Address	Soldiers Field Boston MA 02163 US Tel: +1 (617) 495-6127 E-mail: admissions@hbs.edu Website: www.hbs.edu
Teaching staff	200
Student intake (Class of 2000)	897
No of applicants (Class of 2001)	8,467 10.6% accepted
Average age	26
Estimated annual cost *(tuition fees) – 1999–2000* *Sept. entry*	Single $49,400 ($27,250) Married $56,200 ($27,250)
Average GMAT (Class of 2001)	Mean – 690 Mid 80% range – n/a Mean GPA – 3.5
Median base salary (1999)	$90,000
Student profile (Class of 2001)	Women 31% Minorities 18% International 35%
Notes	January cohort to be closed down.

Why Harvard?

Harvard Business School remains the premier brand in business education. Period. This is reflected in the strength of its MBA program. It also has the most powerful alumni network on the planet. Wharton may top the *Business Week* ranking, it could even be a better all-round program, but Harvard remains the benchmark. With an intake of around 900 students, it is a very large program. At times, the school has been slow to react to changes in the market, notably in the early 1990s, but it nevertheless continues to be the most imposing edifice on the MBA landscape. Under the current dean, Kim Clark, HBS has been reinvigorated, embracing new technology and new ideas.

Founded in 1908, HBS awarded its first Masters degree in management in 1910. Although other schools – notably the Tuck School at Dartmouth College – claim to have had graduate programs in management before that date, HBS was the first business school to require a university degree for entry to its management program.

What the school also had that set it apart from many of the other business schools springing up in America at that time was the Harvard brand. The combination of the Ivy League prestige of Harvard University, the serious approach the new school took to the fledgling discipline of management, and its ability to attract gifted professors – some of them from other parts of the university – soon established the school as the top institution of its kind. The tradition for top faculty continues. HBS faculty members, include dean Kim Clark, Linda Hill, Rosabeth Moss Kanter, Robert Kaplan, John Kotter and Michael Porter. Gary Hamel holds a visiting position.

Many students are attracted initially by the brand. 'In the beginning of the research process – it was obvious that HBS's clearest strengths were the school's brand name and network,' one student told us. 'There are few schools that garner the same type of instant credibility as Harvard. The next point was the format of classes. The case method was truly appealing to me. I get bored in lectures – I need a more interactive environment to keep my attention. Now that I'm here – I'm even more convinced. There's certainly a level of superficial discussion that happens at times – but for the most part, I learn as much from other students as I do from the faculty. It's really a unique way to learn. When I came to HBS to visit a class – that was what really put it over the top for me. Listening to the students interacting – and seeing these incredibly dynamic professors in action was exciting. I visited several other schools – and the HBS professors and classroom environment just stood out.'

HBS is on the Boston side of the Charles River, facing the rest of Harvard University. The large campus blends traditional academic architecture (lots of green doors everywhere) and contemporary buildings. At HBS, the old and the new sit together slightly uncomfortably. To its credit, and despite its Ivy clad image, HBS has shown that it is willing to embrace change, especially the new economy. In 1996, for example, the school introduced a business plan competition, with entries – many of them for internet-related businesses – judged by a panel of venture capitalists, entrepreneurs and business professionals. The winner receives $20,000 in legal and accounting services and cash to support the start-up of the new venture.

As noted, sound brand management is a feature of the school's success. Harvard's onus is on cultivating alumni through relentless communication. Its MBA remains at or near the top of the pile. In recent years the school has revamped its curriculum. Despite some concerns that the case study method provides a superficial view of running a business, the case study has been one of the educational building blocks of MBA programs throughout the world. It was established as the primary method of teaching at HBS as long ago as 1924.

HBS continues to churn out around 600 cases a year and in recent years has taken a digital turn. Harvard put its first electronic case to work in 1996 and now boasts that its MBA curriculum is 'virtually paperless' with an expanding number of electronic cases incorporating on-site video sequences and links to real-time information on the internet.

Getting in

As befits its regal status, admission standards are high. But the size of the program (around 900 students a year), and an average GMAT of around 690, means it is not as tough as Stanford and some other schools. Around 12 per cent of applicants are offered places.

A little name-dropping doesn't hurt, but only if they know you well. One student advises: 'Seek recommendations from individuals that know you well and can really offer informed opinions/assessment of your aptitude/potential. Quality of the recommendation was far more important to me than the title of the individual offering it.'

Some people even seem to enjoy the admissions process. 'Application is certainly time-intensive, but I really enjoyed Harvard's application. The questions were thought-provoking and enabled me to pull from a variety of experiences. The interview was fairly straight-forward, though interesting, provocative questions were asked there, as well. I only applied to Harvard, so I don't have a lens for comparison.'

Academic life

In the mid-1990s, HBS introduced a second MBA intake in January. But in May 2000 the school announced that, following a review, it was to merge its January and September intakes. As of 2001, all MBA students will enter the program in September.

The HBS curriculum, which has seen a number of innovations over recent years, consists of two semesters of required courses followed by two semesters of electives. Students are split into class sections of about 80, who take required courses together. Students select their own study groups, but project work is carried out in assigned teams.

'The beginning of the first year is the worst it gets,' says a student. 'It's very tough starting out because the only real guideline you have is professors telling you you should spend two to three hours a night per case – and you usually have three case days. That makes for an unbearable amount of work. Once you've figured out that you can easily do this much work – it becomes much more pleasant. The key to being here is reading the cases – and getting a good understanding of the subject matter – enough so that you can speak intelligently in class. As you get more experienced with the case method – you know what to focus on – and what you can let slide.'

HBS has a reputation for sharpening competitive instincts. But, say some students, this is exaggerated. 'I was a bit skeptical before coming to HBS about the reputation for a stand-offish, competitive and sometimes arrogant student body. But I didn't find that to be the case at all. In fact, last year I was surprised by the willingness of other students to help out each other in areas where they could. Things definitely get a bit more competitive second year – with jobs and the business plan contest – but more on a superficial level, than in a truly detri-mental way. I have never seen a case of one student sabotaging another.'

In common with other schools, students bemoan the lottery process for second year classes, which means they don't get on all the courses they want. 'The most popular classes with the most popular profs are obviously the hardest to get into,' a student explains. 'You usually get your top two and then have to work down from there. That is, you list your top 20 choices – then you may get 1, 2, 5, 6, 7 etc. so you get a lot of what you want, sometimes, just not always the top 5. Get it?'

The degree is awarded on the basis of grades in each course.

Best teachers: High grades go to Tom Esienmann (managing marketspace), and Andre Perold (investment management). Also ones to watch are Don Sull and branding expert David Arnold.

Social life

About half of the first-year students take advantage of the on-campus accommodation available. Downtown Boston is just a few minutes away by car. The size of the program, and the nearness to Harvard University and MIT make Cambridge a lively student town. There's plenty to do.

'Once you've figured out the work thing – the tough part is just budgeting your time between work and all the other amazing things that are happening in this environment. CEO's, company presentations, political debates at the Kennedy School, etc. – there is always something interesting happening. You have to choose well.'

Cool places to hang out: Restaurants: Number 9 Park (continental food), Mistral (continental food), Olives (Italian), East Coast Grill (seafood). All have great food and great atmosphere,' an HBS gastronome advises. 'Harvest is another one in Cambridge (the only really good restaurant in Harvard Square). The North End has the best Italian. You can have dinner and then go down the street for dessert and coffee. Giaccomo's (no reservations), Euno and Assiago all have good food. Make sure to check about reservations. Parking is a nightmare. Legal Seafood is great seafood – Boston's most famous – though the atmosphere is mediocre. Chang Shoa on Mass Ave in Cambridge is the best Chinese around – including China Town. Tanjore in Harvard Square is good Indian. Claremont Cafe is great for brunch. Armani Cafe also has great food – though the service is 'just the worst'.

Bars: Students recommend: 'Sofia's – Latin dancing. Very fun place. Long lines on weekends. Pravda: Not the same as New York – but not bad. There's a separate bar area in the front – so you can get drinks easily there – and there's a dance floor in the back. Grafton Street: This is the bar that most HBSers hang out in. Located close to campus in Cambridge – it's the nicest of the Cambridge bars. They also have decent food for dinner and late night.'

Social highlights: The 1970s' boat cruise in the spring and the Priscilla Ball in the winter.

PS

Not everyone is convinced that HBS delivers on its brand promise to create better business leaders. As noted elsewhere in *MBA Planet*, the school has also picked up one or two negative endorsements. For some, HBS epitomizes all that is bad about b-schools. Peter Drucker has observed: 'Harvard, to me, combines the worst of German academic arrogance with bad American theological seminary habits.'

Still more opinionated was the late Avis chief and author of *Up the Organization,* Robert Townsend. 'Don't hire Harvard Business School graduates,' he warned. 'This élite, in my opinion, is missing some pretty fundamental requirements for success: humility; respect for people in the firing line; deep understanding of the nature of the business and the kind of people who can enjoy themselves making it prosper; respect from way down the line; a demonstrated record of guts, industry, loyalty down, judgment, fairness, and honesty under pressure.'

But the critics are in the minority. If HBS has an Achilles Heel it lies in its intellectual arrogance. To date it has shown itself to be an adequate if not a spectacular innovator. As the competition continues to intensify, it will have to pick up its feet or risk being overtaken by more agile business school brands.

IESE

Address	Avenida Pearson 21 08030 Barcelona Spain Tel: +34 (93) 253 4229 E-mail: mbainfo@iese.edu Website: www.iese.edu
Teaching staff	75 full-time; 35 part-time
Student intake (Class of 2001)	220
No of applicants	1,300
Average age	28
Estimated annual cost *(tuition fees) – 2000–2001*	€ 17,129
Average GMAT (1998)	620
Median base salary (1998)	11.7 million Pta
Student profile (Class of 2001)	EU 65% N. America 10% Other Americas 15% Asia 2% Women 21%

Why IESE?

With its main campus in Barcelona, IESE is Spain's best-known business school, and one of Europe's top 10. Founded in 1958 on the Harvard case method model, it has diffused the HBS concept in Spain – the first Spanish school to spread the learning environment and management education via case methodology and teamwork. The school's philosophy is to open people's minds, not engage in passive learning, which is more undergrad style and perhaps even Latin-European style – 'We want to develop a critical spirit,' the School says. The HBS style, it believes, brought solidity and stability. IESE launched its first MBA, a Spanish-language course, in 1964.

Five years ago, IESE, by its own admission, was not in the same league as its admitted biggest competitor, the London Business School. But that has changed. IESE now sees itself as competing with LBS, and with the top US schools. In the past, any alumni returning to campus would see that the same professors, and the same buildings, were still there. But today, revisiting alumni who listen to the MBA students will quickly come to the conclusion that their school has changed dramatically.

More professional managers have been brought into the running of the school. Before, IESE was run by professors. Now managers (ex-MBAs who have worked in businesses with multinational firms) handle much of the day-to-day business. Where they were all Spanish before, now they are more international. There is much greater integration across functions and disciplines, and new courses on e-commerce and IT have been added, along with an emphasis on managing in emerging economies and on new initiatives on corporate social responsibilities.

Such changes do not come out of thin air, and IESE made them after company requests. Five years ago, firms said IESE grads were not prepared with enough skills. The school put a conscious effort, with money behind it, into growing more international and selling its product more globally. It had to hire and train an administrative team, create a marketing plan and implement it. IESE began this just after the recession, in 1994. It was a four-year process and the school is harvesting these fruits now. The result is companies – mainly multinationals – are hiring more people, mainly for global jobs.

There is a new focus on internationalism. In 1994 the MBA had 65 per cent Spanish students. The 1999 figure dropped to 40 per cent. Twenty countries were represented in 1994; the number is now around 45, with all global regions represented. The average age of students has risen from 25 to 27, while their average work experience has risen from one to three years.

The school has a strong international reputation in Eastern and Central Europe, and Latin America, which it believes is the second emerging region after Asia. The region, it says, has great potential (350 million people), a relatively stable political scene. Companies recognize this. Spain is integrated into the EU economy but linked to South America. It is also close culturally. The advantage for the MBAs is, eventually, they will benefit from Latin American cases, optional courses and professorial exchange. After Spain, IESE's second largest group of alumni are in Chile, then Mexico.

Getting in

In recent years the admissions office has gone from reactive to proactive. Before, it processed applications; now it is actively looking for candidates. Today it has four managers and a staff of seven, with two of those managers and six of the staff non-Spanish. Incoming GMAT scores have risen to an average of 641, a 50-point improvement over the last four years. Before, a high level of English was not required, but now applicants need a 580–600 TOEFL score.

IESE is owned but not run by Opus Dei, a twentieth-century spin-off of the Catholic Church. It is responsible for IESE's mission. Its emphasis is on the humanistic approach to business – not just making money. This philosophy is woven into the curriculum, without, IESE says, being an indoctrination. IESE doesn't just train general managers, it runs on the basic Catholic principles of the dignity of the individual:

- individual freedom
- participation
- solidarity
- the individual's personal development.

This religious affiliation, the school emphasizes, plays no part in the admissions process. In the curriculum, there is an eight-day ethics course (optional), and a third-term anthropology class (also optional), taught by a priest, but that is all. Says one professor (not an Opus Dei member): 'The school's approach means that there is a more humanistic approach among the staff. There are never any big wars among us.'

Students almost unanimously agree the church has nothing to do with the MBA program.

Academic life

The International MBA came along in the 1980s. Today, it is undergoing a vast redesign to make it more flexible. The first year's required 15 core courses jumped to 18 in 2000. The 30 marginal classes dropped to 22, which will include 18 full courses but with more topics, some half-credit. The 450 classes per year have been reduced to 400. The decrease in hours is minimal and not a drastic change, but it does give more space to add to the core. Classes that have been optional for years, like negotiations, innovation, managing communications and careers management and HR will move into the core, and be mandatory for the 2001 class. The school recently added a Chair for Ethics.

Social life

IESE has no dorms. The school wants its students to live in Barcelona. 'We want them to experience real-life culture, to get familiar with Spanish habits. This means they must live where the real people live. The MBA is already isolated; we don't want to contribute to that or make it worse.' Students rent housing in Barcelona, usually not near campus, but a 20-minute drive downtown. Traffic is not a big problem; Barcelona is not a giant megalopolis like Paris or London. Students have no problem finding places to live. IESE's housing service provides a list with prices, options, etc.

Today, 25 per cent of IESE students go on exchange programs, and the same number come from Latin America, a figure the school wants to maintain. IESE describes itself as a bridge between Europe and the US, and an important gateway for Latin America. It also has a big business school network and a large alumni base there. In addition, CELA, its Center for Enterprise for Latin America, started in 1998–99, a center for research in Latin America, best practices and case writing.

Cool places to hang out: It's Barcelona. No need to ask.

PS

Five years ago, IESE had a good graduate profile for recruiters in the Spanish market. Now, its profile is more attuned to what big multinationals want (more mature managers with international experience). More companies recruit on campus, and more of its students are working abroad. It was strong in domestic executive education; now it is strong in international executive education – something important for the school, and for the MBA program.

IESE has embarked on an ambitious expansion campaign that will double the square footage at its second campus in Madrid by fall 2000. It has also bought land and a new building opposite its Barcelona site. Executive education facilities will move there by 2002, freeing up space for the MBA.

The ambitious expansion campaign is designed to position IESE in the world's top 10 business schools. IESE also has exchange deals with many of the world's top business schools, including Tuck, Columbia, Kellogg, Chicago, LBS, Wharton, Duke, and numerous schools in Latin America. Recently it signed with Darden, UCLA and MIT – this latter school has such deals with LBS and IESE only.

For those whose Spanish is not up to speed, IESE offers a month-long, 125-hour summer intensive pre-program, consisting of four to five hours per day in class, plus company visits and presentations, all in Spanish, to familiarize you with the Iberian environment. Once you start your MBA, you can continue Spanish lessons for an hour a day, Mondays through Thursdays.

IMD – International Institute for Management Development

Address	Ch. De Bellerive 23 PO Box 915 CH-1001 Lausanne Switzerland Tel: +41 21/618 02 98 Fax: +41 21/618 06 15 E-mail: mbainfo@imd.ch Website: www.imd.ch
Teaching staff	Full-time 47
Student intake 2000	85
Average age at entry	31
Estimated annual cost (tuition fees) – 2000–2001	S Fr. 41,000
Average GMAT (2000)	Mean – 650 Mid 80% range – n/a Mean GPA – n/a
Median base salary (1999)	$91,000
Student profile (2000)	Women 20% Minorities n/a International n/a
Notes	One year course – Very high percentage of international students: the 85 students entering the 2000 programme were drawn from 38 countries. Faculty:Student ratio = 1:2

Why IMD?

In Europe, IMD is the little school with the big reputation. Often bracketed with the London Business School and INSEAD, IMD is regarded as one of Europe's top three schools. With an intake of just 85, the program combines intimacy with a diverse range of nationalities. The MBA is, in fact, not the school's main activity – which is executive education. Unlike its much bigger rival INSEAD, IMD has no ambitions to grow the MBA program, believing the small is beautiful dictum. It is a one-year program.

Nestling on the shores of Lake Geneva, IMD enjoys an idyllic, if quiet, location in the small Swiss town of Lausanne. In common with the other leading European schools, IMD is truly international, with no one dominant nationality on the program. Students in 2000 came from 38 different countries, and the school has excellent links with leading European multinationals. Faculty, too, are very international, and drawn from all over the world. Geneva is just a short train or car journey away. Swiss trains are famed for running on time.

Traditionally it has appealed to slightly more mature students – the average age at entry is 31. A student says: 'I was 33 when I decided b-school was the next step for me. I wanted a school with a mature student body. I'm American but most of the schools there have an average age of 28. Some, like Kellogg, are even lower. I didn't want an executive MBA program, I felt I could still afford the "time" and expense of a full-time program, even though classmates on an executive MBA would have an older average age. I was also very interested in IMD because of its one-year program, I didn't want to be out of the working world too long.'

Getting in

Average GMAT is around 650, which is lower than LBS and INSEAD, but IMD is hard to get into. The school says that 80 per cent of students offered places accept them. With just 85 seats to fill, that means the school can be highly selective – it only needs to make offers to 105 applicants a year. A minimum of three years' work experience is an entry requirement. The school also asks applicants to make two presentations to members of the admissions committee – one prepared, and one impromptu.

'If one of your objectives in obtaining an MBA is to have a two-year (or one-year) holiday from the working world, IMD is probably not the place for you. So know what your objectives are before you start writing essays. IMD, like other business schools, wants future leaders as MBA participants, so focus on your leadership experiences in your essays and on your future objectives and goals,' advises a student.

Academic life

The IMD program lasts 11 months. It is intensive, with an onus on individual discipline and self-direction. Students spend around four and a half hours a day in class, with another seven routinely spent on group work. The evaluation of student performance – using a range of indices – is unrelenting.

The program is modular in design, with eight modules, each lasting between four and six weeks. Modules culminate in a group project which aims to pull all the learning together. Groups disband and students are reassigned after each module. In module 1, students spend a week on personal development in the Swiss Alps – known as the Dream Team Week. The school's philosophy emphasizes learning through participation and collaboration rather than teaching *per se*. During modules 6, 7 and 8 students work in groups on an international consultancy project – addressing a real issue in a real company.

'The workload, particularly in the beginning, is intense. Anyone looking to attend IMD should be aware of that. In the first four months a typical day can last from 6 am to midnight, and maybe you still didn't get all the cases read. To manage the workload, its important to set priorities. Ask yourself what courses in particular you are here to learn more about. If it's marketing, then focus on your marketing cases and skim the accounting case or operations case. If you came here to learn more about finance, then focus on those cases. The first few months are all about prioritizing.'

The degree is awarded on the basis of individual participation, group contribution and performance in the international consultancy project.

Best teachers: Leif Sjobolm gets the nod (accounting class in module 1).

Social life

There is no accommodation on campus, but this suits the more mature student population. Lausanne's size means that students see a lot of each other anyway.

'The worst thing about the social life is that you don't have time for one!' says a student. 'The best thing is that the class is small, only 84 participants, and more nationalities than any other school (European or American). This is truly the best, not only are you at IMD to learn, but the cultural exposure you get by working 18 hours plus per day with such a diverse group is a learning experience all on its own.'

Cool places to hang out: For drinks after class, and a 'gorgeous view of the Alps and the lake', outdoors on the upstairs patio at the MGM cafe. For late-night bar hopping, the Bleu Lezard near the center of town. 'The food is good in the restaurant and downstairs is the disco,' a student enthuses.

PS

Unusually, MBA students mingle freely on campus with practising managers on executive education courses. Good networking. Recruiters who come to Lausanne include, among others, blue chip companies like Nestlé, Unilever and Johnson & Johnson.

INSEAD

Address	Boulevard de Constance 77305 Fontainebleau Cedex France Tel: +33 1 60 724005 Fax: +33 1 60 745530 E-mail: mbainfo@yinsead.fr Website: www.insead.fr/mba
Teaching staff	Full-time 124
Student intake – entering 1999	September 1999 – 292 January 2000 – 334
No of applicants	n/a
Average age	28.7
Estimated annual cost (tuition fees) – 1999 – 2000	€ 27,900
Average GMAT (1999)	Mean – 685 Mid 80% range – n/a Average GPA – n/a
Median base salary (1999)	$82,000
Student profile (1999)	Women – 20%
	Non-US – 89%
Notes	One-year course – two intakes – January and September. INSEAD also has a campus in Singapore.

Why INSEAD?

Walk through the main entrance of Europe's most famous business school and you are confronted with a circle of furled national flags. Up the stairs, you enter a long corridor with a balcony overlooking a series of partitioned work rooms. Move on down the corridor and, in Amphitheater B, Professor Anil Gaba is taking his class in applied statistics. The students are searching in their pockets for change as Gaba conducts a spontaneous trial to illustrate the marvels of central limit theorem. He calls out the name of every sixth student. The names are a global roll-call – Ekow, Maha, Filipe, Harumi, Lemeng, Sebastien, Patrice, Massimo. It is then, you realize, that this lecture theater could be anywhere in the world. The only clue to your whereabouts is that the change in the pockets of the students is French francs.

Inside, INSEAD (an acronym derived from the European Institute of Business Administration) is slightly institutional in character, its architecture firmly rooted in the 1960s. There is a matter-of-fact realism; a sureness of INSEAD's place in the world. It is a confident place. If you ask the students and faculty at most business schools about the competitive advantage of their school, you usually draw a blank or PR platitudes. At INSEAD you receive a speedy riposte. 'The whole point of INSEAD is its diversity. No one culture dominates the classroom,' says former dean Antonio Borges. 'More and more Americans are applying to INSEAD. We are, to be honest, getting worried. There is a very powerful Anglo-Saxon component. Everything is in English and there is a risk of Anglo-Saxons taking over the school. There are no quotas so we have to encourage candidates from elsewhere in the world.'

Outside the campus, you are in one of the most striking places in Europe: the forest of Fontainebleau, 65 kilometres outside Paris, complete with its magnificent chateau. The forest is the former hunting ground of French kings, a place inhabited by all the French sovereigns since the Middle Ages. It's the kind of place where the cab drivers are inclined to give you a brisk historical run-through.

It is perhaps paradoxical that an institution in such a unique historical and cultural environment proclaims its statelessness with such enthusiasm. But, while others pay lip-service to internationalism, for INSEAD it is a way of life. A total of 16 per cent of INSEAD's 621 MBA students are from North America (10 per cent from the US). The largest contingent are the British (12 per cent) – hardly surprising when London is a mere 45-minute flight away. The French make up just 11 per cent. Contrast this with Harvard Business School where Americans account for 65 per cent of MBA students; or Wharton where Americans account for 62 per cent of the MBA population.

'There is no concept here of us and foreigners. That richness of cultural diversity is what a truly international b-school offers. This creates a richness of exchange and experience that you can't get if 70 per cent of the class is from one country,' says associate dean of the MBA program, Landis Gabel. The cultural diversity is reflected in the INSEAD faculty drawn as it is from 24 nationalities.

The advantages of such diversity are persistently echoed by students. 'You could go to a US school and learn about Europe, but that's a bit like going to INSEAD to learn about Texas,' says one American MBA student, observing that 'the Americans who come here are a self-selecting bunch.' The 30-year-old arrived armed with a degree from Georgetown University and a law degree from the University of Michigan. Like all INSEAD students he is fluent in another language – in his case, Mandarin – and will add another while at INSEAD. An INSEAD joke is that the language requirement is to keep out more Americans. (French prices may also deter: 'I moved my wife and cat from LA, but still can't get used to paying $5 a gallon for gas,' a US student reflects.)

Getting in

Standards are high. An average GMAT score of 690 for the last student intake, is second only to Stanford, according to Landis Gabel (not actually borne out by other US schools).

But this is impressive when you consider that over 70 per cent are not native English speakers. Nearly all classes are taught in English, but a second language is required for entry.

'They seem to be looking for international and ' interesting' people more than straightforward overachievers as they might in the US. If you have several nationalities emphasize the rare one,' advises one student. 'When here relax and don't let the whole thing stress you.'

Academic life

At INSEAD the mix is the thing. Students work in groups of five or six, chosen to maximize diversity – and tension. Groups work together to produce analyses, reports and presentations. 'You're pushed together in groups which are designed to maximize the potential for conflict,' says one student. 'In my case they succeeded. We have an American male, an Italian male, a Russian female and a Mexican male. That's an interesting combination, but we have to just get on and make it work. You cannot change groups. At INSEAD, the process of learning is as much a lesson as the substance.'

And that is something that companies increasingly value. Ford, for example, has been recruiting MBAs from the top European b-schools for many years. 'INSEAD is known by companies that truly seek global perspectives, but is relatively unknown by the general populace in America,' says Jeffrey Morgan global marketing excellence manager at Ford. 'The true global complexion of the student body and lack of a dominate group are significant. It appears that INSEAD intentionally introduces group conflict – that is a reality in today's business arena – through the use of cross-cultural and functional teams. The language requirements of fluency and two languages at working-knowledge level is unique compared to most b-schools.'

While the global element is central to INSEAD, the second competitive advantage, identified by the school, is intellectual rigor. In the beginning, INSEAD faculty compared poorly with their American counterparts. As recently as 1970, only one member of the INSEAD faculty had a doctorate in business. Now all have. Its faculty includes leading intellectual lights such as the Korean Chan Kim, Yves Doz, and visiting professor Henry Mintzberg.

The INSEAD MBA is tough and intensive – the academic equivalent of lean and mean. It was designed for young managers who want to move into an international career – and don't want to wait two years to do so. The 10½-month program is split into five eight-week sessions, each followed by exams and a short break. There are two intakes a year, in January and September, with each divided into four sections comprised of around 75 students. Students take seven electives (an approved project can be substituted for one elective) and attend topic days on specific subjects such as entrepreneurship and ethics. The degree is awarded on the basis of examination results and continuous assessment of class participation, individual and group assignments, projects and computer simulations.

INSEAD increasingly claims the intellectual high ground, keen to take its place on the mountain top with the luminaries of Harvard, Stanford, Wharton, etc. 'The US schools were very academic a few years back and have had to move the focus and attention back onto what's happening in business. We're moving in the other direction, from being very close to business to being more academic,' says Luk Van Wassenhove, associate dean of research and development.

To an American observer, INSEAD's intellectual positioning sits somewhat uneasily with the fact that its MBA program lasts one year rather than the standard two-year US model. How can a one-year program be as intellectually rigorous and as broad ranging as a two-year program? The response is vigorous. 'We were fortunate to start with a one-year program. American schools would do it if they could. But the two-year tradition is very strong and there are revenue implications,' says Antonio Borges. Students appear unconcerned. Many see the shorter program as part of the school's attraction. 'The subject matter is easily compacted into 12 months. It is not quantum physics,' says an American student.

The MBA program is actually ten months long, points out Landis Gabel. 'That's substantially shorter than to get the same three letters that have a magic to the market. There is no evidence that the recruitment market discriminates against one-year programs in terms of starting salaries etc. If you translate that crassly into a Return on Investment calculation it's very attractive. Do you learn all the same things? All the same subjects are covered. It's a bit like drinking from a fire hydrant.'

Students confirm that such high-pressure knowledge consumption creates a heavy workload. 'Lots of it, do maths class in advance if weak at maths, get the languages under your belt before you come here,' advises a British student.

The final element in INSEAD's competitive armory is a suspicion, in Europe at least, that the American management model has had its day. 'The world is eager to get a non-American view of business and management,' says Antonio Borges. 'Over recent years there has been growing realization that there is more to management than the American approach. The reputation of European management and companies has improved with increasing interest in the business world outside the United States.'

Paradoxically, however, there is also a new interest in the US model. The new economy is all pervasive. The change of emphasis is apparent at INSEAD, too. 'In the past MBA students wrote their strategy reports on traditional industries, most of ours are on start-ups,' says another American studying at the school.

While intellectually European schools may be more influential than in the past there is no doubting a continuing sense of isolation. Fontainebleau, for all its wonders, is not Palo Alto.

Social life

As befits a small place with a large number of MBAs, there is always a lot – sometimes too much – going on. This, students report, is the best and the worst of INSEAD. The size of the program, the largest in Europe at about 600, means that the school lacks the intimacy of some other European schools. 'It means that you'll never know everyone as well as you'd like to,' says one student.

Cool places to hang out: The campus is small and somewhat isolated. Students say that the INSEAD bar is good, especially in summer. There are also a number of bars in town, but most social life takes place at people's houses.

Accommodation can be found in traditional French style, which is a bonus. As one student observes: 'How often do you get to live in a real chateau?'

PS

While it proclaims its global credentials, INSEAD's American connections are manifold. The driving force behind its creation in 1957 was Professor Georges F. Doriot of Harvard Business School. A statue of Doriot in the INSEAD library is accompanied by his observation: 'Without action, the world would still be an idea.' A Ford Foundation grant supported the development of the school and later sponsored doctoral training at Harvard for faculty members. Harvard donated books to help set up INSEAD's library. The former dean was Stanford-trained, and most INSEAD faculty are drawn from American PhD programs.

Today, however, INSEAD is nothing if not global. In January 2000, it became the first truly global business school by opening a full campus in Asia. INSEAD in Singapore will provide the activities and services currently offered in Fontainebleau: MBA and executive education, together with extensive research by permanent faculty. 'One school, two campuses', is the phrase INSEAD is using to promote the new development. According to Antonio Borges, it represents a 'new concept of a business school, responding to a changing world', and one that 'builds on both the international and intellectual influence of the Institute'.

The Singapore campus is located in Buona Vista, the country's educational belt. It will build on INSEAD's multicultural philosophy. Says Borges: 'The Singapore campus offers people options. If you choose an INSEAD MBA you can do it here or there, or a combination of the two. We expect most people to do both though it depends on their career plans. The programs have the same structure, the same curriculum, though the electives may differ. There is no separation of faculty. Faculty can choose where to teach. Singapore and Fontainebleau are two different parts of our campus.'

Richard Ivey School of Business – University of Western Ontario

Address	1151 Richmond Street North London, Ontario Canada, N6A 3K7 Tel: +1 (519) 661 3212 Fax: +1 (519) 661 3431 E-mail: mba@ivey.uwo.ca Website: www.ivey.uwo.ca
Teaching staff	Full-time 98 Others 2
Student intake (Class of 2001)	260
No of applicants	1,065
Average age	29
Estimated annual cost *(tuition fees) – 2000–2001*	C$46,070 (C$20,000)
Average GMAT (Class of 2001)	Mean – 656 Mid range 80% – n/a Average GPA 3.3
Median base salary (1999)	$83,558
Student profile (Class of 2001)	Women 25% Minorities n/a International 36%
Notes	Case method

Why Ivey?

Ivey is Canada's finest b-school – only Montreal's McGill comes close. In the 2000 *Financial Times* ranking it was also ranked nineteenth in the world. It has the advantage of being part of a large university and all the pros and cons of being situated in a college town. 'It was the best school I could attend without having to shell out US-type fees. My interview convinced me that the school had a strong faculty,' says one student.

Ivey's reputation is founded on a dedicated adherence to the case study method of teaching. As we have seen, the case method has its critics – increasingly so – but Ivey continues largely untroubled.

Getting in

'Ivey really focuses on leadership skills/leadership potential. A potential candidate should demonstrate the ability to work in teams quite clearly,' says an Ivey student.

Academic life

The Ivey MBA has no delusions. It is a general management program with minimum frills. Interestingly, Ivey says that most students choose not to specialize in their second year when given the opportunity to do so. Students complain of the early start – some classes start at 8 am. The case approach also raises a few related issues – says one student: 'Ivey has a great management focus. However, due to the 100 per cent case method of education, it has been a challenge for the school to provide a strong quantitative grounding in its program. This should be incorporated into the program.'

The emphasis is also on teamworking. Case-loving loners need not apply.

General agreement among students is that the first year of the MBA is highly demanding with a punishing work schedule. 'You just have to get through that first year. It is a lot of work, not hard, just lots of volume,' observes one. Sylvie Weeks, a 1997 MBA, recounts a typical day as starting at 8 am with a marketing class, followed by a class at 9:40, another at 11:20, case prep in the afternoon and an evening dinner. Not for the faint hearted.

Best teachers: Fernando Olivera gets the vote for his negotiations class.

Social life

Faced with a punishing schedule, students have to ensure they get a life outside school: 'On survival, you must be able to have fun, the best form of stress release. It does not help to be high strung and nervous – everyone goes through the same cycle.' You can do three things at Ivey: socialize, play sports, or study. You only have time to really do two of them,' says one student. The social life is good though alcoholic. The Ivey MBA Association is highly active, has its own website and offers downloadable guides to student life.

Social highlights: 'Too many to identify. At least in our batch, there were important events almost every week,' says an Ivey socialite. However, the Orientation and Disorientation (at end of the second year) are very popular events (week long social events).' Orientation week features the popular Monte Carlo Night.

Cool places to hang out: The main UWO restaurant/bar is The Wave. Also worth visiting because of its name if nothing else is the Outer Mongolian Martini Bar on Richmond Street.

Johnson Graduate School of Management – Cornell

Address	111 Sage Hall Cornell University Ithaca NY 14853-6201 US Tel: +1 (607) 255 4526 Fax: +1 (607) 255 0065 E-mail: mba@cornell.edu Website: www.johnson.cornell.edu
Teaching staff	51 full-time 11 others
Student intake (Class of 2001)	284
No of applicants	1800
Average age	29
Estimated annual cost *(tuition fees) – 2000–2001*	$24,400
Average GMAT (Class of 2001)	647
Median base salary (1999)	$75,000
Student profile (Class of 2001)	Women 27 % Minorities International 32%
Notes	See Johnson in the movie *Any Given Sunday* where Cameron Diaz gets a Cornell MBA.

Why Cornell?

High on a hill above Ithaca, New York, Cornell is the archetypal top American university, complete with 'College Town' and 'Real Town'. There is an air of invincibility and also of some superiority. The Johnson School has recently moved to a new base at historical Sage Hall, thanks to a $35 million renovation project. *Forbes* magazine rated Cornell among the Top 20 b-schools that 'deliver the most for your dollar'. The general tone of the school places an emphasis on education rather than on making fortunes. The b-school is keen to expand the intellectual breadth of its MBA to bring in other university experts and departments.

Its attractions include a strong brand; the lifestyle elements of living in upstate New York; and a relatively small intake.

Academic life

Most recent attention has been paid to the introduction of a 12-month MBA option. This is aimed at scientific and technical professionals and includes a 10-week summer term before the students are fed into the second-year class of the two-year MBA program. The class of 2000 on this one-year program numbers 57 of whom 36 are international students – though a paltry 14 per cent are female. 'Here's what's great. Cornell's brand name; it has great recognition in engineering. The small size of the program,' says one student. 'There is a lot of change going on, people setting goals and achieving them. It's like being in the business world.'

Also notable is the school's use of 'immersion courses' taken during the first year.

Best teachers: Robert Libby is recognized by the American Accounting Association as an outstanding educator. Also worth listening to is decision-making expert J. Edward Russo and David BenDaniel on entrepreneurship.

Social life

Ithaca is a nice place to live. Ithaca is 'gorges' according to local wits. Cornell overlooks Cayuga Lake, and water and forests abound. The arts are also well represented in the town through Cornell's Center for Theater Arts. Local wineries keep thirst at bay.

The usual range of clubs include the engagingly titled Frozen Assets Ice Hockey Team and the Old Ezra Finance Club.

Cool places to hang out: Not that cool perhaps, but try The Chanticleer or O'Leary's Irish Pub on W. Seneca. When it comes to coffee, recommended is Stella's Kitchen and Cocktails – 'Stella's when uttered evokes noble, universal things, placed quite outside of social choices.' Well, yes.

J. L. Kellogg Graduate School of Management – Northwestern University

Address	2001 Sheridan Road Evanston IL 60208-2001 US Tel: +1 847 491 3308 E-mail: kellogg-admissions@nwu.edu Website: www.kellogg.nwu.edu
Teaching staff	Full-time 156 Part-time 50
Student intake (Class of 2001)	Six quarter – 485 Four quarter – 80
No of applicants (Class of 2001)	6070
Average age	27
Estimated annual cost (tuition fees) – 1999–2000	Six quarter $47,538 ($27,273)
Average GMAT (1999)	Mean – 690 Mid 80% range – n/a Mean GPA – 3.5
Median base salary (1999)	$80,000
Student profile (Class of 2001)	Women 31% Minorities 24%
Notes	All applicants are required to attend an interview. Opportunity to complete MBA in one year on the four-quarter program.

Why Kellogg?

Kellogg offers a Master of Management (MM) degree rather than an MBA. The qualification is highly respected in the business world and is just as useful for career progression. The school has a reputation for very bright, high-spirited students. They are an outspoken bunch, as their comments confirm. An average age of around 27 means it is one of the younger MBA programs, and more mature students may find it a little on the rowdy side. There is a strong sense of community, and students are heavily involved in all aspects of the program. The school has more of an undergraduate feel than some others. As one student notes: 'There is some benefit to being in a school with spirit. I think there is a very

strong 'rah-rah Kellogg' atmosphere at the school … and that can annoy some people …
but I enjoy the positive attitude … it's contagious.'

Based in Evanston, a medium-sized town outside Chicago, the school is widely
regarded as *the* place for marketing. Philip Kotler, the marketing guru, is a member of
faculty. But it offers a good general grounding in all management disciplines. 'I wanted to
go to business school to get more of the 'big picture' on business. Kellogg was the right
school for me because it was strong in the areas I was the weakest such as marketing,'
says a student who came from an investment bank. 'Kellogg has a very flexible curriculum
which has given Kellogg students the opportunity to study emerging fields such as
technology. We are the first class of students at Kellogg who can select technology and e-
commerce as one of our majors.'

Getting in

With a mean GMAT of 690, Kellogg attracts very bright students. The school vets applicants assiduously, looking for leadership potential as well as a high IQ. Kellogg takes interviewing very seriously. A student observes: 'I would say that the interview is extremely
important at Kellogg. Candidates should really make sure they come prepared to tell a
coherent, logical story. They need to be able to explain the gaps on their resumes (we all
have them somewhere), explain why they want to go to business school – demonstrating
that they've thought about why Kellogg might be an option for them – and explain what
they want to do after business school and how business school will help them get there. I
think this is where a lot of otherwise good candidates fail … they say something like they
want to work for a dot-com … but they have no logical bridge connecting that to their
previous work experience as a product design engineer … the stories have to make sense!
… remember … the interviewer is sitting there thinking … will this person have a
reasonable chance of getting that job when they leave our school if they tell that same
story to the job interviewer.'

Some find the process somewhat tedious. 'It's a complete pain in the ass, especially as
an international student,' one student complains. 'I didn't realize that the process would
take so long, and I only had 24 hours to do my applications, also the GMAT required some
advance thought. On the upside, at least you can apply and pay on line.'

'Start early,' advises another. 'Be creative with your essays and make sure you have a
good "story" on why you are pursing an MBA. Make sure some of your essays talk about
accomplishments or projects you worked on in teams.'

Academic life

The Masters in Management is a flexible program. In year one students take core subjects
and three electives. Year two is entirely devoted to electives – with a minimum of 14
required over the two years. The post core curriculum is broad in scope, offering a solid
grounding in most aspects of general management. Students must major in at least one

functional area, but are encouraged to take several, and a high percentage major in at least two. The school also offers four professional fields of study – health services management, public and non-profit management, transportation, and real estate management. In-company project work is also emphasized.

'Once you get in … well, unless you really fooled the admissions committee … you should be able to handle it … just be diligent and balanced … I think most accepted candidates can survive just fine …,' says a student about the academic side. Classes are big, which some students say reduces the learning. 'While most classes have 60 people in them, some professors of oversubscribed classes open up their classes to 100+ people. This class size is too large to facilitate any meaningful discussion,' says one student.

Another adds: 'Kellogg is more time-consuming than difficult. Working in teams is a great learning experience. However, it is brutal to your schedule. Some days, I have group meetings for six or seven hours in a row. It seems that every class has a group component to it. I makes a lot of sense for cases. However, I believe some things such as problem sets would be more of a learning activity if done individually rather than in groups.'

The MM degree is awarded on the basis of assessment of courses taken. There is no thesis or final comprehensive examination.

Best teachers: Students give good grades to Professors Chopra and Novak (operations), and David Besanko (management & strategy).

Social life

Kellogg students are a lively lot who approach social activities with gusto. Most first-year students live on campus. It is convenient, they say, if overpriced. Off-campus accommodation is hard to find – 'impossible if you want to live in a nice place'. With so many students living on campus, some students are reminded of college days.

'The best thing about the social life at Kellogg: everyone is social. It seems that there weren't many people who slipped through the admissions committee with less than strong interpersonal skills and a desire to meet new people. The worst thing about the social life at Kellogg: too many people wanting social time. I never try to forget that I'm at business school for a purpose, but there are definitely temptations to think that I'm a freshman in college again. I found that I know too many people to hang out with all of them … so I've made an effort to make sure to have some close friends whom I see on a regular basis. I've told non-business-school friends that being at Kellogg is just like being at my own wedding … there are so many people I would love to spend more time with talking to … but I only have 15 minutes to spend with each of them.'

Another adds: 'Sometimes I think Kellogg is too social. There are a percentage of people here who are trying to relive their undergraduate years. Most people go on a KOA trip (outdoor adventures) before they start school. They form KOA cliques for the rest of their time at Kellogg. Those who don't go on a trip can feel very left out,' says one student.

Cool places to hang out: There are only about seven or eight bars in Evanston, which means a limited choice of places to hang out. 'Evanston is not really the Mecca for nightlife,' a student says. 'I live in the city (Chicago) because the restaurants and nightlife are much better. For some people, Kellogg is their life. However, I have many other friends and activities I participate in outside of Kellogg. That makes me very anti-social, I guess. Sometimes, I feel like an outsider. However, I wouldn't change my situation for the world.'

Another concurs: 'My advice would be make sure you force yourself to go downtown some weekends,' says one more student. 'My wife and I often invite other couples out to Lincoln Park or Michigan Ave on the weekend and they seem to really enjoy it. I recommend just getting off the L at Belmont and walking up and down Clark Street … there are tons of places to go out or eat … it's only a thirty minute ride from Kellogg … and you'll get to see lots of b-school aged people.'

PS

Students have been cramped for study space, but a recent refurbishment of the main buildings and another new addition should improve things.

The Kenan-Flagler Business School – University of North Carolina

Address	Campus Box 3490 McColl Building Chapel Hill, NC 27599-3490 US Tel: +1 (919) 963 3236 Fax: +1 (919) 962 0898 E-mail: mba-info@unc.edu Website: www.kenanflagler.unc.edu/
Teaching staff	Full-time 104 Others 15
Student intake (Class of 2001)	Full time MBA – 260
No of applicants	n/a
Average age	28
Estimated annual cost *(tuition fees) – 2000–2001*	$32,989 ($20,353)
Average GMAT (Class of 2001)	Mean – 671 Mid 80% range – n/a Mean GPA – 3.3
Online application	Yes
Media base salary (1999)	$75,000
Student profile (Class of 2001)	Women 34% Minorities 10% International 30%
Curriculum	Core curriculum revised for fall 2000.
Notes	Case studies major component of class work.

Why Kenan-Flagler?

Kenan-Flagler Business School is putting a lot of effort into boosting its international image. It is actively encouraging hiring organizations to interview all students, whether they are US or international. The aim is for every company that recruits at Kenan-Flagler to be willing to evaluate students based on qualifications and regardless of residency status. Many more companies now interview international students. The Office of Career Services has provided support for organizations that want to hire international students, by helping them to become familiar with the legal steps required. The school has also organized job fairs for international students with neighboring schools at Duke and Virginia universities.

Dean Robert Sullivan wants to build on the school's technology base and to increase its global thrust. KFBS has key strengths in general management, entrepreneurship and economic development, and, increasingly, environmental management.

The school is housed in the $44 million McColl building, opened in 1997, which has facilities for undergraduate and masters programs as well as students, faculty and staff. It has all the latest high tech equipment, including a trading room, putting KFBS among the top-ranking US schools in terms of facilities.

The McColl building is on the edge of the campus of the University of North Carolina. On-campus accommodation is available but most students live off campus in Chapel Hill. The university is also in the middle of the Raleigh–Durham–Chapel Hill Triangle area, a part of North Carolina that has attracted many leading US companies.

'The school is constantly changing to meet the needs of a changing business environment,' says a student. 'From this perspective, there are lots of little things that are constantly being addressed and tweaked. Honestly, KFBS is an outstanding institution that has found a good blend. I would hate to spend two years at business school always looking over my back. Here at KFBS we work hard together and learn a lot. We also realize that life is more than just work.'

Getting in

KFBS is a school on the move. It has bucked the trend toward falling MBA admissions with a 50 per cent rise in applications, so getting in is starting to get tough. It likes to interview applicants so interpersonal skills are key.

'The school looks for team players and go-getters so the best way to get in is to highlight your team skills and the fact that you go out of your way to get things done. They look for people who go that extra mile to ensure success,' says a student.

'I think our school really emphasizes well-rounded intelligent students,' adds another. 'It is not enough just to have diverse experiences, I think you have to have demonstrated a strong academic background or a good GMAT score. Apply in the first or second round to maximize chances of being accepted. This year our applications were up more than 50 per cent so it can't hurt to get it in early.'

Academic life

First-year students are assigned to study groups of five or six that stay together for the year. One to two international students from different countries are assigned to every first-year study team. There are a variety of teaching methods including simulation, experiential, and 'immersion learning,' as well as more traditional case studies and lectures. Core course work in the first year is divided into four seven-week modules, although the two-semester system is retained. Some courses run for more than one module. Soft skills workshops run throughout the first year.

The second year was revised in 1999. Strategic areas were chosen and curriculum, placement, and admissions were aligned around them to enhance students' career opportunities. Students follow a series of electives designed into 'career concentrations', which lead to particular career paths. These include corporate finance; customer and product management; e-commerce; entrepreneurship and venture development; global supply chain management; investment management; management consulting; and real estate.

Two 'enrichment concentrations' – sustainable enterprise and international business – cut across different career paths and are not as closely aligned with specific job targets immediately after graduation.

Redesign of a new first-year core curriculum began in summer 1999 with the new program introduced in fall 2000.

The framework for the core is the business process model and it uses four organizing themes: analyzing capabilities and resources; monitoring the marketplace and external environment; formulating and implementing strategy; and assessing firm performance. During the year, four modules of varying lengths are organized around these themes. Integrative exercises in each module pull together what students learn across courses. The exercises are evaluating a company, deciding whether to enter or exit a country or market, the business plan and a business simulation.

The new design creates more flexibility by providing an additional elective opportunity in the first year. Students may go into more depth in a specific area, such as finance or marketing, and build functional skills before their summer internships.

E-commerce is a required course and there is a mandatory leadership course at the start of the MBA program. 'The workload is entirely dependent on how serious you are about learning all the material and getting high pass grades (approx. the top 15 per cent of every class),' says one student.

Best teachers: Mark Lang (cost accounting); David Ravenscraft (strategic economics); Stuart 'Stu' Hart (sustainable business). Special plaudits to Joseph Bylinski's first-year core curriculum, cost accounting.

Social life

Chapel Hill is a charming, attractive, and typically American college town with loads of places to eat and drink. The school and university also provide lots of entertainment.

'Arguably Chapel Hill is one of the best atmospheres for learning and relaxing in the US,' says one student. 'Along Franklin Street you can find a full range of college-type eating places and bars. Also, being a major university, there are many arts available. Additionally, sports at UNC are exciting. For personal sporting, it is hard to find better golf courses concentrated within 45 minutes and the university offers a full range of intramural sports. I golfed every month of the year and played ultimate Frisbee throughout the year. The weather in Chapel Hill is great.'

But another adds, 'the worst thing is without a doubt the restaurants. The school does have every kind of college eating imaginable. But coming from DC before school, I am hard pressed to find good foods from other places.'

Cool places to hang out: Spanky's (a refurbished UNC institution); beer on the terrace at Top of the Hill; ACME grill (good food); Thai Palace; Carburitos. Best bars for MBAs include Woody's (sports bar); Henderson Street Bar and Grill (called H-Street); He's Not Here (outside deck); the Spotted Dog in Carrboro is one of the best restaurants for students on a budget.

Social highlights: 'Asia Night' party where the Asian students cook food, do skits, play music, wear traditional dress, etc.

PS

Top recruiters include Ernst & Young, IBM and Deloitte Consulting.

London Business School

Address	Regent's Park London NW1 4SA UK Tel: +44 (0)20 7262 5050 Fax: +44 (0)20 7724 7875 E-mail: ohutton@london.edu Website: www.lbs.ac.uk
Teaching staff	Full-time 144 Others n/a
Student intake (Class of 2001)	271
No of applicants	n/a
Average age	29
Estimated annual cost (tuition fees) – 2000–2001	Tuition year one – £15,450 [$24,720]
Average GMAT (Class of 2001)	Mean – 690 Mid 80% range – n/a Mean GPA – n/a
Median base salary (1999)	£53,000
Student profile (Class of 2001)	Women 22% International 79%
Notes	Two-year course. Bulk of teaching lecture based. Emphasis on group work – students work in same group throughout first year. All students must be competent in a second language in order to graduate.

Why LBS?

The word international means different things to different business schools. To the US schools, 30 per cent of foreign students is being international. In Europe, it's different. LBS, along with INSEAD and IMD, is one of the world's truly international schools. Non-students make up 80 per cent of the MBA intake. This is not a coincidence. It is LBS policy. The faculty, too, is truly international in origin. Many of the professors did their training at US schools but are drawn from a wide range of nationalities and cultural traditions. This, and a strong reputation for finance, is LBS's great strength.

As one student with a first degree from a top American university said: 'The composition of diverse personalities, backgrounds, and specialities creates an incredible learning environment. In particular, I felt that I would learn more at LBS than at schools dominated by similar background MBAs, such as Stanford and MIT. I was right.'

Another explained: 'I wanted to pursue a career in general management and strategy. I compiled a list of b-schools world-wide that were strong in these subjects. LBS was one of the top schools in the list. However, what finally drove me to LBS was its world-renowned strength in finance (which is a very important complement to strategy) and its unmatched internationalism (80 per cent of the MBA class of 2001 is non-UK with nearly 50 countries represented in the class). Working in a team where no two members come from the same country, professional or academic background, I reckoned would indeed be an invaluable learning experience. Since no other school in the US or anywhere offered me such a combination, LBS won hands-down.'

LBS is unusual, too, among European schools because it offers a two-year MBA program, which appeals to Americans. This, says dean John Quelch, is not about to change. 'Our mantra is "transforming futures". I just don't believe in an MBA course where you are recruiting four weeks after arriving. There just isn't the time for reflection that is part of the MBA experience. The market for the 21-month MBA will remain robust. I have no intention of presiding over a move to a one-year program. We are looking at the second year curriculum to make it more supportive of business-plan writing and putting some entrepreneurial courses over the summer into blocks so people can accelerate the second year learning if they want.'

Students say the school excels at finance, international sensitivity and global strategy, entrepreneurship, and management research, and that LBS has a very strong program for consulting, finance, and entrepreneurial MBAs.

Being slap bang in the middle of one of the great cities of the world also attracts students. LBS is actually closer to London's entertainment center, the West End, than to the financial center – the City. Architecture is impressive regency style. 'Location (London is fantastic!), atmosphere …,' gushes one student.

Getting in

'No more burdensome than other schools', is how one student described the LBS admissions process. Students spoke highly of the school's admissions staff, however. 'LBS was one of the few top programs that encouraged prospective students to ask the admissions staff questions and offered ample opportunities to speak with existing students. I thought this spoke greatly of the school's commitment to its MBA students,' said one student. 'Other programs did not offer this; in fact, they discouraged questions and requests for information beyond what could be had in the brochure. I thought that was a bit ridiculous – after all, I would not buy an $80,000 car from a salesman that did not let me ask questions.'

LBS requires all graduates to be fluent in two languages (one must be English) to graduate. If you don't have this requirement covered, then you better start studying a second language.

Academic life

The LBS curriculum is academic with a practical bent, and with an accent on the international dimension. The first year consists of a large number of core courses, a number of soft skills and language workshops, and a week-long shadowing project observing a practising manager at work. In the second year, students take 12 electives from the 75 or so on offer. They also have to complete a consultancy project with another student including a full report.

Dean John Quelch has overseen a re-evaluation and reorientation of the program. LBS now drives four themes through the MBA curriculum:

- becoming a leader
- becoming an international citizen
- becoming a strategic thinker
- becoming a great implementor.

These four themes, says Quelch, are desired by the leading recruiting companies. LBS is now looking at the core curriculum as well as all electives, and how teachers deliver against these themes.

Students report that the program keeps them pretty busy. 'The workload is quite heavy if one wants to get the best out of the MBA. Nearly all the classes have a case study discussion which means that you have to prepare for the case study and also the related readings. Other than that there are several group assignments that you have to take care of.'

'Workload depends on: your background, i.e. it will be harder for someone from a humanistic background to learn finance; how fast you adapt to the teaching style – people come from different countries that have different ways of teaching, which is a major issue at school; and how well you work in groups. Group work is a key component for LBS and, thus, the better you do it, the lower the workload and the more you will learn from others.'

London, along with Stockholm, is also the European center for dot-com activity. This is reflected in the MBA. The school has 10 new elective courses that didn't exist two years ago, mostly dealing with e-commerce and the new economy. For example, the managing.com course is now well established and very popular. It brings together four faculty members from different disciplines.

Best teachers: Kudos goes to: Costas Markides (strategy); Kent Grayson (marketing); John Bates and John Mullins (entrepreneurship); Terry Hill (operations); and Ian Cooper, Julian Franks, David Goldreich (finance).

Social life

Socially, there's lots to do in London generally. At the school, students recommend Sundowners on a Thursday evening after class.

And there are plenty of bars around. Be aware that the UK still suffers from draconian drinking hours – pubs close early. This can be annoying, but may be beneficial to studying. There is no MBA accommodation at LBS (space is tight), so students tend to be scattered around the city. Most say that London is a great place to live, but expensive. 'It's very tough, especially in London! After years of working and maintaining a certain lifestyle it is difficult to return to student life,' says one.

'It is simple enough to find accommodation in London but one must be prepared to pay a premium,' adds another.

Social highlights: The Latin American party, and the Summer Ball got high marks.

Cool places to hang out: 'Windsor Castle (bar), which has a back-door entry for LBS students is a cool place to hang out given its proximity to the school,' says an LBS pub afficionado. 'Other than that my favorite is Biz, which is the MBA pub on campus and the Buzz, which is the MBA restaurant on campus. Reason: They are not far and not very expensive, making it easy to quickly grab a drink after classes!' Then there is the rest of London.

PS

LBS has been rated the top b-school in Europe for two years running in the *Financial Times* global rankings (eighth in the world in the 2000 league table). A criticism made of LBS is that it has not leveraged its brand as strenuously as US schools. 'The only area of improvement that I felt was a stronger push to the School's brand. This, I believe, is also being taken care of now.' (John Quelch, the current dean, came from Harvard and is widely regarded as a global branding guru.)

Some students feel that the summer internship process should be brought forward. 'The recruitment process for summer internships begins in January, which places LBS students at a few months' disadvantage to US-based MBAs,' said one. 'But all the Top 10 consulting and investment bank firms make it to LBS.' LBS had 22 graduates going to Goldman Sachs in 2000. For LBS students, most of the opportunities are in Europe because employers target the school for these positions.

University of Michigan Business School

Address	701 Tappan Street Ann Arbor, MI 48109-1234 US Tel: +1 (734) 763 5796 Fax: +1 (734) 763 7804 E-mail: umbusmba@umich.edu Website: www.bus.umich.edu
Teaching staff	Full-time 130+ Others n/a
Student intake – (Class of 2001)	429
No of applicants	3,987
Average age	28
Estimated annual cost *(tuition fees) – 2000–2001*	Non resident $41,023 ($26,500)
Average GMAT (Class of 2001)	Mean – 675 Mid 80% range – 620–730 Mean GPA – 3.34
Median base salary (1999)	$77,714
Student profile (Class of 2001)	Women 26% Minorities 19% International 33%
Notes	Teaching methods – mix of lectures, case study and project work.

Why Michigan?

Michigan is a 'full range' school teaching management and business at undergraduate, masters, and doctoral levels and through short executive programs and company-specific programs. It is particularly strong in general management, international business, and leadership development. Its strong executive education arm gives the school particularly good links with industry, especially the automobile industry – not surprising given its location near Detroit. It does not, however, specialize in the motor industry.

Michigan operates from a six-building complex on the university campus and is one of the most lavishly equipped business schools in the US. It has large classrooms, study rooms, computer labs and a superb 211,000-volume library (one of the biggest business libraries in the country). That stems partly from the school's strong financial base, in 1997–98 revenues were over $90 million and endowments in the year totaled $15.8 million.

In 1999 the school received $10 million to create the Samuel Zell and Robert H. Lurie Institute for Entrepreneurial Studies, which among other things fosters a school-run venture capital fund and in-company experiential learning for students at locations from Michigan to Israel. This is typical of alumni backing for the school.

In 1992 a $30 million endowment from alumnus and business entrepreneur William Davidson funded the Davidson Institute. Researching and facilitating the transition of former state-run economies to free-market economies, the institute has had a major impact on the internationalization of the MBA program. During the summer MBA students work in small teams, which often include students from other schools of the university, with institute partner companies.

The school has also been in the forefront of innovations in management education. It was, for example, the first major US school to embrace distance learning technology back in the early 1990s and also the first to accept the academic integrity of company-specific MBA programs. This has continued. In January 2000 it agreed a joint venture with FT Knowledge (part of the Pearson Group – publisher of *MBA Planet*) to produce co-branded on-line executive education programs.

Michigan's student body is reasonably diverse. 'I was looking for a program with a strong general management focus, superb facilities and resources, and a diverse student body. I found all that at UMBS,' says one student. '[The people] in the program are the kind that you like to be around: competitive but no backstabbers, smart, team workers with a lot of energy,' adds another.

Getting in

Michigan has a typically high average GMAT and GPA so getting in isn't that easy. But students advise not to be put off. 'Apply even if you think you won't get in because it doesn't cost you anything and you never know. If it's what you want to do, you should do it. If you have good work experiences let the admissions people know, talk to counselors about what they are looking for, get your essays etc. read over by as many people as possible,' one says.

Another advises taking the GMAT seriously – whatever the admissions office says: 'I know many admissions people tend to downplay the GMAT. However, I would say that taking a prep course and spending a lot of time preparing for the GMAT is an important step that will improve your chances of getting in. The other things like work experience are tough to change as quickly as one can improve/prepare for the GMAT.'

Academic life

The MBA first-year core curriculum emphasizes integration and self-managed learning. In the second year students take elective courses (an elective course in either ethics or business law is required) and one mandatory course. Students are assessed on their writing ability on entry and may have to take a managerial writing course. They also take part in the seven-week multidisciplinary action program (MAP), an in-company case study that ends the first year. MAP teams of half-a-dozen students work together in a company (in the US or overseas) and multidisciplinary faculty teams act as consultants and mentors. Skills workshops, based on action-learning techniques, run throughout the year to develop managerial skills such as multicultural awareness and conflict resolution. They are based on students' performance during the five-day leadership-development program, a wide-ranging series of events that is Michigan's version of an orientation week.

Electives can be drawn from a variety of areas or grouped into concentrations. Some may be taken in other graduate schools of the university. There are three specialist concentrations with group-related electives: the entrepreneurial track; the environmental track (the corporate environmental management program, a three-year joint degree); and the manufacturing track (MBA with manufacturing concentration).

'The first year is the most intense one, the core course,' says one student. 'Expect at least six hours of work every day. The worst time is when recruiting and study coincides during the first year. In order to survive at those times, you should focus on what you want to do for your internship and manage your time very efficiently since there are tons of companies that come to campus for interviews. There are a lot of second/third rounds out of campus that keep you very busy, sometimes in other cities. My tip would be do your homework about your professional goals before hand and interact with recruiters from the first day of the program in order to be more relaxed when recruitment actually begins.'

Best teachers: Strategy guru C.K. Prahalad gets good marks for approachability. He and his wife invite his students to dinner at his home when his course is over.

Social life

Most students live in rented accommodation in Ann Arbor. Accommodation is plentiful but can be expensive. Ann Arbor is a college town stuffed with appropriate bars and restaurants so no difficulty in finding places to hang out or other amusements.

Cool places to hang out: Students recommend Pancheros for 'real people'.

PS

Michigan is not a specialized school with a strong marketing or finance ethos and so recruiters tend to come from a wide range of industries, including, of course, the management consultancies and investment banks.

MIT Sloan School of Management – Massachusetts Institute of Technology

Address	50 Memorial Drive Cambridge MA 02142 US Tel: +1 617 253 3730 E-mail: mbaadmissions@sloan.mit.edu Website: http://mitsloan.mit.edu
Teaching staff	Full-time 89
Student intake – (Class of 2001)	361
No of applicants (Class of 2000)	3500+
Average age	27.4
Estimated annual cost *(tuition fees) – 1999–2000*	Single $48,200 ($28,200)
Average GMAT (Class of 2001)	Mean – 700 Mid 80% range – n/a Mean GPA – 3.5
Median base salary (1999)	$84,000
Student profile (Class of 2001)	Women 27% Minorities 15% International 38%
Notes	Electronic application only.

Why MIT Sloan?

Located on the Cambridge side of the Charles River, north of Boston, and within walking distance of neighboring Harvard, the Sloan School of Management is part of MIT, probably the top technology university in the world. The functional rather than beautiful look and feel of the school is in sharp contrast to the majesty of the Harvard campus. But MIT Sloan prides itself on being functional. 'The only disappointing aspects are the facilities of Sloan. The buildings are just not very beautiful. Clearly, that is not a major problem,' one student observes.

Although MIT's reputation for technology and engineering is reflected in the Sloan School's program, and a high concentration of engineers on the MBA program, it also attracts non-engineers. It is also among the most progressive MBA programs in the US, with major innovations to the curriculum in recent years. The school boasts a $3.5 million trading floor, modeled on those found in financial centers around the world. It is also home to some of the leading thinkers in management, including Peter Senge, who popularized the learning organization idea; Edgar Schein, who has done ground-breaking work on organizational culture; and Lester Thurow. The Black-Scholes mathematical model for pricing options, much beloved by MBA students everywhere, originated at the school.

'One aspect that sets Sloan apart from other b-schools is the fact that it is part of MIT. Sloan also has an excellent general reputation and seemed to be serious about the internet and e-Business,' one student says, explaining his reasons for choosing the school. Adds another: 'The location in Cambridge is fantastic – you are really part of a larger academic community in a cool location. I have cross-registered at Harvard Business School, and I have friends from the Fletcher School of Law and Diplomacy, the Kennedy School of Government and Harvard Law School who have cross-registered at Sloan. Moreover, I have been able to take advantage of opportunities throughout MIT to expand my education beyond business. Plus, given the "new economy", it was important to me to be at a school that took technology seriously.'

The school is a Mecca for those with internet-based ambitions, and is a magnet for VCs and new-economy companies. The school also hosts one of the most prestigious – and serious – business plan competitions with a $50,000 prize. Says one student: 'The MIT 50K business plan competition is a major event on the MIT campus, and an opportunity for many business students to work with students from the engineering departments on business ideas.'

Students say the school's strengths are entrepreneurship, finance, and, not surprisingly, IT. However, some students believe the school could be more integrated with the rest of the institute. 'Actually I was most disappointed with how little Sloan interacts with MIT. There is little to no interaction with the other graduate students,' said one.

Getting in

With a mean GMAT score of around 700, MIT Sloan is one of the toughest schools to get into. Applications from non-engineers who are good at math and economics, are likely to be well received, as the school wants more diversity.

'GMAT scores matter,' advises a student. 'The school is dominated by former engineers, but they are definitely on the look-out for strong liberal arts candidates who can prove that they have strong quant skills.'

Academic life

The school prides itself on turning theory into practical applications. It has also taken strides to marry academic study with longer-term career aspirations. Central to the Sloan philosophy is the belief that MBA graduates should be adding value from the moment they step off campus into the work environment.

The core curriculum is made up of six interconnected subjects completed in the fall semester of year one. Once that's under their belts, students can pursue their own self-managed track. This involves a bunch of functional management courses and electives. Or, they can take a management track, designed to support their future career aspirations and meant to provide a more in-depth immersion than the traditional majors at other schools. Based on the school's proven leaders for manufacturing program, they are a blend of required courses, electives, workshops, field work, and presentations from industry experts. Summer internships, too, are geared to career goals.

The workload is heavy. Although 'not nearly as bad as undergraduate days', one student told us. 'The best thing to do is not read everything – you have to learn to manage your time.'

Teachers: Michael Scott Morton (intro to strategy) gets plaudits.

Social life

Students can take advantage of campus accommodation, although many prefer to live off-site. MIT Sloan is a comfortable stroll from downtown Boston, which offers most distractions and plenty of historical interest. Plenty of scope, too, for messing about in boats. Cold in the winter.

On campus, consumption functions are popular. 'Best thing – C-functions. Worst, not enough opportunities for interaction between first- and second-year students,' says one student.

Social highlights: 'Compared to MIT, not many besides the C-functions and Galas.'

Cool places to hang out: 'Au Bon Pain because everyone comes by there and I love the cookies, and the orange juice.'

PS

MIT Sloan is in the thick of the internet revolution, and many students are looking to get into new-economy companies – or start their own. 'For a lot of students starting or joining a dot-com is now a serious option,' a student told us. 'We had over 100 students visit Silicon Valley in January, and the most popular management track at Sloan right now is the "new product and venture development" track.' Naturally, the consulting firms and old-economy outfits are also keen to hire Sloan MBAs as they move to clicks-and-bricks models. 'There's a very structured process for the established firms, that also includes many social events, like dinners with partners etc. Then the Career Development Office sends out information on job postings on an *ad hoc* basis about job postings at companies. This can be from any type of company (start-up, VC, high tech, etc.).' The school also attracts first-rate guest speakers on campus, many of them alumni who are successful entrepreneurs. They include the principals of Akamai, a company that was founded about two years ago by a MIT computer science professor and a Sloan MBA who dropped out. The company is now worth more than $20 billion.

Owen GSM – Vanderbilt University

Address	401 21st Avenue S Nashville, TN 37203 US Tel: +1 615 322 6469 Fax: +1 615 343 1175 E-mail: admissions@owen.vanderbilt.edu Website: www.mba.vanderbilt.edu
Teaching staff	Full-time 47 Others 17
Student intake (Class of 2001)	210
No of applicants	n/a
Average age	28
Estimated annual cost (tuition fees) – 2000–2001	Single student $39,950 ($25,100)
Average GMAT (Class of 2000)	Mean – 631 Mid 80% range n/a
Median base salary (1998)	$73,000
Student profile (Class of 2000)	Women 26% Minorities 5% International 31%
Notes	Tuition based on case method.

Why Owen?

A relative newcomer to the b-school parade, the Owen School at Vanderbilt University was founded in 1969 by local Tennessee businesses as a regional center of excellence. It has succeeded beyond all expectations. It is not as well known as other US schools, but offers an interesting alternative. From humble beginnings – just ten students and ten faculty – the school's stature has grown in recent years. Its position as twenty-seventh in the world in the 2000 *Financial Times* global rankings confirms its growing reputation overseas. It is a good school, with an enthusiastic student body. In particular, the ratio of faculty to students is high, which provides good access to professors.

Based in Nashville, Tennessee, the home of country music, today the school offers a little over 200 MBA places. Students say it is a friendly, collaborative place, and the wearing of Stetsons and cowboy boots is not mandatory. The main school is located in

Management Hall, a pleasant amalgam of modern interior with a Victorian exterior (the Mechanical Engineering Hall which dates back to the 1880s).

Students say the sense of community is especially strong, as befits a small program. 'I was looking for a small program that would enable me to interact a great deal with the faculty and cultivate lasting friendships. Owen provided both. The program I chose had to be competitively ranked but still have a co-operative and supportive student body,' says one.

Students are also enthusiastic about its approach to all things new economy. 'The school's focus on e-business really sets it apart from other b-schools. There is a philosophical split among b-schools about how to handle the need to teach e-business skills to MBAs. Owen was the first to set up a separate "emphasis" and "concentration" to address these issues, bringing in dedicated faculty. Other schools have tried to put a PR spin on their existing curriculum, arguing that they weave e-business into all their concentrations. How can this be done with the same professors who have been teaching for 30 years? Is that really who you want to teach you e-business?'

It's a good question.

Getting in

With an average GMAT around 630, Owen is not necessarily attracting the academically brilliant – but the correlation between GMAT scores and business performance is tenuous anyway. The school's admission procedures are demanding, however. With only 210 or so MBA places the school can afford to be selective. The typical Harvard or Wharton profile probably wouldn't fit the Owen template. Again, the emphasis is on the personal touch.

'Owen's recruiting program was very thorough. Many students called me once I was accepted to congratulate me and assist me in the decision-making process by answering questions. In addition, I was able to communicate directly with the director of admissions (who always took my calls or returned them promptly) throughout my decision process. Other groups, such as financial aid and career planning and placement, were equally responsive.'

The school is looking for balanced, but ambitious, people. 'I feel applicants that can weave their prior education, past work experience and future career path into a logical reason for why they choose Owen will have a better chance at admittance. Apply early. I believe that it helped in my case,' says one student.

Academic life

The MBA is based on a solid core curriculum, with a combination of elective concentrations (about six courses) and free electives – some of which can be taken in other parts of the university. Concentrations may start in the second semester of the first year.

Students agree that the core curriculum is demanding. 'The core workload (during the first semester) is heavier, as is probably the case at most b-schools. Handling it is not particularly difficult, so long as you understand that late nights are a part of business school. The most important lessons to learn regarding workload are time management and group management. Get to the point, divide the work and come together to polish off the finished product,' says one.

Another adds: 'At the start, it was common for me to spend 80 hours a week doing school work. Granted you learn techniques and short-cuts as the year progresses but in the beginning it was a bit overwhelming.'

The school takes number crunching very seriously. Students need to be proficient at calculus, statistics, and basic computing – and the school offers pre-school 'camps' to help them get up to speed. Group assignments require students to evaluate each other's performance as well as the team as a whole.

As one student observes: 'Students should not expect that since Owen is ranked lower than other programs, the school work will be easier. I feel that sometimes it is the opposite; as students are always having to prove that Owen graduates are equal and at times superior to those at the top 10 schools.'

The degree is awarded on the basis of grades in all courses.

Best teachers: Kudos goes to Emeritus Professor Tom Mahoney (HR strategy), Visiting Professor Brooks Holtom (human resources), Gary Scudder (strategy), and Alex Brown (operations).

Cat calls for Dick Daft (change management) 'because we didn't really get to get our hands into any change initiatives,' and unnamed statistics and marketing professors.

Social life

Nashville is unique. Depending on your point of view, it could be either one of the coolest places in the world to spend some time, or the nightmare from a B-movie Western. Those with a healthy curiosity and a sense of humor will probably enjoy it.

Owen, students say, is a social place. Kegs in the lobby, student association-sponsored parties and activities, and the like. There are plenty of temptations. But some students say they would like more opportunities to mix with undergraduates.

'The best thing about the social life is that you are all in the same boat and understand what is going on with each other. Also, you meet some really great friends because since you all came to business school, your interests are usually pretty well aligned,' says a student. 'Also, you get one last chance to act like a college student again. The worst thing is making such good friends and then being spread across the country after graduation.'

Another adds: 'With Owen being a small school, people generally know what other people are doing socially. Perhaps this is the price to pay for a close-knit, small community. In my opinion, the amount of gossiping that occurs is offset by the support that a friendly, small class provides. Many people probably wonder about life in Nashville. For two years, it's a blast! For a West-Coaster like me, heading down to the honky-tonk bars after a tough week of studying is a great time. Don't worry, there are plenty of non-country activities around Nashville as well.'

Social highlights: The Owen Follies – a tongue-in-cheek talent show held towards the end of school. It's a chance for students to blow off a year or two's worth of steam and put on some great skits. Some skits address school issues and poke fun at professors and other students. Beer is plentiful and some of the faculty/staff come as well. Faculty members have been known to participate, performing on the guitar and imitating Seinfeld. The Follies also mark the beginning of the weekend of the formal dance, the Capitalist Ball (known affectionately as the Owen Prom).

Bar crawls, global cocktail parties, Halloween party, marketing madness, are also popular ways to unwind. Kegs in the lobby on Monday also draw a good following.

Cool places to hang out: Close to the school, students recommend Jonathan's, a sports bar that has Two-for-Tuesdays. Downtown is also popular with hangouts like Buffalo Billiards, where most people just hang out at the bar, and Banana Joe's, a dance club. Also worth a mention, they say, is Silverado's, 'a country dance club that has a cover charge but offers free bottled beer until 11 pm.' Green Hills Grille is a popular restaurant. Sole Mio is good for Italian, and Davinci's has excellent pizza.

Or, advises one student who likes to get about, you could head out to Green Hills and check out the Green Hills Grill and then have a drink at the Green House – an actual greenhouse converted to a bar with lots of greenery and a fireplace outside. Closer to school, Broadway Brewhouse is a good time. For more expensive food, head west on West End to Zola, or try Boundry – very close to campus and also has a nice bar. A good casual restaurant is 12th and Porter (which also has a bar and live music) or Tin Angel. Satco is a tex-mex place to sit outside and have a couple of beers and Bongo Java and Fido are favorite coffee bars.'

PS

Most students seem very happy with Owen. But there are the usual grumbles: 'My expectations were that a business school would be run like a business,' says one innocent. 'I have realized that academic politics still outweigh the reasonability of business sense at times. The business challenges the school faces seem crazy with the wealth of experts at the school (from what I have heard, this is typical of most business schools).'

The size of the MBA program and its relatively short existence also means that the number of Owen alumni is small compared to the big schools. The flipside of this, say some, is that alumni tend to lean over backwards to help if they can. 'I think the alumni network is extremely important, especially for a small school like Owen,' says a former student. 'Being small, everyone appreciates having someone else out there familiar with Owen.'

Experiences are mixed, however. One student says: 'I've found that many of the recent graduates are very enthusiastic about the school and assisting fellow Owen students in finding jobs, giving tips on interview tactics or general advice. I used the alumni network to make contact with a (non-Owen recruiting) company and was able to schedule an interview, and called another recent graduate for advice on how to prepare for a difficult interview process. He not only gave me some great advice on how to prepare for the interview and gave me insight on his internship, but also offered the opportunity to be considered for opportunities within his company. In addition, I called a local alumnus from my city for housing advice for moving to Nashville.'

But, another adds: 'The alumni network is very important. I utilized our alumni database which was very resourceful; however, I didn't get the response or help I had anticipated and was a little disappointed.'

SDA Bocconi

Address	Master's Division Via Balilla 20136 Milan Italy Tel: +39 2 5836 3281/98 E-mail: reception@sda.uni-bocconi.it Website: www.sda.uni-bocconi.it
Teaching staff	Full-time 83 Others 59
Student intake (1999)	140
No of applicants	750
Average age	29
Estimated annual cost *(tuition fees) – 1999–2000*	Tuition $20,250
Average GMAT (1999)	Mean – 630 Mid 80% range – n/a Average GPA n/a
Median base salary (1999)	n/a
Student profile (1999)	Women – 19% Non-Italian – 43%

Why Bocconi?

Look, you're in Italy. And that means being sophisticated and cool even if you are an MBA student. OK, so Bocconi isn't the best-known MBA school in the world but it brings Latin flair to the subject, combining a romantically fanciful program structure with a hard-headed business approach. The SDA in the title (Scuola di Direzione Aziendale) means this is the graduate teaching arm of Bocconi University, Italy's top-notch business university, founded in 1902. It may not have guru-level teachers *à la* Anglo-Saxon model but you can be sure of getting a first-rate business education and the chance to become fluent in one of the world's top languages.

Bocconi is well plugged into the global business school scene and offers an extensive exchange program. Key strengths are in information systems, entrepreneurship, and marketing.

The school used to be based in some typically Italian dowdy rooms in the main university building, but some years ago moved a few blocks to its own more stylish building (once a convent school and chapel). New buildings are promised that will offer larger and technologically advanced facilities.

Bocconi University has one of the largest economics and business libraries in the world with over 500,000 volumes, and MBA students have access to the university mainframe and all university facilities. Milan dominates Italy's main industrial and commercial region and is a financial, cultural and fashion center for the whole of Europe. The city is a great winter and summer base within easy reach of the Alps for skiing and the Italian Riviera for beach weekends. It's also near Verona, Florence, Venice, and the wine regions of Tuscany and Piedmont. There are excellent transport links throughout Italy and with the rest of Europe. The school is in the center of the city and there is no on-campus accommodation. Bocconi helps with accommodation. Living is fairly cheap; expect to spend up to € 600 a month on a one-bed apartment.

Getting in

Bocconi has a small intake but the GMAT is relatively low. You need to have an interest in Italy to really make the most of this unusual but attractive school.

Academic life

Unsurprisingly perhaps, the SDA Bocconi MBA has one of the more baroque structures, though its 16-month program is among the toughest and most innovative in the world. Minimal holidays means that the ground covered is immense.

The MBA is divided into five sections, roughly meant to equate to a physical or spiritual journey. The initial 'Prelude' is a period of pre-program home study of materials supplied by Bocconi. Once on campus this is followed by 'Pillars', an introduction to basic management concepts. Students have to pass an exam before they can proceed. The next stages, 'Functional Management' and 'General Management', form the basis of the program. The following 'Exploration Itineraries' are a mixture of electives, in-company projects and workshops in which students can choose two from a range of specializations on offer. At present these are: international accounting and tax planning; privatization of public services; systems thinking and management; the internationalization itinerary; management of small and medium enterprises; management consulting; the fashion system (this *is* Milan); design-oriented sectors and design management (ditto); merchant and investment banking; value management; client-knowledge-based marketing; and product innovation and development.

As an alternative, students may opt for one of two specialized focus options – information systems or entrepreneurship – under the 'Focuses' banner. (These also involve electives, workshops and projects.) These need to be specified on application. An exchange with another business school is an option in the last four months of the program.

A guest-speaker series involving distinguished people inside and outside the business sector is held under the title Horizons – Management Testimonies. As well as senior executives, participants have included comedians, astrophysicists, journalists and singers.

The first part of the program has both English and Italian tracks and students are expected to study the other language. The second part can be in either language depending on subject matter and lecturer.

As well as the bilingual MBA and various Italian-language masters programs, Bocconi also offers a Master in International Economics and Management degree, an MBA-like, full-time, 12-month interdisciplinary program in English.

Best teachers: Alas, none highlighted, though finance teaching gets a pretty good rating.

Social life

You're in Milan, so it has to be good. There's lots on offer and a lot of it close to the university in the Navigli/Tichinese or Brera districts. (Navigli is the canal district near the university and has a wide variety of restaurants, bars, and cafes.)

Cool places to hang out: Premita (one of the best pizzerias in town and great for parties); Sant Eustorgio (popular local restaurant); BeBop (fantastic all-rounder, say students); Joe Penas (Mexican and music, especially at weekends). Still around Navilgi/Tichinese, Capo Horn, Lighthouse and Shu are all favorite bars for MBAs. Further afield in Brera: Dell Anoglo, Tropico Latino and Radinsky (restaurants) and Bar Victoria, Bar Brera and YAR (bars). Students recommend Sempione for a good old student night out with a crowd; Hollywood or Shocking to get a feel for Milan's model and fashion set; as well as Propaganda for a selection of styles depending on which day it is.

PS

Top recruiters include McKinsey, Boston Consulting Group and General Electric.

Stanford Graduate School of Business – Stanford University

Address	Master's Division Stanford CA 94305-5015 US Tel: +1 650 723 2146 E-mail: mba@gsb.stanford.edu Website: www.gsb.stanford.edu
Teaching staff	Full-time 120
Student intake	365
No of applicants (Class of 2001)	6606
Average age	26
Estimated annual cost (tuition fees) – 9 months 2000 – 2001	Single, on campus $44,000 ($28,896) Single, off campus $49,000 ($27,243)
Average GMAT (Class of 2001)	Mean – 725
Median base salary (1999)	$80,000
Student profile (Class of 2001)	Women 39% Minorities 27% International 32%

Why Stanford?

Where do you start? Let's see: There's the fact that it's on America's West Coast, within easy reach of San Francisco and the Bay Area, and Palo Alto. There's the fact that it has a great academic reputation and is internationally renowned for its research. Then there's its links with the Pacific Rim, which attracts Asian, especially Japanese, students. The school also has good links with Silicon Valley, which means excellent job placement opportunities and a procession of new-economy luminaries and CEOs giving presentations. For those who like to follow in famous footsteps, Phil Knight, CEO of Nike, Scott McNeally, CEO of Sun Microsystems, and Charles Schwab, all did degrees at Stanford.

One student explained that his choice was based on: 'Reputation, location, and most importantly students. Not only are the students very bright but they are extremely friendly, helpful, and know how to have fun. There is zero competition among students.' Another told us: 'Its "relaxed" reputation compared to Harvard, and its proximity to Silicon Valley all factored into my decision.'

Executives from the fabled Valley also teach on some elective courses. Venture capitalists have also been known to stray onto the campus – just in case you wondered. 'Access to VCs is available,' a student confirms. 'Every major VC firm in the Valley has a Stanford GSB alumnus as a partner. Some of the access, though, reminds me of Hollywood – everyone has their script (a b-plan) and access to valuable contacts (VCs, angels), but getting the pitch into full gear is another matter. '

Students say the school excels in entrepreneurship, finance, and accounting. And, there's also the aesthetics and architectural interest to think about – the school is built in a low-rise Spanish style, making it one of the most interesting in America.

But despite its manifold attractions, Stanford isn't for everybody – the stringent admissions procedure sees to that. There is also a certain irony in the fact that the school associated with being close to the vortex of Silicon Valley is also one of the most academic, and analytically retentive, in North America. The Stanford MBA emphasizes analytical rather than functional skills. It offers education rather than practical training. Peter Robinson, a former speech writer for President Reagan, wrote a chronicle of his MBA experience at Stanford. It was called *Snapshots From Hell*, and in it he described, among other dull adventures, how he and other 'poets', a Stanford term for mathematically challenged students, struggled with the quantitative part of the course. But before you rush out and buy the book, one student pointed out that '*Snapshots* is nothing like life at Stanford unless you a) have no business background whatsoever, b) are a ridiculous over-achiever.'

Getting in

Stanford is probably the toughest business school of all to get into. The acceptance rate is around 7 per cent. In 1999/ 2000, Stanford received some 6,606 applications for 365 MBA places. The average GMAT score of successful applicants was 725 out of a maximum 800 score. Pretty harsh.

'Writing the essays were a pain and required the positioning of yourself as a balanced, complete person, which, in fact, you're decidedly not if you've applied to HBS or Stanford,' one student said. 'On the whole, though, I'd describe the process as healthy in that it forces you into brief moments of introspection.'

Academic life

The academic side, students say, is not as bad as Peter Robinson made it out to be. '*Snapshots from Hell* is something of a joke,' said one. 'I was an English major in college, and had never taken economics or calculus prior to coming here and have not had major problems. Last semester, I studied three to four hours a day, and now I study much less. I do believe some people have problems with the quant nature of the program, but they are in the minority (under 10 per cent). I believe that the author was exaggerating for comedic effect.' Robinson, it seems, was using a little poetic licence – or was really bad at math.

'At Stanford it's very hard to get really good grades but very easy to pass,' another student observed.

The Stanford approach, as noted above, is to instruct students in the use of analytical tools rather than the basic skills of marketing and finance. Students start in the fall and study over six academic quarters. There are 14 core courses in the first three quarters and a minimum of 13 electives in the final three. The b-school offers around 100 elective courses and four can be taken in other schools within Stanford University. It is very much a general management program with no requirement to specialize. But there is the option to take the public management program, which is aimed at the public and not-for-profit sectors. Also on offer is the global management program, which was established in response to student demand.

Best teachers: Teaching in general got very good reviews, although students complained about 'a few mediocre profs in the core'. Sadly, they didn't name names.

Social life

Cool places to hang out: San Francisco and the Bay Area cater for most tastes. You will find what you want.

Social highlights: Tuesday night all-you-can drink at a local bar (f.o.a.m) and Friday evening kegs at the b-school after class (l.p.f.).

By all accounts Stanford also has a fair rugby team.

PS

Leading recruiters of Stanford graduates are McKinsey and Company, BCG and Goldman Sachs. But many other MBAs skip off to seek their fortune in the Valley. 'A large proportion of [my] classmates are either joining internet companies or starting their own,' says one MBA.

Stern School of Business – New York University

Address	Henry Kaufmann Management Center 44 West Fourth Street New York, NY 10012 US Tel: +1 (212) 998 0100 E-mail: sternmba@stern.nyu.edu Website: www.stern.nyu.edu
Teaching staff	Full-time 208 Others 104
Student intake (Class of 2001)	420
No of applicants	n/a
Average age	27
Estimated annual cost (tuition fees) – 1999–2000	$48,664 ($28,593)
Average GMAT (Class of 2001)	Mean – 686 Mid 80% range – 640–740 GPA –3.40
Median base salary (1999)	$77,722
Student profile (Class of 2001)	Women 39% Minorities 21% International 32%
Notes	From fall 1999 Stern's core curriculum was revised to incorporate an international perspective. Collaborative team-based approach to learning. 30% of students on merit-based scholarships.

Why Stern?

Like fellow NYC school, Columbia, Stern makes the most of its location. And since it's a stone's throw from Wall Street you won't be surprised to hear that it makes the most of the close bonds between it and New York's financial community. Stern excels at finance and its finance department is often leading the way in developing and spreading knowledge of the latest techniques and concepts. You'll probably want to go to Stern because you want a finance job (American Express, Chase Manhattan, Goldman Sachs, and Deloitte Consulting are top recruiters) but it has strengths in other areas, most notably international business, information systems, and entrepreneurship.

Stern has an even higher percentage of women students than Columbia and there is a good mix of nationalities in both the faculty and the student body. Its exchange program is comprehensive and its guest-speaker series attracts some of the world's leading executives. Alumni support perhaps could be improved. One student, admittedly wryly, laments the chance not to have had a drink with Federal Reserve chairman Alan Greenspan, a Stern alumnus. And as with many big city, non-campus schools, some students miss the socializing. 'Socially, I really wish it were a closer-knit school. Although I'm meeting great people and making great contacts, I don't know if I've had the opportunity to develop deep friendships,' says one. Even so, Stern students have a reputation for being involved with the school, organizing many major events such as conferences.

The Stern School is based in two buildings, the Henry Kaufman Management Center and Tisch Hall, in Washington Square in the Village. It shares Tisch Hall with the undergraduate business program. There are plans to expand into Shimkin Hall, next to Kaufman. Facilities are modern and well designed. Stern is building graduate housing for 120 students with the opening scheduled for fall 2001. It also owns a number of apartment buildings in the surrounding area for students to rent.

Getting in

With just over 400 full-time places and 11 applicants for each of those, getting into Stern is as tough as any other top school. The usual rules apply.

Academic life

Stern redesigned its MBA program in 1999 to boost the integration of courses and generate more cross-functional links. A key part of the program is an intensive two-week required pre-program session covering ethics, computing, mathematics, and data analysis as well as teambuilding and social events. During this session the annual intake is divided into blocks (or classes) of around 65 students, who spend the first year together. Students further organize themselves into study groups of about five people.

In the second semester there is an integrated strategy exercise, an in-depth case study that combines strategy analysis with communications workshops and written assignments. Stern's MBA is quantitative and rigorous and a good prior knowledge of most of the quantitative disciplines is assumed. It is recommended that students have their own laptop.

Students moan about Stern's '35 per cent' rule, which means that any assignment/test/project will yield only 35 per cent A-grades. The rest are B+, B, B-, and sometimes even C.

'In the mentality of a b-school student,' says one, 'a B or B- is pretty much a failing grade. Some of the faculty and students are fighting to change the 35 per cent rule so that any student who deserves an A gets it. However, much of the administration believe that this will hurt Stern's placement in the b-school rankings.'

Best teachers: Aswath Damodaran (associate professor of finance) gets high marks.

Social life

As one Stern student says, the best thing about being at the school is the opportunity to do cool things in NYC; but the worst thing is that no one does them because they are so busy working. Stern is in the Greenwich Village area of Manhattan, one of its most diverse and lively areas, but because Stern and parent NYU do not have a campus most students commute in from Brooklyn, New Jersey, and elsewhere and so the physical distance between school and home makes it hard for students to socialize.

That said, there seems to be plenty going on, not least the regular Thursday night 'Beer Blasts'.

Social highlights: Halloween party; Charity Ball (spring); Stern Follies (summer).

Cool places to hang out: There's the whole of Manahattan to choose from but in the NYU area the best bars are Swift's, the Scratcher, and the Stoned Crow. Best restaurants are said to be Harry's Burritos, Corner Bistro, John's Pizzeria (cheap, serves pitchers of beer – rare for NYC), Tortilla Flats (1 am happy hour)

PS

Stern is a traditional MBA 'finance' school but has moved quickly to add new areas of expertise to attract students interested in dot-coms and related start-ups. To a large extent, however, it still relies on servicing the needs of its near-neighbors, the giant recruiters of Wall Street such as Goldman Sachs.

Stern students, however, are suggesting that the internet revolution is having a major impact that perhaps reduces the school's ability to do so. Many are sacrificing traditional jobs offering security and high pay to pursue start-ups and even the 'traditional' students want to take at least one or two courses in e-commerce so that they can see how it will effect their jobs. Students also aren't as worried about landing jobs quickly. Many delay accepting a job because the opportunities at small start-ups are 'real-time'. There is no longer the expectation that you have to get a job by December. Expectations for salary are also going down slightly, but the expectations for early retirement and huge stock option packages are on the rise.

'Everyone,' says one student, 'thinks they'll be the next millionaire.'

Tuck School of Business – Dartmouth

Address	100 Tuck Hall
	Dartmouth College
	Hanover, NH 03755
	US
	Tel: 603 646 2369
	Fax: 603 646 1308
	E-mail: tuck.admissions@dartmouth.edu
	Website: www.dartmouth.edu/tuck
Contact name	n/a
Teaching staff	Full-time 40
	Others 14
Student intake (Class of 2001)	189
No of applicants (Class of 2001)	2,689
Average age	27
Estimated annual cost	$43,500 (27,150) excluding cost of laptop
(tuition fees) – 1999–2000	
Average GMAT (Class of 2001)	690 Range – 540-780
Median base salary (1999)	$80,000
Student profile (Class of 2001)	Women 31%
	Minorities 16%
	International 28%
Notes	Tuck has one of the highest participation rates for annual alumni giving at 63%.
	A new core curriculum introduced for the fall 2000.

Why Tuck?

Tuck (formerly Amos Tuck but now keen to drop the Amos) is one of the oldest b-schools in the world. Established in 1900, it launched the world's first graduate business program – the forerunner of the modern MBA. Students say Tuck's strengths are operations, strategy, and internet technology. Tuck appeals to those with a yen for small college towns. Located on the western side of the Dartmouth College campus in Hanover, New

Hampshire, it is a beautiful if somewhat rural setting. Hanover is a two-hour drive from Boston, and offers a small-town college idyll – if you like that sort of thing. With fraternity houses lining the campus, it looks like the set of a Hollywood college film *circa* 1975. (The John Belushi film *Animal House* is said to have been based on the goings-on at Dartmouth, and the whole frat issue is a bit of a touchy subject).

One student listed the reasons for choosing Tuck as: 'Good reputation, in the northeast, and general management school. A lot of the schools 'ranked' higher than Tuck are too focused in their reputations for me. MIT = geeks, Kellogg = marketing, Columbia = bankers.'

Dean Paul Danos is an internet evangelist, and the school has invested heavily in technology, providing a modern counterpoint to the folksy old-world charm.

Of interest, too, the school recently established the John H. Foster Center for Private Equity. Phil Ferneau, a very bright assistant professor, is heading up research into early stage investment, and has opened a branch office in Silicon Valley.

The business school combines a close-knit community (about 190 MBA students) with traditional Ivy League ambiance and values. It is, one student informed us, 'a magnet for rich white Connecticut kids and wannabees'. 'Tuckies', as they refer to themselves, are a tight-knit, and generally well-connected, bunch. They talk about having green blood (the Dartmouth colors) in their veins. Minorities are thin on the ground – about 16 per cent, but there is a good mix of international students. The 6000 strong alumni association is very active, with many former students closely involved with the school. It's friendly, if a bit WASPish.

Getting in

The school looks for good team players. GMAT scores average about 690, which isn't as high as some other Ivy League schools. It is also supportive of cash-strapped students, with a school loan system. 'Writing the essays was the hardest part,' says a student. 'Visit the school, and talk to alumni,' advises another.

Academic life

Unlike some of the more dog-eat-dog US schools, the Tuck philosophy emphasizes collaboration. Almost all work is done in designated teams. Students say professors are very accessible. The degree is awarded on the basis of grades for each course. Overall, Tuck's reputation is not as fiercely academic as some other schools.

Tuck is currently revamping its core curriculum, which is all covered in the first year. Second-year MBA students act as mentors to first-year study groups. The second year is entirely devoted to electives. About 50 are on offer, and don't have to be grouped into a concentration. In year two, students are encouraged to take a wide range of electives but they can choose to focus on a particular area. Up to three courses can be taken at other Dartmouth College departments. An approved study project can be substituted for one elective. Mini electives can also be used in pairs to make up a single course.

The atmosphere is pretty relaxed. Compared to some of the more angst-ridden MBA students at other schools, Tuck MBAs are positively chilled. But some students say class participation could be keener.

'Class participation could be better (more diverse); a lot of the same people are raising their hands and speaking, for the most part. I found many of the HBS cases that we've used to be painful and meaningless.'

Best teachers: Tuck has some excellent professors, a number of them world class. Students report that there are one or two clunkers, as well. 'Most professors have been great, but a couple have sucked.'

Students rate Vijay Govindarajan, a second-year strategy prof. 'Very eloquent and great for the spring – you can get as much or as little out of the class as you want,' says one student. John Shank, who teaches first- and second-year managerial accounting, also gets a good grade from some. 'Puts you on the spot, pushes your thinking to the limit, teaches you things such as "the long run starts now" that are as applicable to life as they are to business.'

IT guru Phil Andersen also gets good marks.

Social life

Social life at Tuck revolves around other students and the b-school – there isn't much else in Hanover. Outdoor pursuits are a feature. Late-night ice skating is also popular. Inevitably, the time students get to spend on such activities is constrained by the odd class and reading assignment. 'I thought I'd have more personal time to hike, ski, etc. but I've found it very easy to get oversubscribed in both academics and activities,' one student told us.

The close-knit community also means that everybody pretty much knows everybody else. This is good if you enjoy being part of a small community, not so good if you favor a bit of social diversity. 'Some people complain that Tuck is too cliquey – and in a way it is (mostly the younger, single dorm-dwellers), but the majority of students are not cliquey and are very approachable, warm and friendly.'

Social highlights: Include the winter carnival – a ski competition attended by other schools like Harvard, Wharton and Columbia. The skiing is followed by copious amounts of drinking. 'Great parties', says one student. Talent shows are also popular.

Cool places to hang out: Limited. Hanover is small. 'Basically there's CBGs, a restaurant that's only a bar on Thursday nights, specifically for Tuck,' says one student. 'Murphys, a pub, and 5 Olde, a basement dive that's usually frequented by locals who look like they came down from the hills except on the Wednesdays when Tuckies go there to get buffalo wings.'

PS

Despite its remoteness, Tuck attracts a good number of recruiters. Regulars include the great and the good of the consulting world, Bain & Co, the Boston Consulting Group and

Andersen Consulting among them. With Boston within easy reach, it also has good links with the city's investment banking community and is reaching out to the high tech community. A drawback is that the small MBA program makes the trip out to Hanover unrewarding for some recruiters.

Comments one student: 'The only downside, which affects some people, is that Tuck doesn't get as wide an array of recruiters as other schools because of its size. In other words, if recruiters have previously gone back empty-handed (with no one taking their offers), they are less likely to invest in recruiting the following year. So a small student body means fewer overall offers accepted.'

The Wharton School – University of Pennsylvania

Address	102 Vance Hall 3733 Spruce Street Philadelphia, PA 19104.6361 US Tel: +1 (215) 898 6183 Fax: +1 (215) 898 0120 E-mail: mba.admissions@wharton.upenn.edu Website: www.wharton.upenn.edu
Teaching staff	Full-time 194 Others 65
Student intake (Class of 2001)	790
No of applicants	8434 – 12% accepted
Average age	28
Estimated annual cost *(tuition fees) – 1999–2000*	Single student $47,456 ($31,279)
Average GMAT (Class of 2001)	Mean – 692 Mid 80% range – 580–750 Average GPA – 3.5
Median base salary (1999)	$80,000
Student profile (Class of 2001)	Women 30% Minorities 17% International 38%
Notes	Wharton has consistently ranked in the top three business schools in the world.

Why Wharton?

Wharton has topped *Business Week*'s influential business school rankings since 1994. (It was rated second to Harvard in the 2000 *Financial Times* global rankings). Much of the credit has to go to Thomas Gerrity. During his nine-year deanship, he revamped and revitalized the MBA program to the point that Wharton's place at the top of the *BW* poll looked increasingly impregnable. Gerrity has now stepped down to spend more time with his family – and his portfolio of non-executive directorships – but plans to continue teaching. His legacy is impressive.

In particular he seems to have inculcated a willingness to innovate, not usually seen among traditional b-schools. Founded in 1881, Wharton is the oldest business school in the world. Yet, despite its age, Wharton in recent years has become one of the most progressive schools in the US – and probably anywhere. Under Gerrity, subject areas were integrated to create a more holistic learning experience. While Wharton, under Gerrity, has been highly proactive in changing its program, other leading schools have struggled in Wharton's wake. Most famously, Harvard Business School began changing its MBA program long after Wharton had already completed the task, and has appeared a reluctant convert to new technology.

'I think that Gerrity's fundamental insight about Wharton was that there could be a way to get different academic disciplines to work together so that Wharton graduates would develop well-rounded skills and be more effective business leaders,' says Wharton MBA Peter Cohan (now a successful author and consultant). 'Gerrity's academic credibility with the faculty was so strong that he was able to get different departments to work effectively in teams. While Wharton had many strong individual departments, it was the teamwork among them that enabled the school to rise to the top.'

This view is reflected in student comments. 'The Wharton administration recognizes that the business landscape is morphing faster than the club scene in New York City. To this end, they have taken fast, and I believe decisive, steps, to embrace change! This level of responsiveness is critical in keeping the MBA relevant in the internet age,' says one.

With an annual intake close to 800, Wharton is a big school. It is, by US standards, also international in outlook, with almost 40 per cent foreign students. Location-wise, Philadelphia lacks the pizzazz and glamor of some other schools, although the campus is OK and facilities are good.

Getting in

It's tough. Just over 12 per cent of applicants are accepted. Average GMAT score is 692.

Academic life

In the early 1990s, Wharton was the first school to adopt an integrative approach to the MBA. An intensive four-week pre-program session aims to get students to base level in core disciplines – including statistics and accounting – and ends with a two-day retreat. The main program is split between core courses in the first year and electives in the second (Wharton has one of the largest selections of electives among b-schools). For core courses, students work individually and in teams of five, and the first year includes a 12-week team company project. The first year culminates in an (optional) four-week international study tour.

Second-year students choose a major from 30 or so on offer, opt for joint majors or pursue individualized programs – and complete a project in their chosen area. Throughout the program, there is a high emphasis on integrating subject areas.

'You cannot graduate from Wharton without understanding the complete business system', says a student. 'Regardless of whether you will ever see a production line or sit in the marketing department, the Wharton curriculum forces you to understand how these and other related business sub-cycles are interrelated. Wharton also allows its students to develop incredibly deep skills in their areas of interest.'

Despite the focus on group working, individual competition is fierce. Some humility is required. 'The greatest piece of advice I can give is to temper your expectations. Everyone who comes to Wharton, or any top business school for that matter, has been in the top 1 per cent of their company or field. When you get all those people together not everyone can be the star or the valedictorian. Many people, smart people, have trouble accepting that there are other people out there who could beat them like a drum in a given class. What these people don't necessarily digest is that you can't expect to compete with a CPA in an advanced accounting class if you haven't had considerable work experience in the field. Unless you have perspective and humility you will fight this unsuccessfully your entire MBA career.'

Social life

'The best things about my experience to date are swing dancing lessons, scuba diving and flying lessons – and I have only been here for two months,' says one student. Most suggest that the combination of Philadelphia and the close proximity of New York, makes for a myriad of social possibilities. 'From a social perspective, Wharton has been phenomenal,' says one student. 'Philly is a neat city with great dining and NYC is two hours away and I make it up there as often as possible.'

Cool places to hang out: The MBA Pub.

Social highlights: The Welcome Weekend; Follies, Wharton's musical comedy show.

PS

Wharton attracts the leading recruiters. It has also recently added a full-time post dedicated to organizing treks – tours of recruiters in Silicon Valley and other hot spots. 'Everyone who wanted a job in a given field got one, maybe not with the top firm or in their city of choice but if you wanted to be a VC or buy-side stock picker those jobs were available to you,' says a student. 'The quality of leads at Wharton and HBS are without peer. People come here to hire as many good people as they can get and then go to other schools to round out their recruiting needs or regional offices. Sometimes I would see stuff that would require a double take it was so amazing.'

Yale School of Management

Address	Boulevard de Constance PO Box 208200 New Haven, CT 06520-8200 US Tel: +1 (203) 432 5932 Fax: +1 (203) 432 7004 E-mail: mba.admissions@yale.edu Website: www.yale.edu/som
Teaching staff	Full-time 54 Others 26
Student intake (Class of 2001)	216
No of applicants	n/a
Average age	27.9
Estimated annual cost *(tuition fees) – 1999–2000*	$40,660 ($26,380)
Average GMAT (1999)	Mean – 682 Mid 80% range – 640-740 Average GPA – 3.47
Median base salary (1999)	$75,000
Student profile (Class of 2001)	Women 31% Minorities 18% International 29%
Notes	Yale has an impressive line up of speakers for its Leaders' Forums at the school. Lined up for the 2000–2001 academic year for example are Leon Brittan, Steve Case, Michael Dell, Jurgen Schremp and Harvey Golub.

Why Yale?

Academically a big name, but not in the b-school firmament. Yale only started offering an MBA – in name at least – in 1998. The brand, however, is a formidable thing. The brightest brains from past and present are on tap – and not just those from the b-school. The Yale network is a potent attraction. 'The alumni network seems to be incredibly important,' concludes one student. 'SOM is a small, new school. The environment is intimate, and alumni have struck me as very loyal and helpful. Several alumni have come to speak in classes and for presentations, and I contacted some people for advice and contacts in marketing for my summer internship. I was interviewed by returning alumni for my first-choice internship, which I eventually took. I imagine this is a self-perpetuating cycle; I have deepened my business school experience by frequently interacting with alumni; so, when I become one, I will return the favor.'

Aside from the mutual back-scratching, Yale School of Management offers an MBA with a thoughtful twist. 'The SOM is trying to look at management in a broader context. Hard to explain exactly what it is – you have to be here to feel it,' says one Yallie. 'Maybe a more thoughtful MBA is the right expression. It manifests itself in various ways – such as the emphasis the curriculum places on the social responsibility of business leaders. The large number of students with non-profit background changes the approach we take on almost every case – and there is a very collegial feeling among the students – which you don't always find in other schools.'

The slightly different – almost off-beat – culture is helped by the relatively small size of the school. 'Having a class of 200+ students means that students get to have meaningful relation-ships with the faculty and the other members of the class. It is not uncommon to have lunch with professors, or even an occasional drink at a local bar,' says one student.

Getting in

Small intake; high standards. The admission process includes two essays and three referees.

Academic life

Yale's academic approach is, perhaps surprisingly, innovative. The first year includes 'Perspectives on management' which is based around a series of guest speakers.

Among the most distinctive elements is its grading scale, which is not the typical A–F. Instead, 80 per cent of the class receives a 'Proficient'; 10 per cent a 'Distinction'; and the remainder, 'Pass' or 'Fail'. 'Practically, Yale SOM has no grades so it's really up to you to decide how much you want to put into each class,' says one student.

The grading system means that, according to students, competitiveness between students is less than at some other schools: 'Because the environment is very friendly, and due to the lessening of pressure because of the grading system, people are able to work together and support one another during the overwhelming times, rather than increasing the already existing stress by elbowing one another and fighting for coveted A grades.'

The debate about the merits of Yale's approach to grading continues. This is not, according to some, altogether helpful – 'If I have been disappointed with anything, it has been the battle going on over whether to implement a grading system that will supposedly increase our competitiveness in the global MBA market. The philosophy behind SOM was what drew me here, and I fervently hope that nothing will change that philosophy so that SOM becomes like all other business schools.'

Rather than concentrating on dominant majors, Yale offers more of a smorgasbord of 18 courses.

Best teachers: Jeff Sonnenfeld's 'Managing strategic change' gets rave reviews as does Sigal Barsade on 'Designing and managing organization', and Barry Nalebuff on decision analysis and game theory. Yale faculty hold focus groups to see how they can improve classes.

Social life

With an average age of 26, Yale students are on the youthful side and show commendable dedication to their social lives.

Small is usually beautiful. Says one student: 'The best thing about the social life is the ability to have a lot of friends rather quickly. You're all thrown into a difficult situation together, so it's equivalent to boot camp in that respect. Yale is a small school, so it's easy to know (and feel friendly towards) a majority of your classmates, plus the class above you. On the downside, a school as small as Yale doesn't allow for much privacy. Everyone knows everybody's business (kind of like a small town).'

The schedule can be hectic: 'Friday is the small party night – get a dinner at Hot Tomato or Zinc and then maybe go to BAR. Saturday somebody is hosting a party (by definition). Sunday is for small dinners. Monday is Anna Liffeys. Tuesday is study sessions and maybe Pizza at Naples. Wednesday is when you get some much needed sleep.'

Social highlights: The internship auction, in which members of the Yale community, professors and students volunteer items for auction. The proceeds go towards paying for students taking non-profit jobs for the summer. 'You have to be there to realize the sheer madness of the event.'

Cool places to hang out: The grad student pub is GPSCY ('Where you discover that your classmates can dance – if you have any extra energy that is.'). Also popular are Gypsy, BAR, Anchor, and Anna Liffey's. New Haven has a wide selection of interesting restaurants. Good Thai food can be had at Bangkok Gardens; then there is Scuzi, the Union League Café and Samba.

PS

Recruiters are the usual suspects.

index

Note: Bold indicates main entries on schools in Chapter 9